150 Shades *of* Play

# Also *by* Em & Lo

SEX: How to Do Everything

Buh Bye: The Ultimate Guide to Dumping and Getting Dumped

Rec Sex: An A-Z Guide to Hooking Up

Sex Toy: An A-Z Guide to Bedside Accessories

Sex Etiquette for Ladies and Gentlemen

The Big Bang: Nerve's Guide to the New Sexual Universe

# 150 Shades *of* Play

## A Beginner's Guide to Kink

**by** EM & LO

**illustrated by** Arthur Mount

BETTER
HALF
BOOKS

Jacket design by LELO and Lorelei Sharkey
Jacket photographs provided by LELO
Author photo by David Jacobs

ISBN 13: 978-0615735108
ISBN-10: 061573510X

Better Half Books
www.BetterHalfBooks.com

# Advance Praise for *150 Shades of Play* by Em & Lo

"Unlike *Fifty Shades of Grey*, this was fun to read, informative, and didn't take eight chapters to get to the sex part. Em & Lo have yet again taught me more about sex than all the extensive research I've done by watching porn."
— **Joel Stein**, *Time* magazine columnist & author of *Man Made*

"For readers looking to tap their erotic potential, *Fifty Shades of Grey* is only the tip of the sexual iceberg. With their signature sense of humor and commitment to educate, Em & Lo take readers on a guided journey into titillating, and often taboo, territories and expertly navigate a diverse landscape of thrilling possibility."
— **Ian Kerner**, PhD, GoodInBed.com founder & CNN columnist

"I consider Em & Lo my adopted sex daughters, and they have made me proud once again with *150 Shades of Play*. Their sound advice, smart writing, and sense of humor empower women to give kink a try, safely and realistically—in ways that awful book *Fifty Shades of Grey* never could."
— **Betty Dodson**, sex educator icon & author of *Sex for One*

"Em & Lo mix the perfect quantities of smart and saucy; *150 Shades of Play* is a spirited, comprehensive guide to the kaleidoscopic possibilities of sex and sensuality. You won't find hipper, savvier, or more fun sexperts anywhere."
— **Jack Murnighan**, PhD, author of *Much Ado About Loving* & *The Naughty Bits*

"For over a decade, Em & Lo have helped millions navigate new sexual frontiers. And now, with kink on everyone's mind thanks to *Fifty Shades of Grey*, there's simply no one better to help us learn and laugh about what a sexually fascinating species of ape we are. *150 Shades of Play* is both humanizing and hilarious!"
— **Grant Stoddard**, author of *Good in Bed* and *Working Stiff*

"Em & Lo have distilled kink into its finest, funniest, smartest, and sauciest points. This is a delightful dictionary of debauchery for all persuasions. Throw out *Fifty Shades* and replace it with this, Em & Lo's encyclopedia that doubles as a kinky lightning rod for your sex life."
— **Violet Blue**, author of *Lust* and *Total Flirt*

## Praise for *SEX: How to Do Everything* by Em & Lo

"[One of] the 10 best sex guides."

— The Guardian (UK)

"If you are young and sassy…you might enjoy *Sex: How to Do Everything*, by two women who call themselves Em & Lo and have a penchant for frisky wordplay."

— The New Yorker

"Em and Lo have achieved the quite impressive trick of professionally dispensing advice without it sounding at all *de haut en bas*. Beneath their irreverent manner is an undeniably feminist agenda, in that they are both passionate about encouraging women to enjoy their sexual nature and own it more confidently. The ultimate 'how to do it' book, *How to Do Everything* is guaranteed to be a talking point if you're bold enough to display it on your coffee table."

— The Observer (UK)

## Praise for *The Big Bang* by Em & Lo

"*The Big Bang* is this generation's smarter, funnier and raunchier version of *The Joy of Sex*."
— Time magazine

"*The Big Bang* is the hippest, the funniest and the funkiest [of the four best sex manuals out there]; lots of frank language and a general air of cool, heterosexual downtown-ness pervades. Ideal for a young adult or your sister who just got a tiny tattoo that no one can see."

— O, The Oprah Magazine

"The hottest book on bonking for years."

— The Sun (UK)

"Em & Lo definitely know the ups and downs of sex and dating, but what makes them special in the advice world is their willingness to take it from readers. The result is that everyone gets edified and hopefully, in the end, satisfied."

— Austin Chronicle

"It doesn't matter what you do in the bedroom as long as you
don't do it in the street and frighten the horses."

—Daphne Fielding, *The Duchess of Jermyn Street*

# Table *of* Contents

= referred to in the *Fifty Shades of Grey* trilogy

**bold** = an entry in the A-to-Z section of this book

## Introduction
# A Case *for* Kink

What is **kink**? It's the opposite of plain ol' **vanilla** sex, the opposite of doing it in the same position 2.4 times a month, the opposite of just lying back and thinking of England. Kink is dramatic, deliberate, and dirty. When people talk about spicing things up, kink is Tabasco sauce. It's the kind of extracurricular activity **Christian Grey** enjoys in the bestselling *Fifty Shades of Grey* trilogy by E.L. James, give or take a **Red Room of Pain**. Being kinky might mean bringing props into the bedroom, it might mean acting out dark fantasies, it might even mean wearing something absolutely ridiculous—but then again, being kinky might just mean using a swear word or two when you're makin' lurve.

Most people define kink as anything *they'd* never do in bed—whether that means dressing up like a puppy dog (complete with **collar, leash**, and bone-**gag**) or simply doing it doggy style. Stuffy types will say that kinky means deviant, implying that those who do things a little differently in bed are touched in the head. We prefer the term *unconventional*—or better yet, *creative*—implying that those who do things a little differently in bed are just doing things a little differently in bed. When you compare it to the alternative—doing things the same way in bed for the next half century or so, potentially with the same person —who *wouldn't* want to get their kink on?

A more technical term for kink is **BDSM**, which is short for **bondage & discipline**, **domination & submission**, and **sadism & masochism**. In layman's terms, that includes tying each other up (**rope**, **handcuffs**, etc.), dressing up, **role-playing**, headgames, **mindfucks**, exploring fantasies, exploring orifices, exploring **pain**, exchanging **power**, wearing (p)**leather**, wearing **rubber**, wearing spandex, **whipping**, **spanking**, **paddling**, **tickling**, playing with **food** (see also **sploshing**), playing with **temperature**, playing doctor (see **medical toys**)...we could go on (we do, actually—just keep reading: Every bolded word leads to an entry in this encyclopedia of sorts).

Of course, one book couldn't possibly cover every single **fetish** out there (that's what the Internets is for!). You name a body part, inanimate object, substance, or item of clothing, and someone out there has fetishized it. You name an activity, and someone has sexualized it. But while your particular interest or inclination might not be specifically addressed, we hope you'll at least feel at home in one of the more general entries. You've got a thing for Crisco? Then camp out at the **sploshing** entry. You like to meow? Try **animalism**. And so on.

The list above might remind you of the things you do in bed, or the things you would *like* to do in bed, or the things you would never dream of doing in bed, or the things you think *nobody* should ever do in bed. And these categories are ever shifting—we bet there's at least one thing that grossed you out a decade or two ago that you now engage in on a regular basis (and if there isn't, you were either a very kinky teenager or you need to get out more). If this book tempts you to muddle your categories even further, then we've done our job—but even if it just gives you a proxy thrill spying on Other People's Kink, then we've done our job, too. Because we're not here to tell you exactly where you should draw your boundaries—everyone draws theirs in a different place, and what does it matter, so long as we all draw the shades? (And keep things **safe, sane, and consensual**, of course.) Rather, we just want to remind you that leaving your comfort zone and crossing your own personal boundaries every now and then—wherever they may lie—is one of the best ways to keep things hot 'n' heavy. Or at least entertaining.

This book is intended to be a fairly light-hearted introduction to kink, and was written with beginners in mind—beginners who may have had their curiosity piqued by *Fifty Shades of Grey* and are looking for a little more information, inspiration, and guidance. If that's the case, you may want to start with all the entries marked with the **tie** icon 🖉 (symbolic of the famous woven tie **Christian Grey** uses to restrain **Anastasia Steele**)—they will give you *a lot* more information on all the activities and toys you read about in the famous erotica series. From there, make it a choose-your-own-adventure book by following any bolded words you're interested in to their own dedicated entry. Or just start at A and don't stop 'til you get to Z—or 'til you're compelled to try something out with your partner, whichever comes first. If you'd like to purchase any of the accessories we discuss, always go for quality: that means safe materials, ergonomic design, care and cleaning instructions, and warranties. We recommend LELO products throughout this book because their pleasure objects always meet—and exceed—these standards (plus they're gorgeous to boot!). Encourage your friendly neighborhood sex shop to stock these kinds of well-made products—that way, you'll boost your sex life *and* the local economy! (For more shopping advice, see Appendix A at the back of this book.)

But a word of warning: we cover topics E.L. James wouldn't touch with a ten-foot vibrator, such as **watersports** and **scat play**. We know the majority of our readers will never be interested in these things, even if **Christian Grey** paid them to be. But we've included them to help illustrate just how wide the world of sexuality is, maybe open up your mind a little in the process, and—we'll admit it —give you something bat-shit crazy to talk about at your next cocktail party. As newbies, if none of the entries in the book shock or **squick** you, then you've got stronger stomachs than we do. And if none of the entries crack you up, then you're better people than we are.

Yes, this book probably won't be of much use to people *already* in the BDSM **scene**, i.e. people who have made kink a lifestyle choice, many of whom tend to take their kink very seriously. (Never let it be said that getting whipped on a weekly basis automatically gives you a thick skin.)  But we didn't set out to earn any awards from the **Eulenspiegel Society**—those folks have long outgrown this kind of introductory manual. (For more advanced—and more earnest— reading, check out any one of the titles recommended in Appendix C.)

We have nothing against such learned kinksters, bless their assless chaps, we just don't think that you have to become one of them in order to get a little pervy every now and then. You also don't have to be a former theater major to get into **role-playing**, you don't have to use the "official" lingo if you're bad at second languages, you don't have to wear a **gimp suit** if you're more the fleece hoodie type, you don't have to join an online support group for your **fetish** of choice, you don't have to like **pain** to enjoy a light spanking, you don't need baggage to like being **dominated**, and you don't have to embrace goth style to appreciate **vampirism** (that said, "Bela Lugosi's Dead" by Bauhaus is a seriously good soundtrack for kink). But if you *do* do any of the above, that's cool, too. After all, how will you know for sure you don't like something unless you try it?

But before you try something kinky, you need to bone up on it, as it were—because many kinky endeavors are dangerous if not done correctly. Yes, there is a wrong way to have sex, especially when it comes to BDSM. And the *Fifty Shades of Grey* trilogy certainly doesn't spell it out for you. So while our book is far from comprehensive (you're not going to be able to wield a 12-foot **bullwhip** after reading it, so don't even think about it), it *will* help learn you a naughty trick or two.

Yes, we said "learn." We know there are purists out there who think that the best sex occurs naturally, spontaneously, and without any props or planning. We say, dry spells occur pretty naturally, too. And if you think the planning spoils the fun, then you're not doing it right—it's long-term foreplay, people, not homework! (See **communication**.) Besides, what's so unsexy about putting a little effort and forethought into your sex life?

Those same purists also like to claim that kink is just a way to avoid true intimacy. And sure, if you can't ever get in the mood unless your one-and-only has a ball-gag in place, then we might start to wonder. But as an element of a healthy sex life, exploring your dirtier, darker fantasies with a partner requires a boatload (or a buttload, if that's your thing) of trust and communication, which can bring you closer than even the most teary-eyed, face-holding, make-up sex. Think of kink as the X-rated version of that trust-falling game they used to make you play at camp. Sure, you could get kinky with a near stranger, but we think that most of the activities in this book are best practiced—or hottest—with a long-term partner (then again, we're kind of stuffy). After all, you can't brew a little **sadistic** hate without its opposite: true wuv (or something like it). And what's the fun of breaking a taboo if you're with a stranger who has no idea you just crossed the line? Who's gonna high-five you?

It comes down to this: We believe that every person's sex life should contain at least one act they'd never share over brunch or beers—if nothing you currently do makes you blush that much, then keep reading (either that or shut up and let everyone else enjoy their pancakes, would ya?). John Waters once said, "I thank God I was raised Catholic, so sex will always be dirty." In the absence of a vengeful higher power, consider this book a friendly reminder of how dirty sex can be.

EM & LO
EMandLO.com

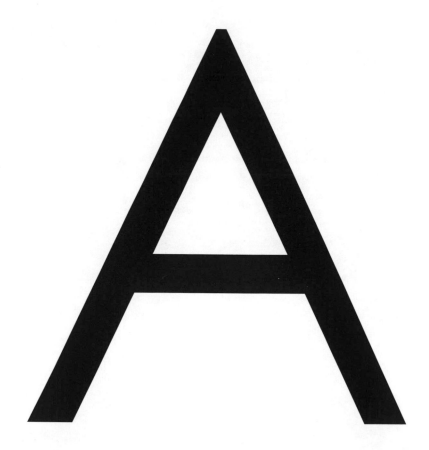

## aftercare

The care given to a **bottom** by their **top** after a **scene**. This includes, but is not limited to: fetching them some water; warming them up with a blankie; soothing body parts with **ice** or creams (e.g. **arnica cream**), or heck, maybe even some ice cream; helping them get up, get to the bathroom, and/or get dressed (perhaps in a silky robe, e.g. from the Sussurra Collection—soothing *and* sensual); **communicating** with them (to make sure they had as much fun as they seemed to be having, and to ensure that the next go-around is even more to their liking); **cuddling** them; offering words of encouragement, emotional support, and/or high fives; giving them some quiet time and space to collect their thoughts or themselves (a room of their own, if you're **Christian Grey**); making them breakfast (or having your maid serve breakfast, if you're Grey).

## age play

A brand of **role-playing** wherein one party does not act his or her age. Usually it's a case of the **sub** pretending to be way younger—a wide-eyed tween in knee socks, say (it may **squick** you, but there's no **law** against play-acting, remember). If the sub likes to regress all the way back to baby status, then he or she is what's known as an adult baby. See also **baby (adult)**, **scat play**, **tickling**, and **watersports**.

## airport security

1) The people who *will* insist on searching your hand luggage if you're so brazen (read: pea-brained) as to carry on your mouth **gag**, **bullwhip**, police-issue **handcuffs**, **gimp suit**, and vibrating **nipple clamps**. Come on—they confiscate nail clippers and don't think twice about full-body-searching dear old grandma...Do you really think they're going to turn a blind eye to your bag o' tricks? (Perhaps this is why **Christian Grey** always takes his private jet.) If you're into long-distance kink, save yourself the hassle and check everything in. Just be sure to remove all batteries first—vibrating devices can easily turn themselves on in transit, and you don't want to be the passenger responsible for an emergency deplaning after a baggage handler comes across an ominously buzzing suitcase. Better yet, if your BDSM props are more menacing than a pair of pink fuzzy **cuffs**, ship all your stuff via Fed Ex, et al. Or, when you get where you're going, just visit the local **hardware store** to create a satellite **dungeon** (see **D.I.Y.** for a suggested shopping list).

2) Common post-9/11 **role-playing** scenario, wherein the person full-body-

groping you isn't *actually* a pisspot wearing government-issue nylon pants two sizes too small…unless that's your bag, of course. Note: This **scene** should be played out in the privacy of your own home, not at an actual airport. *You* may think it's hot to make your **slave** walk through the metal detector wearing his weighted steel ball stretcher (featuring removable spikes for optional **cock torture**), and we're sure your slave agrees that he's a weasel who deserves to be put in his place by the National Guard (then again, he has to agree with you, he's your slave!)—but the three hundred Spring Breakers waiting behind you to board the plane to Cancun beg to differ. And we don't think that telling them, "If we stop wearing our titanium **butt plugs** during international flights, then the terrorists have won" would appease them, either.

## anal beads

Anal beads look like a snapped-together kids' plastic necklace—in other words, totally *unlike* something you should stick in your behind. But they feel really good, both on the way in and on the way out. Insert the string slowly, one bead at a time, pausing for permission after each bead like a dirty game of Mother May I? Then pull the beads out—gently but not quite as slowly—either just before, or at, the moment of orgasm. Do not—repeat, do not—yank the beads out: This is not an area where you want rug burn. The cheapie kind of anal beads are made of plastic (which can have rough seams) and are attached on a nylon cord (which is hard to clean). So throw down a bit more money and go for high quality beads built on a stalk of the same material (instead of on a string)—ideally silicone. And remember, as with any anal toy: **Lube** is your friend. For more on safe **anal play** (with or without toys), see the next entry.

## anal play

Stimulation (which usually includes penetration) of the anus with a finger, penis, or **dildo**. (Use your tongue, and it's called rimming.) For some, it's as-kinky-as-it-gets sex; for others, it's just a nice way to wake up every morning. A gentle poke in the rear isn't anywhere near as kinky as, say, adult **baby** play—but we wouldn't go so far as to say that Greek love has become mainstream, either. After all, it was still a crime in some U.S. states up until 2003 (still is in some countries). We can thank the Bible for making it a sin, at least between fellas: "Men with men working that which is unseemly." (Of course, eating oysters is also an abomination according to the Good Book, but plenty of God-fearing Christians enjoy guilt-free shellfish-sucking every now and then.)

Anal sex can make for great kinky play for a number of reasons. Because of its association with literal dirtiness, anal play can make the sex figuratively dirtier. You can play around with gender roles and domination: A gal can wear a **strap-on** and "take" her boyfriend. It can also be a form of play punishment or **humiliation**, if it's not usually the recipient's bag (though **consent** is always key!). And with anal sex, if you're not careful and don't know what you're doing, you could really hurt someone, so it also takes a lot of trust, which can foster intimacy.

Unlike most **vanilla** sex, there *is* a wrong way to have anal sex. In fact, there is a wrong way to engage in most of the play in this book, which is why safety is so important. When it comes to good old-fashioned backdoor lovin', understand that the anus and rectum are not like the vagina: They are not self-lubricating, their tissue is much more delicate, and they don't expand to fit the penetrator. So keep the following in mind:

1. To prep, no need for an **enema**, just make sure you've got enough fiber in your diet for solid deposits, avoid beans and such 24 hours prior, drop the kids off at the pool, and shower *thoroughly* beforehand.
2. It would be downright deviant *not* to use the ass-istance of manmade **lube** (try Liquid Silk, Maximus, or Probe Classic)—be liberal in its application.
3. Don't go in like gangbusters: Work your way up slowly and gently, first with a pinkie, then with a **butt plug**, then with a small (okay, average) penis or **dildo** —there are no anal sex starter kits that come with 12-inch dongs.
4. Once you're in just past the two ring-like sphincters of the anus, angle your penetrator towards their bellybutton to avoid hitting the rectal wall.
5. When using something other than your own finger or penis, make sure it was *made* for assplay (i.e. has a tapered tip for smooth entry, no rough seams, and a flared base so it doesn't get lost up there).
6. Keep anything that's been in the butt away from the vagina and, we'd say, the mouth to avoid infection (see **scat**).

Anal sex is one of the highest risk activities for transmitting STDs, including HIV, so always use condoms, both on flesh penises and fake ones (that'll help keep everything cleaner anyway).

A.k.a. buggery, crime against nature, sodomy. See also **anal beads**, **butt plugs**, **fisting**.


## Anastasia Steele 🐾

The heroine/reluctant **sub**/damsel in distress (**D.i.D.**) of the *Fifty Shades of Grey* trilogy, who falls hard (literally) for romantic bad-boy billionaire **dom**, **Christian Grey**. She has two imaginary friends: her snarky, cartwheel-twirling Inner Goddess and her finger-drumming Subconscious (yes, yes, if this character were truly *subconscious*, then Ana wouldn't be aware of her, but let's not let literary accuracy get in the way of a good time, shall we?). All three appear to be virgins at the start of the series—and none of them ever met an adverb she didn't like. By the end (spoiler alert!), they're all on board for a little **BDSM** play in a custom-designed **Red Room of Pain** with now hubby/baby-daddy Christian.

## animalism

Human animal **role-playing**, with one person adopting the mannerisms of a particular animal and another acting as "trainer" and/or "owner." In other words, playing piggyback, grown-up style. The most common form of animalism is **pony play**, which typically focuses on training. Other activities include puppy or pup play, which is mostly about discipline (with a kennel or doghouse), cow play (think milking fantasies), and pig play, perhaps for **sploshing** fans. As with much of **BDSM**, the appeal is in the power exchange: The animal gets to give up control (even the ability to communicate verbally) and the trainer gets to wield it, by feeding, grooming, walking, or riding them. And what would playing pretend be without the props? There are **butt plugs** with fluffy tails, animal masks and hoods, muzzles and bits, leashes and reins and riding **crops**, and gloves and **boots** which transform hands into paws and hooves. It gives a whole new meaning to the term "animal lover." But while sex may occur while in character, it's usually a "breeding" scene between two people acting like the same animal—because a trainer fucking their pony would be an act of bestiality, and that ain't what animalism is all about. Similarly, and most importantly, sex does not—repeat, *does not*—occur between these "animals" and real animals. Don't make us call P.E.T.A. A.k.a. pet play. See also **furries**.

## armbinders 🖊

Never know where to put your hands when you're standing there naked being verbally abused by your **master**? Try armbinders! As with any **bondage** accessory, there are about a million different variations on the theme, but the basic gist of the armbinder is this: either one big conical sleeve or two sleeves (sometimes called bondage opera gloves), usually with mittens for hands, which can be laced, zippered, or buckled to each other and/or to other objects. The most popular version brings your hands and arms together behind you, as if you're about to stretch for yoga. Except, in this case, your instructor gently pulls up on a **D-ring** (usually at the base of the contraption where your hands come together) to turn you into his or her own downward facing dog. The more minimalist version of the armbinder is two bicep **cuffs** which attach via a short strap across your upper back, like **Christian** and **Anastasia** use in *Fifty Shades*. (You can also improvise with a set of wrist cuffs, as

long as they're big enough for your biceps, fit comfortably without cutting off circulation, and don't keep falling down around your elbows.) Whatever kind of armbinder you employ, the pleasant result is your best involuntary impersonation of Dolly Parton. But they should be worn only by the most flexible of people for a limited amount of time, as the extreme position can cause shoulder problems and poor hand circulation. A.k.a. monoglove, singleglove. See also **endurance bondage** and **reverse prayer position**.

## arnica cream

This is a pain-relieving gel for bumps, bruises, sprains, sports injuries, and over-exercising—at least, that's what the packaging says. Applied after a bottom spanking (as **Christian** did on **Anastasia**'s red tush in *Fifty Shades*), this ointment may reduce bruising. You can also try applying beforehand as well. Either way, you get a nice sensual butt **massage** out of it. See also **aftercare**.

## autoerotic asphyxiation

Intentionally strangling yourself while masturbating in an attempt to heighten sexual pleasure by limiting the oxygen supply to the brain. Some practitioners prefer a bag over the head to a hangman's noose. Possible side effects include memory loss, windpipe rupture, brain damage, cardiac arrest, stroke, and, oh yeah, *death*. (In the annals of tragi-comic demises, this ranks somewhere between being crushed by a falling safe and cracking your skull open after slipping on a banana peel.) Our lawyers and your moms insist you not attempt this activity, which is mostly enjoyed by young dudes. And this isn't one of our half-assed "Don't engage in this behavior without further research" bans. We mean don't do it *ever*. If you really like to live on the edge, why don't you do something safer, like jam your elbow in your own ear? A.k.a. AeA, breath control, pulling a Hutchence. See also **bondage (self)**, **edge play**, **erotic asphyxiation**.

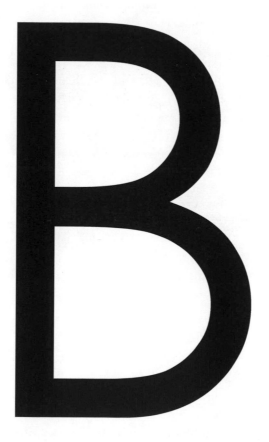

## B&D

Bondage and **discipline**, the "B" and "D" of **BDSM**.

## baby, adult

Adult baby is a form of role-playing wherein one partner (typically a straight guy) plays baby and the other plays grownup (typically **mommy**). The "baby" wears man-sized diapers and might accessorize with a frilly bonnet or noise-maker; if his tastes run to girlish pink dresses, then he is known as a "sissy baby." Infantilists—as adult babies are also known—enjoy being bathed, bottle-fed, burped, **spanked**, **tickled**, put in diapers, and generally babied. Some of them even take full advantage of their man-diapers…or simply poop in the bathtub, we shit you not (see **scat** and **watersports**). Infantilism doesn't get a lot of respect in the **vanilla** world, probably because (a) outsiders assume that the "baby" in question is psychologically mangled due to a lack of love from his real mommy, and (b) big hairy men look ridiculous in diapers and a pacifier.

By the way, diaper **fetishism** is not the same thing as infantilism, though most adult babies are also diaper fetishists: Some kinky types just get off on wearing diapers and doing naughty things (whereas adult babies often don't do anything sexual at all, as that would be considered "breaking character," though the occasional baby has been known to "nurse"). Diaper fetishists who aren't into infantilism (still with us?) don't bother with a mommy or any of that baby talk— they might be a **bottom** who just feels more subservient in Huggies, or they might have a diaper buddy they meet up with for play dates (see **wrestling**). For the record, however, baby talk as a stand-alone practice has not been proven to be a gateway drug to infantilism (though it might still **squick** some people). And as for frat boys who don diapers so they don't have to get up and pee during the "big game"? We're gonna go out on a judgmental limb and say, that's just plain wrong. A.k.a. infantilism. See also **age play**, **scat play**, **tickling**, and **watersports**.

## "back massagers"

See **wand vibrators**.

## ball gags 🐾
See **gags (mouth)**.

## ball stretchers
Wide leather cuffs, worn around the top of the scrotal sack, which push the testicles away from the body; heavy metal rings, worn around the top of the scrotal sack, which weigh the testicles down; or leather collars or "parachutes," worn at the top of the scrotal sack, with chains hanging off to which weights can be added. The resultant tugging can be pleasurable to painful (depending on how heavy the weights are), and if worn repeatedly for long enough can noticeably and permanently stretch your sack, causing cruel tops to sing in your presence, "Do your balls hang low, do they wobble to and fro, can you tie 'em in a knot, can you tie 'em in a bow, can you throw 'em o'er your shoulder like a continental soldier? Do your balls hang low? Now suck my cock!"

## balls, vaginal 🐾
See **vaginal balls**.

## bath toys 🐾
Waterproof props to help you get dirty while you're getting clean. Bath toys tend to skew toward the vanilla end of the kink spectrum—think: bath oils and bubbles, vibrating rubber **duckies** and loofahs, edible chocolate soaps—so they're perfect for newbies and/or those who require a shower before any hanky panky. But even the intensely dominant **Christian Greys** of the world have been known to enjoy a little soft and soapy sensual play in the tub.

Of course, bath toys don't have to be cutesy and/or disguised as innocent bathroom accessories—hundreds of sex toys these days are fully waterproof. Sex toy design has improved vastly in the past decade, and a broader selection of waterproof toys is one of the most exciting developments. Just check the packaging when you browse for a new toy for "fully waterproof" (*not* "water resistant")— you'd be surprised how many toys are happy to go for a dip with you. For example, most of LELO's toys are fully waterproof.

So try substituting a bath—whether solo or *à deux*—for all that mindless TV you've come to rely on for winding down. Pick out a toy or two, light some candles, play some music, and leave the freakin' Blackberry in the kitchen. Hunt down a copy of the book *Hot & Steamy: Erotic Baths for Two* by Annalise Witberg for some saucy suggestions—it's waterproof, so you can actually read it in the bath, *and* it's designed to fit in your soap dish! Or, for some wet and wild erotic fiction, check out the adults-only waterproof book *Aqua Erotica*.

But here's the rub (or, rather, the rope burn): Being *squeaky* clean means bath or shower water will wash all your natural lube away, and regular water-based lubes will slide right off, too. You're going to need some waterproof (i.e., silicone) **lube** if you're planning on doing more than just washing behind your ears. See the **lube** entry for specific suggestions.

## BDSM

One-size-fits-all acronym for six activities which usually travel in pairs (think of it as the kink buddy system): **bondage** and **discipline** (B&D), **domination** and **submission** (D/s), and **sadism** and **masochism** (a.k.a. sadomasochism, SM, or S&M). While each of these six activities has its own definition, "SM" can also be used as an umbrella term for anything kink-related, and "B&D" can be used as a synonym for "SM" (especially if you think that "SM" sounds too hardcore). "D/s," on the other hand, refers mostly to the psychological **power exchange** element of kinky **play**. Confused yet?

## beads, vaginal

See **vaginal beads**.

## belts

*Not* a good flagellation tool for beginners, even if you're **role-playing** an erotic beating from your **daddy** after you broke curfew. They're just too hard to control. Plus, buckles are dangerous with a capital D. Best to stick with quality, **made-for-play** products like **paddles**, **slappers**, **crops**, **canes**, and **floggers**. Or, for a purpose-made option that actually *looks* like a belt, try the slapper called "Daddy's Belt"—you can't wear it (its two ends have been glued together so it's more like a slapper that you can't unfurl), but you can certainly give your "kid" something to cry about. We would guess that this is the kind of thing **Christian Grey** used to **spank** the crap out of **Anastasia Steele** in the final, climactic kink scene of the first *Fifty Shades of Grey* book (*He opens the door, and still grasping my arm, grabs what looks like a belt....*) A.k.a. straps. See also **bondage belt**.

## Bend Over Beginner Kit

A starter **strap-on** kit for beginners—usually women who want to try being the penetrator for a change. The kit comes with two very approachable silicone dildos (one small, one medium), an adjustable two-strap nylon **harness** that fits hips up to 60 inches in circumference (which looks wholesome and crunchy, kind of like climbing gear or backpack straps), and a miniature **bullet vibrator** that fits snugly into a pocket located on the front of the harness, meaning she might get a little clitoral stimulation while riding him like a bucking bronco and whooping, "Who's your daddy now?" (Okay, so maybe the whooping comes later, after you've graduated from this kit.) Warning: The triangular section of the harness that covers the mons is available in purple velvet (which just happens to match the purple dildos). We know some people can't get enough purple velvet in their lives, but if you're not one of them, opt for basic black. See also **anal play** and **kits (kinky)**.

## blanket consent 🦇

Long-term kinky permission, either for a specific act, or for an entire relationship (see **slave**). For example, in a **taken in hand** relationship, a woman may give her husband blanket **consent** to bend her over his knee and **spank** her whenever he thinks she deserves it (burnt toast, missed PTA meeting, etc.). In other words, the go-ahead extends beyond the bedroom and is employed as a form of domestic **discipline**. It's still a form of foreplay, of course, but it won't necessarily always lead directly to sex—rather, it's ongoing foreplay as a sort of erotic undercurrent to your sex life.

Blanket consent in this context means that you don't have to talk everything to death—you trust each other enough that you don't need to negotiate a **scene** or settle on a **safeword**. It's not that you *can't* "break scene" in an **edge play** kind of way—rather, the blanket consent is based on a good will understanding that you probably won't *need* to. This is particularly handy for couples who find all that **communication** a bit of a buzzkill.

Of course, you don't *have* to be in a taken in hand set-up to give blanket consent for something—you might just really like a certain activity (like, say, **cock and ball torture**) and agree to be down with it whenever, wherever, just to increase the element of surprise. That said, blanket consent, even in a limited sense, is likely to cause a little bleed-through—in other words, if your partner has permission to goose you at any time, chances are goosing is never going to be far from the back of your mind, even when you're trimming your nose hair.

A more general form of blanket consent is when you give your partner permission to **top** you at any time, in any way—if you're a taken in hand wife, this is based on an understanding that you want to be married to Alpha Ken, and if you're a slave, this is based on the **contract** you signed. See the **slave** and **taken in hand** entries for more on how the hell people make these things work.

## blindfolds

The only kink accessory guaranteed to make it past judgmental cleaning ladies, visiting parents, and **airport security** (hell, the airline might even give you a blindfold for free if it's an overnight flight!). It's also a must-have for beginners: If you're having trouble embracing your inner kinkster, then making your partner don a blindfold will make everything seem less, well, silly. Not sure that a latex **catsuit** is "you"? Blindfold your partner and make them guess what you're wearing with their hands. Afraid that your **paddle** action is lackluster and limp-wristed? Keep your victim in the dark while you work on your swing. Does eye contact keep taking you out of the moment whenever you try to **role-play**? It's much easier to stay in character (and avoid the giggles) if only one of you can see. Basically, when your partner wears a blindfold, your inhibitions are lowered, much like having sex on tequila—but without the raging hangover or diminished hand-eye coordination (and five minutes with this book should tell you that many of the activities described herein require advanced hand-eye coordination…sloppy **cock and ball torture**, anyone?). And when *you* wear the blindfold? It's a legitimate excuse to just lie back, relax, and be attended to—simply enjoying the heightened sense of touch that results from another of your senses (in this case sight) being restricted. For special occasions, check out LELO's pure silk Intima version (pictured on the back cover). See also **sensory deprivation**.

## bloodplay

Any kinky activity that involves blood—*intentionally*, not because you were running with scissors—usually as a result of breaking the skin by cutting, play **piercing**, **whipping**, or playing with **medical** equipment. (Some milder blood fetishists may simply get off on period sex, while others may just get a tingly feeling in their special place when they give blood.) The cutting is usually performed with a sterile razor blade or scalpel, and may be intended to be temporary (you just like the look of blood on a naked bod) or more permanent (you think **scarification** is hot). Or maybe you just get off on the **pain**. If you're really hardcore, you might find gory car crashes a turn on (in which case, here's a dime—call J.G. Ballard and tell him all about it). Blood fetishists are sometimes referred to (incorrectly) as **vampirists**—while there is a natural degree of overlap, you can like blood and hate *Twilight*, and you can be into goth and white face makeup without wanting to get all crime-scene.

We would tell you about all the safety rules of bloodplay, but that would imply that we think there *is* a safe way to engage in it. WE DON'T. It's **edge play** of the highest order—sure, you could wear latex **gloves**, but they won't protect you from anything (like, say, HIV) if you accidentally cut yourself. And your gloves certainly won't be any help if you cut your partner too deeply and they require stitches. We understand that some people like the whole tribal bonding notion of blood—in which case, may we recommend a little cunnilingus next time Aunt Flow is over? (If you join the Hell's Angels, they'll even give you a Red Wings badge for that act of "bravery.") Just bring the dental dams if you're not body-fluid committed. A.k.a. bloodsports.

## body bags

**Mummification** made easy. These are *not* the real McCoy for corpses, so don't even think about calling Morgues "R" Us. Real medical body bags don't bother with a breathing mechanism (for obvious reasons) so you've got to get yourself a **made-for-play** BDSM version: either a headless version with a collar or one with breathing holes. They're often made of canvas (though sometimes leather or rubber), with adjustable belts along their lengths for added security and/or D-rings for lashing them to the ground or **suspending** them in the air. The term is often used interchangeably with **sleepsacks**. See also **straitjackets** and **vacuum bed**.

## body modification

Permanently or semi-permanently decorating or altering your body via tightly laced **corsets**, **branding**, **scarification**, plastic surgery, **piercings**, and tattoos. You don't have to be into kink to be into body modification, but the two go together like *The Bachelor* and broken engagements. Mainstream patron saints include Angelina Jolie, Dave Navarro, and that crazy cat lady Jocelyn Wildenstein. Arch enemies include God ("your body is a temple") and John Mayer ("your body is a wonderland"). A.k.a. body art (at least by those going through with it).

## body service 🐾

A warm fuzzy way to be the **bottom**: bathing, massaging, fanning, toe-nail clipping, or otherwise grooming your **top** (rubber **duckie** optional). A top may also administer some body service, ordering the bottom to sit still while their is hair is lovingly washed/body sensually rubbed down/enema gently inserted, etc. See also **service kink**.

## body stockings

More breathable, flexible, and see-through versions of **catsuits** (which tend to be made of latex or rubber). In other words, pantyhose for your entire body without the panties (many have open crotches for convenience). Some have open busts for breast play. Sometimes made of fishnet material, lace, or crocheted lycra, for when you want to be a Playboy model or just look like one! A.k.a. unitard (a decidedly unsexy synonym that should never be used to refer to such apparel if you want to stay in the mood).

## bondage, about 🐾

Bondage is the "B" of **BDSM**. Restraining a loved one or being restrained in an erotic context is one of the cornerstones of kink. Bondage is a great on-ramp to kinky play because you don't have to get into character or find your **motivation** in order to do it. In fact, quite the opposite—the ties that bind can actually bring on a kinky mood: There's nothing like a **spreader bar** and a pair of **handcuffs** (even the fuzzy animal-print kind) to help you lie back and indulge that bad cop fantasy ("Hands up and spread 'em!"). And when you tie up your partner with the Ted Baker silk **tie** that he wore all day while slaving for the Man? Let's just say that someone's in a *lot* of trouble for screwing up the Powerpoint presentation (Dilbert never had it so good...er, we mean, bad).

Not that bondage has to be accompanied by a fantasy that "explains" the situation at hand, of course. Sometimes the appeal is purely aesthetic—there's a reason why the thick leather wristband (donned by rebels and wannabes from Colin Farrell to Avril Lavigne) has outlasted just about every other rockstar trend...save for having sex with groupies. Besides looking good, it can feel good, too—like a cozy heavy blanket.

Other times, the simple fact of being rendered helpless—or being responsible for this state of affairs—is enough to send you over the edge. If you tend to be too much of a giver in bed (especially true of women who worry about how long their partner spends chasing down their elusive orgasm), then a dose of bondage will force you to lie back and enjoy that partner's administrations. It's hard to stress about returning the favor when you've got about thirty feet of intricately wound rope between you and your "turn." Alternatively, if you're a bit of a sheep in the sack and always let your partner set the pace, then tying up your shepherd will force you to make some damn decisions for a change. It's the best way to find out what you really like (speed, position, depth, angle, mayo vs. Miracle Whip, etc.). You may think you're not confident enough to fly solo like this, but there's nothing like being the only one who can move to make you feel like you've got *all* the moves. Aw yeah.

The most common form of bondage is the kind that you'll be familiar with from cop movies, old westerns, and the lesbian-lite film, *Bound*: tying various parts of the body to each other or to foreign objects (a chair, a bed, a large house guest, etc.) to restrict movement, using **rope**, **cuffs** and straps, **chains**, neckties, **bondage tape**, **harnesses**, duct tape over clothes (if you're nasty), etc. But technically, the term bondage also encompasses several other activities— variations on the theme, if you will—typically reserved for more advanced players: 1. spreading (pulling apart various body parts such as arms and legs by attaching ankle and wrist cuffs to distant objects or using a cleverly named **spreader bar**); 2. **suspension** (suspending body parts from the ceiling or another object, e.g. using door jamb **cuffs**); 3. binding or **mummification** (when the whole body is wrapped, e.g. in cloth, **Saran Wrap**, a **body bag** or a **sleepsack**); and 4. bondage clothing that restricts movement (e.g. a **straitjacket** or a Geisha-inspired **hobble skirt**).

And as for bondage's frequent traveling companion, **discipline**? Let's just say that there's nothing like a pair of door jamb cuffs to make sure your partner stays put while you give them the spanking (verbal or otherwise) that they deserve. See also the various **bondage** entries immediately below (especially **bondage safety**).

## bondage belt

A bad-ass leather belt that transforms into an easily adjustable figure-eight **restraint** and can be used as a wrist, ankle, or neck restraint. For those days when you need to cinch your pants *and* tie up an errant love slave.

## bondage, breast

Binding the (usually female) breasts with **rope**, leather straps, **Saran Wrap**, etc. For simplicity's sake, we'll restrict our discussion to lady breasts here, since with men, there usually isn't any *there* there to bind—unless you've got man boobies, a.k.a. manneries, in which case, bind away!

Breast bondage, unlike most other forms of bondage, is primarily an aesthetic, rather than a restrictive, pursuit—after all, it's not like a rope bra is going to prevent you from going anywhere (except, perhaps, out in public). Sure, there's an aesthetic element to *any* kind of bondage (especially if you're a master in the art of **Japanese rope bondage**), but when it comes to lassoing the twins, you pretty much do it for the view. That said, this practice is not entirely without fringe benefits: Breast bondage done right can feel really good, and oddly comforting, too—like a **massage** bra. Plus, some women find that the bondage makes their breasts, and especially their nipples, extra sensitive. (So watch what you're doing with that **nipple clamp**!) Breast bondage is also key to **suspension** play, though that should NOT be a concern—or a goal—of beginners.

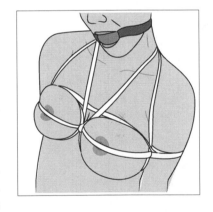

There are copious tata tying tricks, most of them too complicated to explain here. Some focus on breast exhibition (e.g. the "presentation rope shelf") while others are more about binding and hiding (think Gwynnie in *Shakespeare in Love* or Hilary Swank in *Boys Don't Cry*—the patron saints of breast bondage); **Saran Wrap** or **bondage tape** come in handy for this kind of plain tube-top-esque binding. Some rope methods require at least a C-cup to work properly, while others are easier to maneuver if you're working with a little less in the mammary department (good for the fellas, too!). Some **BDSM** enthusiasts claim to be turned on by the color purple in the context of breast bondage (wrapping multiple times around each breast so they almost look like disembodied eggplants), but you should consider it a major WARNING sign that the girls are being deprived of oxygen and could suffer nerve and tissue damage. To explore a decent beginner's range of breast bondage options, check out Jay Wiseman's excellent *The Erotic Bondage Handbook*. And as with any form of restraint, abide by the **bondage safety** guidelines.

Of course, if all this sounds too much like hard work, you could always invest in a pre-made body or chest **harness**—consider them the automatic cars of the breast bondage world. Or just try the super simple **D.I.Y.** rope harnesses outlined in the **harness** entry: so quick and easy to learn, even the butter-fingered could master them.

## bondage, casual

Casual bondage is just what it sounds like—the bondage equivalent of a one-night stand or booty call. Except instead of meeting at a random dive bar, you probably hooked up at a BDSM **club**, a **play party**, BDSM-related **online personals**, or a set-up thanks to a mutual friend in the **scene**. And frequently, casual bondage encounters end in masturbation, or even no happy ending at all (see **nonsexual BDSM**). Which is not to say they're without risk—after all, you're letting a complete stranger tie you up and possibly **whip** or **flog** you. You would, therefore, be well advised to indulge in such play with someone who comes with a personal recommendation, or at least someone who has a rep to protect in the scene—the latter is kind of like eBay's self-regulating "power seller" scheme, except you're trading in kink instead of collectibles. Just don't leave home without your **safeword**. See also **bondage safety, clubs, play parties**.

## bondage, endurance

1) Bondage that's meant to feel uncomfortable as well as restrictive, i.e. the opposite of sensual bondage (see **bondage [sensual]**). Endurance bondage should be practiced for very limited periods of time, and is for *advanced players only*, i.e. not you. A.k.a. punishment tie.

2) Tying up your partner and forcing them to watch the entire Miley Cyrus oeuvre (including "Hannah Montana").

## bondage, hair 🖎

The use of one's tresses (often in a ponytail) as part of a restraint system (or just as a means of steering the **sub** in the right direction, à la **Christian Grey**). For instance, a ponytail may be connected to a cord which is then tightly secured to a **D-ring** (perhaps one that is attached to an ankle **cuff**, a **dungeon** floor, even the external end of a **butt-plug** hook) so that the bound person's head is forced back and must remain that way for the duration of play. Whatever you do, don't sneeze! A.k.a. hair tie.

## bondage materials 🐾

See **bondage tape**, **chains**, **cuffs**, **rope**, **Saran Wrap**, and **tie**. Steer clear of scarves, household twine, and thin rope—the knots will tighten with stress ("stress" being a euphemism for "your partner writhing around in torturous ecstasy") and will be hard to undo in a pinch. Plus, the thinner bindings will cut into the skin and can cut off circulation or cause nerve damage. Also, no **cable ties**. And as for duct tape, it can take off hair and skin—so play nice and always duct tape *over* clothing. See also **bondage safety**.

## bondage mittens

The boxing gloves of the **BDSM** world—except they're not intended for aggressive violence, but rather passive submission. Plus, they're thumbless. (Other versions look more like the flat loofah mitts **massage** therapists use at spas.) Have your partner put them on you and you'll suddenly realize how helpless you are when you can't type, hitchhike, or bite your nails. Helpless and yet sexually liberated! Often available with handy **D-rings** for further restraint. A.k.a. bondage mitts.

## bondage, object 🐾

Restraining some*one* to some*thing*, like a chair or a bed. The challenge with this is to make sure that tugging won't result in (a) tightening the bondage around the limb, and (b) the object falling over on top of them. For this reason, your safest beginner bet is to stick with restraining someone lying on a bed *to* that bed: They'll be in a comfortable position, they won't fall should they faint or trip or get tired, and, assuming there's no earthquake, the bed isn't going anywhere. **Made-for-play** cuffs often come with straps that can be tied or Velcroed around sturdy bed-posts, -frames or -legs; if not, they should at least have **D-rings**—loop some rope through these rings, wrap the two tails around the post a few times, and finish with a bow **knot**. Sportsheets' "Under the Bed" restraints, available at most sex shops, include two pairs of Velcro cuffs, each attached via snap hooks to a long, adjustable strap that fits under any mattress, so you can quickly and easily secure all four limbs in a spread-eagle position without needing the right length of rope, knot knowledge, or a secure post; the downside of these is that Velcro cuffs can be weaseled out of fairly easily, and the hooks are fairly cheap, making them less than ideal for heavy tugging.

If you have the time and the inclination, rope is much more secure—plus, it's got that whole **D.i.D.** (damsel in distress) aesthetic. There are innumerable options with rope, but here are two quick and easy methods to master:

1. Take about 10 to 15 feet of rope and tie two limbs together with a "rope **cuff**" (see that entry for details); then wrap the two ends of the rope, or the "tails," around a bed-post, -frame or -leg a few times, and tie with a bow **knot** if out of reach of the bottom (a square knot if within their reach, which is harder for them to undo).

2. For securing a single limb in one place (i.e. for spread-eagled position), start coiling the middle of the rope around one wrist or ankle three or four times, wrapping evenly so the rope doesn't bunch or overlap. Tie the two ends in a "granny **knot**" against the cuff (see entry for details), then take the knot's two ends and loop them underneath the cuff coils in opposite directions (this will prevent the coils from cinching when tugged upon). Or, before you tie the granny knot, cross the two tails so they run perpendicular to the wraps in opposite directions, then tuck them underneath the cuff coils until they come out under either side of the cuff and *then* tie the granny knot. In either case, wrap the two long remaining tails around the post a few times and tie with a bow **knot** if out of reach of the bottom, a square knot if within their reach.

## bondage, predicament

A form of **edge play** bondage wherein the bound one is forced to choose between a limited number (usually two) of equally uncomfortable positions; in order to ease one aspect of their "predicament," they end up making another aspect of it worse. For example, a **bottom** may be bound so that they are forced to choose between standing on tippy-toe or having their genitals tugged on. Pretty sneaky, sis!

## bondage safety 🖐

Keep all your extremities intact with these eleven bondage do's and don'ts:

1. There's no rule that says bondage should be uncomfortable—it's not like you're illegally detaining someone at Guantanamo. In fact, if something hurts (and not in a good-**pain** kind of way), stop immediately. You should be playing with drama, not death—think David Copperfield rather than Houdini. And leave the **endurance bondage** to the experts.

2.  If something turns blue, purple, numb, or cold to the touch, it is the body's cry for help (and oxygen): *Release the bondage immediately!* The **top** should check for these symptoms frequently, and the **bottom** should report any numbness or tingling immediately.

3.  Distribute the tension evenly over a wide area of flesh with the appropriate materials. Good = padded cuffs, several coils of thick **rope** tied properly, **straitjackets**. Bad = a single coil of rope, silk scarves, stockings, twine, electrical cord, cable ties—all of which can cut off circulation and are a bitch to untie.

4.  The more of a newbie you are, the briefer the bondage should be. Start out at 10 to 15 minutes, tops—less if you spot any symptoms listed in #2, obviously. Once you've worked on your craft and form, you can keep a healthy, willing play partner in a comfortable position for up to an hour.

5.  Don't start something that you can't finish: You need to be able to release someone quickly and safely in case of an emergency (see #2). So make sure you have **medical scissors** handy for cutting bondage; use the kind of rope **knots** that are secure but can be untied quickly; use **panic snaps** for standing positions in case of fainting; and keep keys for locks nearby. Actually, you don't want to end up nervously fumbling with your keys during an emergency the way victims in horror movies always do when the serial killer is right around the corner, so why not stick with heavy-duty Velcro?

6.  To avoid nerve or circulation damage, always leave a finger's width between skin and the ties that bind. And when binding two body parts together (e.g. wrist-to-wrist), leave a little space between those parts, too.

7.  Bondage doesn't have to be actually inescapable (e.g., your captive could probably undo two Velcro cuffs that are hook-snapped together). But while you don't want the bondage too tight, you definitely want it to be secure and stable. If it's too loose, it can cause chafing. Plus, if your captive is struggling against their bonds and they suddenly come undone, they might hurt themselves or you—an accidental punch in the face is neither kinky nor cool.

8.  Never restrain someone by the neck.

9.  Agree on a **safeword** *beforehand*.

10. Don't ever abandon someone who's all tied up (you can *pretend* to abandon them for a bit of a **mindfuck**, but never actually let them out of your sight or earshot).

11. Don't ever agree to be tied up by a stranger you met on the internet (or a stranger you met anywhere, for that matter), anyone who fails the finger-to-nose sobriety test, or a vengeful ex. See also **safety kit**.

## bondage, self

It's not just for attention-starved illusionists anymore. Some people like to tie themselves up before getting off; the rest of us are left wondering, "So who's in charge of the **medical scissors**?" According to bondage pro Jay Wiseman of *The Erotic Bondage Handbook*, it's the number one kinky killer out there (a.k.a. "failed self-rescue mechanism" in the pathology reports). That's enough for us to say, *Avoid death by solo **edge play** and use the buddy system!* Unless, of course, your "self-bondage" is sitting on your dominant hand and wanking with the other.

## bondage, sensual

When the ties that bind feel pretty comfortable, actually—like you could settle in for a Julia Roberts flick and a tub of ice cream (though your **top** might have to spoon-feed you). The opposite of endurance bondage (see page 22).

## bondage tape

Soft, stretchy, reusable PVC tape that sticks only to itself (i.e. *not* to skin, clothes, back hair, etc.), typically sold in red or black. Did you ever wonder what office life might be like if nobody had gotten around to inventing Post-Its? Not nearly so pleasingly yellow or easily adhesive, that's for sure. And that's how we feel about bondage tape: Sure, people have been tying themselves up since the *Kama Sutra* without it (see **history of kink**), but was it ever this much fun? And because bondage tape binds only to itself, it doesn't get tighter once it's in place—plus, no need for knots! Oh yeah, and it's waterproof, too. Use it for binding, **gagging**, tying up, or **mummification** (see mummification illustration). See also **bondage safety**.

## bondage, verbal

When the only thing holding you down is a mild threat from your partner (said in a *murmur*, of course, if you're **Christian Grey**): *If you move an inch the cunnilingus stops now; If you open your eyes I'll start over back down at your toes; If you make a peep the Rabbit gets it*; etc. A.k.a. psychological bondage. See also **gags (mouth)**.

## bondage wheels

The human-sized rat-exercise wheels of the **BDSM** world—except instead of running inside the wheel, you're strapped to the outside, either facing inward for flogging or outward for sexual manipulation by passersby. It can also be a flat wheel, like a vertical table top: You are strapped to one side, so the visual effect is not unlike da Vinci's Vitruvian Man,

except you may be spun upside-down. This is not the kind of thing a mere dabbler in BDSM picks up one day at Home Depot; no, this large and expensive piece of **dungeon** equipment is for the serious pro only, usually one who has (a) a dungeon to begin with and (b) their own pay-per-view bondage site to make this a tax-deductible expense. Featured on said site would be photos and videos of the wheel in action, i.e. some person bound, **cuffed**, or **Saran Wrapped** to the contraption with their naughty bits hanging out as they're spun around by a perv with a Pat Sajak **fetish**. Whee! See also furniture and **Saint Andrew's Cross**.

## boots, fuck-me or otherwise

Requisite accessory for most kinky sex. A pair of boots can convey either power and dominance (oftentimes with lots of buckles and either uber-thick platform **heels**, a.k.a. shitkickers, or pointy stiletto daggers) or submission (usually with heels so high and delicate they're nearly impossible to walk around in).

Take the ballet boot (illustrated), which practically forces the wearer *en pointe* with only the skinniest of seven-inch heels for support. There are even boots designed to look like horse hooves which force dedicated **pony players** to walk on the balls of their **feet** only (look ma, no heels!)—they go great with

riding boots and tight riding breeches worn by the pony trainer. For bad cop fantasies, forget **handcuffs**: A pair of police boots *make* the **role-playing**. For general kink, the old standby is, of course, the thigh-high boot, designed to elongate the legs and thus accentuate sexiness. Great—indeed *essential*—for when you've invited a **submissive** shoe shiner or boot licker for snacks and **humiliation**. Browse at BootDungeon.com for ideas.

# bottom 🐾

1) (*Noun: the bottom*) The one being "done to" in any **BDSM** scenario (the **top** does the doing). The term bottom derives from the gay male community, wherein "bottom" means "receptive one," i.e. the partner being penetrated. In BDSM, the bottom won't *automatically* be penetrated; won't necessarily be *literally* on the bottom, à la missionary sex; and doesn't have to be in a particularly **submissive** mood either (though the two frequently go hand in hand, kinda like Scientology and vacant stares). Rather, the bottom is simply the one receiving the orders. This usually involves receiving some sort of stimulation too, whether that "stimulation" takes the form of a **whip**, a **flogger**, a teasing tongue (physical and/or verbal), 30 feet of **rope**, a pinkie finger, **nipple clamps**, or a 12-inch silicone **dildo** (see **strap-ons**). A bossy or non-submissive bottom may bark out (or purr) instructions to their top while being slapped upside the butt cheek (see **topping from the bottom**, and consider an attitude adjustment).

**Bottoming** doesn't have to be a permanent state: Partners frequently trade places from one session to the next, or even—for particularly versatile **switch**-hitters—mid-sesh. That said, some kinksters (especially those deep into the **scene**) consider their top/bottom role to be a fixed state—in fact, their role might even trump their sexuality (e.g. a gay female bottom may not mind playing with a man, so long as he's a top). Bottoms tend to far outnumber tops in the BDSM community, probably because it's the easier role to learn, especially for newbies (it's not your fault you don't know what to do, you're just a poor little bottom waiting for your top's instructions!). And given a choice, who *wouldn't* rather receive than give in bed? (C'mon, be honest…) However, bottoms who take this attention for granted tend to be frowned upon in the community (see **do me queen**). After all, if a bottom is pantsed in a forest and there's no one there to spank them… .

Besides, being a bottom isn't all free orgasms and flowers: Some tops will give you orders to focus the attention on them—they'll make you shave their legs, lick their **boots**, clean their toilets, perform non-reciprocated oral sex, etc. See also **body service**, **bottoming**, **service kink**, and **submission**.

2) (*Proper Noun: Bottom*) Actor-fool character in Shakespeare's *Midsummer Night's Dream* who is turned into an ass by a fairy and grows to quite like his new role; when he eventually comes to, he realizes he has had "a most rare vision." In the same vein, many BDSM bottoms like to be made asses of, either figuratively (by being humiliated) or literally (by engaging in pony play).

## bottoming

Being the **bottom**.

## boy toys

1) Props and tools designed with the male anatomy in mind. While there are certainly plenty of equal opportunity accessories for both men and women looking to get their kink on—**butt plugs**, **anal beads**, **strap-on dildos**, **nipple clamps**, **rope**, and **floggers**, to name a few—these days it's understandable why many men might think toys just aren't for them: Get caught in an earthquake while visiting a sex shop and you'd be buried beneath a never-ending avalanche of women's vibrators! Not that that's necessarily a bad thing. But it can leave the guys feeling a little left out—or worse: feeling like using toys makes them unmanly sissies.

   Fortunately, designers of high-end, well-made toys are making men a priority, producing plenty of cool gadgets for the penis in your life. There are some beautiful **butt plugs** (did you ever think you'd hear those words together?) designed with the prostate gland in mind, like the elegant Billy massager by LELO. There's a rainbow of **cock rings**, from the kinder, gentler, vibrating **love rings** for couples to the scarier metal cock-and-ball contraptions that look like something straight out of the *Saw* franchise. For a man's alone time, he can shop for masturbation sleeves, the most famous (and perhaps silliest) being the Fleshlight; the Japanese Tenga line of products is a funkier option. And the Koa Ring vibrator can be looped around a penis. But we would also posit that there's absolutely nothing wrong with a fella turning his girlfriend's vibrator on himself. In fact, we often thought **Christian Grey** would have benefited from trying out some of the items in his treasure chest on his own person.
2) The human male playthings of **doms** (and Madonna).

## branding

Body art created by burning the shit out of your skin. Kinky **slaves** are very into getting branded as property, a fact that is usually blamed on the popularity of the *Story of O* (*hello?* Fiction, people!). Branding was once just the realm of kinksters and tough motherfuckers (think jail, army, bike gangs), but these days teens who hate their parents are getting in on the third-degree burn action, too. See also **body modification** and **edge play**.

## breath control

See **autoerotic asphyxiation** and **erotic asphyxiation**.

## bukkake

A form of erotic humiliation, popularized by Japanese porn—and, later, by Howard Stern—in which a group of people take it in turns ejaculating on one lucky volunteer (usually on their face or in their mouth). In lesbian bukkake porn, a group of ladies will female-ejaculate on the piggy in the middle. One of the reasons bukkake became such a motif in Japanese porn (besides the obvious one: *It's Japanese porn*) is that Japanese law bans the depiction of penetration—it has to be blurred out—and thus the porn mongers learned to get creative with the whole "money shot" thing. In Japan, it turns out that censorship is the mother of invention. See also **tamakeri**.

## bullet vibrators

Miniature **vibrators** shaped more like an elongated egg or a symmetrical OB tampon than an actual bullet. Typically 1 to 2 inches long and less than 1 inch across, these vibes *can* be used on their own—for external stimulation only—but they're much more commonly employed to add vibrations to something else: a **butt plug**, a cock **ring**, a **dildo**, a **harness**, **nipple clamps**, etc.

Cordless bullets with watch batteries give you freedom of mobility, but the batteries can be expensive and tend to run out quickly (though here's a handy hint: Buy the batteries at sex stores, where they tend to be much cheaper than at watch stores). Bullets with regular battery packs usually give you more control options and come with a belt clip, but there are some drawbacks: The cord can easily get tangled between two moving bodies, there's always a temptation to tug on the cord (which risks damaging the vibe), and regular batteries, though cheaper than watch batteries, can wear out the vibe motor faster.

But best of all is a *rechargeable* bullet vibrator with a *wireless* remote control, like the Lyla 2. By the way, if you do want to use a bullet vibe internally, check out the Honi Mini Vibe—its attached loop means you can insert it vaginally and then pull it out (not for anal use, however). See also **remote control toys**.

## bullwhips

See **whips (single-tail)**.

## butt plugs 🔌

These are small or, if you're feeling brave, not-so-small **dildos** designed specifically for rear entry—i.e. they have a flared base, which means they won't get sucked in. (Because that is one E.R. visit you do not want to make, Obamacare notwithstanding.)

We know the name isn't exactly appealing, but trust us: If you've ever enjoyed a well-lubed pinkie in the behind—if you've ever even *entertained* the notion of enjoying it one day—you can handle a butt plug. You insert the plug during either sex or masturbation, then you pretty much just get on with your business and enjoy its company.

The anal area is chock-full of nerve endings just dying for some attention. And a butt plug can do that for you—filling you up, giving your sphincter something to contract around, and raising all-over goose bumps when it's finally removed (you *know* you know that feeling). Either way, "filled up" is a gender-neutral diversion no matter what your sexual orientation—and, no, a guy can't make his anal nerve endings go on strike by voting Republican. Plus, for women, getting filled up back there during vaginal penetration can cause a knock-on effect, causing the penis or dildo in the front door to stimulate her in brand-new places.

You've got to start small with a little finger and then work up to an inanimate object, *but only one designed specifically for the tush*. As with any toy, go for safe, hygienic materials (like silicone), quality design, and durability. The Little Flirt is a good start for both guys and gals. As you get more comfortable with the idea, you can graduate to larger plugs, or rippled plugs, or even vibrating plugs. And if you really want to kink things up, consider a plug with horsetails or feather plumes sticking out the end. And you thought *your* Halloween costume went the extra mile.

By the way, some butt plugs are designed specifically for men: the Aneros is white and medical looking and was originally manufactured to relieve congested prostate fluid (sexy, we know), but it had serendipitous side effects because of the way it moves in response to the ass muscles relaxing and contracting. Others are more stylish: the Bob by LELO would look right at home in the pages of *GQ* magazine. The Tano by PicoBong is colorful and simple—almost athletic looking. Or, for the kinky billionaire in your life, the Earl by LELO comes in stainless steel ($1,590!) or 24K gold plate ($2,590!!!)—see the Luxe collection pictured on the back cover. Hey, if spending an entire paycheck on a butt plug makes you feel more comfortable exploring your tush, go for it.

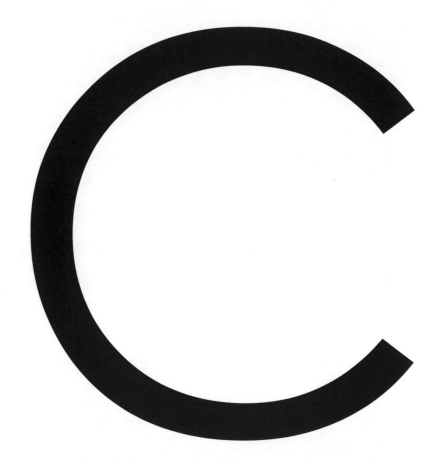

## cable ties

Something that should *never* be used during **BDSM seshes**—unless, of course, you're just using them to organize the cords of all your plugged-in electric **vibrators**. While it's never explicitly stated in *Fifty Shades of Grey*, the implication of Christian Grey buying cable ties from the hardware store where Anastasia works is that he's planning on using them as restraining devices for ankles and wrists. Terrible, novice, irresponsible, bad, bad idea! Did we mention this is a bad idea? Plastic cable ties can cut, cause nerve damage, and leave scars. What you want to use instead are purpose-made **cuffs** or, if you know how to tie and knot properly, then soft, thick **rope**.

## canes

Like walking sticks, except they're much narrower, flexible, usually (preferably) without a curved handle, and meant for whipping instead of leisurely strolls. Canes are the Powerpuff Girls of the **BDSM** world: Don't be deceived by how delicate and innocent they look, because they will kick your ass (literally). A cane immediately instills the holder with authority, like a kinky (or kinkier) version of the school teacher's pointer. Even if you take your **role-playing** lightly, you should take using a cane very, very seriously. These intense flagellation tools are usually made of rattan, fiberglass, Derlin, or bamboo (though bamboo breaks easily and should be avoided). Because canes are so narrow, light, and stiff, their sting is super strong and hurts *a lot*...more than most whippings. Experts use 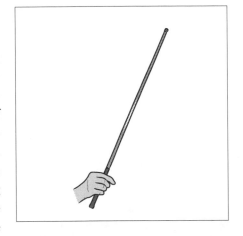 strokes that start in the shoulder and follow through the elbow and wrist, but if you're not the Roger Federer of Whipledom, then limit your stroke to a simple wrist-flick—the cane is much easier to control this way. All the **flagellation** safety rules are in play and then turned up to eleven when it comes to caning: Your **sub** needs much more recovery time between strokes; you should limit blows to the fleshiest parts of the buttocks and thighs only (forget about the upper back!); and no fancy Zorro moves—just a straight-down snap. A.k.a. rod, switch. See also **crop (riding)**.

## cats (or cat o' nine tails) 🐾

Multi-tailed whips much like **floggers** but with a slightly longer handle and *braided* "tails" knotted at the ends. (The ones specifically called cat o' nine tails have, you guessed it, nine tails!) They're probably called cats because of the clawing sensation they deliver (but don't ask us why the tails aren't then called claws) and were originally intended for the severe punishment of naughty sailors by captains of the British Royal Navy centuries ago. Cats made for BDSM purposes today are much more user- (and recipient-) friendly. Still, braided (and knotted) tails hurt more than unbraided ones, and round braids hurt more than flat ones. Work your way up to cats only after you've mastered floggers. And you can only really master floggers after you've read more on **BDSM** than this book has to offer (like the book *SM 101* by Jay Wiseman). See **flagellation** for more important safety information.

## catsuits

Skin-tight, body-conscious jumpsuits usually made of shiny latex or PVC, sometimes leather or Spandex. Originating in the Batman comics of the late '40s, the Catwoman catsuit has morphed into various real-life iterations over the past several decades, from the '60s sparkly version worn by Julie Newmar on the Batman TV show, to what most would consider the "authentic" version worn by Michelle Pfeiffer in Tim Burton's *Batman Returns*, to the simple, sleek style featured in the 1996 French flick with a cat-burglar subplot, *Irma Vep*, to the more guido bikini-top number donned by Razzie-award winner Halle Berry, to the latex sheath worn by Anne Hathaway in *The Dark Knight Rises* (apparently Obama was a fan). We wouldn't recommend wearing one to the office, but if you can squeeze yourself into a catsuit for a little Gotham **role-playing** or a serious Halloween party, more power to you. They retail anywhere from 25 bucks for the plastic versions that'll look only slightly better than a Glad trash bag, to close to a grand for custom-made jobbies that'll look like a million bucks. Seriously, all the **fetish-wear** enthusiasts insist that if you're going to go catsuit, go custom-made. Try WinterFetish.com or Baroness.com for your own personal take on the classic costume. Don't forget to request a zipper crotch if genital stimulation or peeing is important to you. See also **bodystocking**.

## CFNM

Short for "clothed female, naked male"—a fantasy, **fetish**, or porn genre with a distinctly straight male following. There are two kinds of CFNM: humiliation (man is caught masturbating or forced to strip by female doctor/coach/porn director) and exhibitionism (bachelorette parties, flashers). See also **CMNF**.

## chains

While you can't make any pretty knots when you put Alice in chains, they do offer a certain *je-ne-sais-quoi* when it comes to **bondage**—the punk-meets-Houdini vibe, the feel of cold metal on skin, the clanging, **dungeon**-esque sound they make as you writhe around trying to "escape." (Yeah right, like you'd want to be any place but here right now.) Heavy chains can be used to attach **cuffs** to bedposts or to each other or to ceiling hooks for **suspension** bondage and standing positions (remember **Anastasia**'s first **Red Room of Pain** session in *Fifty Shades*?); smaller chains that look more like necklaces are the norm on **nipple** and **cock-and-ball torture** devices. Then there's chain-related **fetish wear** (mostly for her): bras, thongs, and negligees made out chain mail (not the forwarded email kind)—perfect for that knight-in-see-through-armor fantasy.

## chastity devices

1) Lockable garments designed to prevent the wearer from having sex, masturbating, and/or becoming erect. Depending on the context, the wearer may or may not be down with said device. Chastity belts date back to at least 1400, when wives might have worn them while their husbands fought wars and hunted for bacon. Then, in the Victorian era, men got their, er, come-uppance when masturbation suddenly fell out of favor, and children and teens (especially the salami slappers) were forced to sleep in torturous chastity devices. These days, the padlocked undies industry is mostly underwritten by kinksters, who recognized the devices' potential as a **bondage** accessory.

The devices sold at **BDSM** outlets are designed for long-term wear (there goes that midday wank) and come in two basic styles: cages that enclose his twig and berries (preventing erections while allowing urinal visits) and shields that run between the legs, covering the naughty bits (mostly hers). The latter usually have some kind of built in-mechanism allowing the wearer to answer nature's call. And while leather and metal are the most common materials for these devices, they can also be found in plastic if, say, you want to get your **sub** past **airport security** while making sure they don't join the mile-high club on their next business trip (but don't blame us when they get randomly selected for a TSA rub-down and miss their flight). Some chastity devices even attach to genital piercings, if you're the dead-bolting type. As to *why* you might want to go all medieval like this? Think of it as long-term foreplay to a kinky domination **scene**

—there's nothing like an all-day reminder that you can't get off to prep you for some big-time begging that night. A.k.a. chastity belts. See also **humiliation**.

2) Religious right daddies (*not* kink **daddies**) who enforce their daughters' lapsed virginity pledges with shotguns.

3) Stuffed animal *tableau vivant* on one's bed (women); bed sheets depicting a favorite superhero (men).


## Christian Grey 🐾

The billionaire/romantic lead/**dom** of the *Fifty Shades of Grey* trilogy. His "crack whore" mother didn't love him enough (e.g. she allowed somebody to use his chest as an ashtray before she kicked the bucket) so now to get his rocks off he has to tie up women who look like her and then spank the shit out of them (a fact that many kinksters *without baggage* take issue with). But deep down, Grey's got a heart of gold. You shall know him by his steely grey gaze and the ubiquitous smirk lingering at the corner of his mouth.


## clamps 🐾

Pinchers (besides your fingertips) to place on naughty bits. Popular models include wood or plastic clothespins, tweezer clamps (specially made adjustable rubber-tipped clips that look like, you guessed it, tweezers), and even "chip clips" (for keeping your opened bags of Baked Lays fresh). Clamps are cheap, easy to come by, and completely silent (assuming the wearer doesn't yelp when you put them on or take them off). The idea here is constant stimulation, ranging from a gentle erotic reminder to full-on erotic **pain**. Don't you remember when Johnny pinched you really hard in 6th grade, but you kinda liked it 'cause you had a crush on him? Same diff. And once the clamps are off, the newly liberated bits will be super sensitive and/or slightly sore for a while, which is a good thing if you're into it.

The most popular resting places for clamps are the gender neutral nipples (**nipple torture**); a man's scrotal *sack* (NOT the testes themselves!), penis, and perineum (**cock and ball torture**); and a woman's outer labia (**cunt torture**). Other areas some people also find painfully erotic are the earlobes (NOT the upper ear cartilage!), lips, neck, chest/breasts, belly button, butt, arms, legs, and back. If we haven't mentioned a body part yet, chances are you shouldn't clamp it. And remember, teen makeout sessions aren't the only way to get hickeys: If you don't want something to bruise, don't clamp it too long or too tightly (or at all).

A quick search online and you'll find photos of bound subs wearing so many clothespins they look like human porcupines. But need we tell you the only thing that should have that many clothespins on it is a clothesline? First-timers should start with *one clip at a time*. Newbies can gradually work up to two at a time. And most people are quite happily pained to the max with no more than a handful at once (or at least in one area at once).

Test any clamps on yourself first, so you know just how (un)forgiving they are. Many are adjustable; with clothespins, you can even jimmy the spring or use rubber bands (on either side of the spring) to loosen or tighten their grip. Avoid alligator style clamps or anything that might break skin (no jumper cables!). Don't go pinching willy nilly—move slowly, deliberately, and gently. First take a bit of dry (non-lubricated, unlicked) flesh—remember, the bigger the area

pinched, the less intense the pinch—and apply the clamp, oh-so slowly increasing its grip around that bit of flesh to the desired tension. Give your pinchee time to acclimate to the sensation. Light grips may not hurt at all; tight grips will. If it doesn't become "good" pain for them after a few minutes (i.e. they haven't stopped clenching their teeth or their butt cheeks), slowly remove the clamp. If, however, your sub has relaxed into the sensation, you can move on 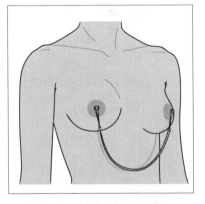 to other fun torture, like **teasing** oral sex! But don't forget about the clamps— unlike spanking or flogging, the sensation is constant, and if the clamped area doesn't become numb, the pain may get to be too much to bear.

The first time, don't exceed fifteen minutes. We'd say dabblers shouldn't *ever* exceed 30 minutes. (Experts say an hour is a good maximum play time for those who know they can handle it.) Remember, the erotic pain comes from cutting off circulation: You don't want gangrene setting in. So don't wear your clamps under a big sweater to a party, have one too many, then come home and pass out without taking them off.

If you don't want the clamped area to get numb (maybe your bottom doesn't deserve the break!), you can increase the pain by gently tapping or twisting the clamps. But don't go readjusting them or accidentally bumping them askew—that's crossing into "bad" pain territory. Once you're ready to remove the clamp(s), have your sub brace for the rush of blood about to flow back into the spot with the power of Niagara Falls: It's going to hurt. For that reason, taking off one at a time is a good policy. If your partner's a newbie or you're nice, you'll do this slowly and gently. If not, you'll slap the clamps off and hope you have soundproof walls. Dabblers should work only with clamps that remove easily, and not the metal clover-style clamps which actually pinch harder when tugged on. (And *never* connect clover clamps to a line connected to another object, especially if there's any chance the wearer may get bumped or fall down.) It's a good idea to synchronize this removal pain with some serious pleasure, like an orgasm. Talk about a **mindfuck**. See also **nipple suction cups**, **pumps (nipple)**, and **zippers**.


## clubs

**BDSM** or **fetish** clubs are for people who like to take their kink beyond the bedroom, and are typically named something like "Hellfire" or "Sweet Torments." What you'll find behind the leather rope varies widely: Some spots are pretty much just dance clubs with a strict dress code (think pleather, **leather**, et al—see **fetish wear**), while others boast an entire kinky jungle gym for guests to play on: **dungeon** equipment, vaulting horses (all the better to **flog** you on), **swings**, **slings**, etc. At the latter, you'll witness couples (or more) engaging in **scenes**, though penetrative sex is often frowned upon (as is flagrant masturbation at someone else's scene).

As a general rule, your pick-up behavior at any kind of fetish club should be even more restrained and respectful than it would be at a **vanilla** nightspot— you should be practicing something like work-related cocktail party etiquette. And while not all fetish clubs are dry affairs, drunk and disorderly behavior is a party foul. Thus, never touch someone without permission, even if they're wearing nothing but **chains** (no dry-humping the **gimp**, either), and never assume that anyone wants to play with you. Ask politely if you can join in, and be prepared for a no—many people attend clubs with a partner or group and aren't interested in working out their **daddy** issues with a complete stranger (they just want to be watched by one). Also, it's a big no-no to boss around someone else's **bottom**—you have to get their **consent** to do that, remember? (If a bottom is already "taken," you will need to ask permission of them both; but even if the bottom is a free agent, you still need their consent to step in.) And don't point and laugh, kids.

Finally, you should always, *always* dress the part—not only will you be a massive buzz kill if you show up in khakis and a button down (at fetish clubs, **suspension of disbelief** is a group effort), but you'll also feel like a complete twat. There's no need to don a **hobble skirt**, but you should at least wear some form-fitting latex (that goes for you dudes, too). You'll probably find clubs listed in your local alternative weekly—if that doesn't work, try posting a request on a kink-related message board for suggestions (see website suggestions in Appendix B). If you're looking for something more festive, many cities hold elaborate fetish balls (Google "fetish ball" for an event near you). The perfect occasion to break out those elbow-length leather **gloves**! See also **munch** and **play party**.

## CMNF

Short for "clothed male, naked female"—often found at strip clubs, **Christian Grey's Red Room of Pain**, and pretty much every **BDSM** site on the web. See also **CFNM**.

## cock and ball play

1) *(Without props)* Manual or oral sex on him.
2) *(With props)* Fun with **boy toys** like **love rings**!
3) *(With props and cruel intentions)* A friendlier, more palatable term for **cock and ball torture** (see immediately below).

## cock and ball torture (C.B.T.)

Erotically painful, humiliating, decorative, and/or sensual attention paid to the male genital protuberances in any number of ways, including **slapping**, flicking, waxing (**hair removal**), hot **waxing, icing, mentholating, teasing**, or applying any of the following devices: penis **pumps, e-stim** electrodes, **clamps**, latex strips for binding, **rope** for bondage, **cock rings** (worn around the penis or the penis and testicles), glans or head rings (worn during intercourse), cock (and ball) harnesses, cock cages or "the Gates of Hell" (usually a series of steel rings attached to a leather strap so your penis looks like one of the legs of the "Lost in Space" robot), snug **latex** bondage sheaths (like kinky socks) for the twig and/or two berries (some of which come with urine tubes for going long, and most of which aren't intended to be worn during sex), **ball stretchers** (which push the testicles away from the body), ball splitters (which separate the balls from one another), ball weights and parachutes (which tug on the balls with heavy objects dangling between the legs), permanent piercing (as opposed to play **piercing**, which generally isn't done to the genitals), leashes, **chastity devices**, urethral plugs or "sounds" (also known as penis plugs: yes, they go *in* your pee hole—see **medical toys**), and even C.B.T. boards to which the cock and balls can be strapped and worked on like Frankenstein's monster. These devices might make you want to start a "People for the Ethical Treatment of Penises" organization, but for many guys, just *mentioning* such tools gives them half-chub. Like with most **subspace**, the appeal is in the extreme vulnerability—and there's nothing more vulnerable than a bound man's sausage in the hands of a sadistic **top**.

While we don't have the space, skill, or stomach to tell you how to practice *all* of these activities safely (besides, our guinea pigs wouldn't let us come *near* their jammies with most of this stuff), please keep in mind a few points of safety before you start to delve and dabble (but *after* you've conducted further research on your own):

1. The penis and testicles are very delicate organs which can be permanently and severely damaged without a lot of force. So please go slowly and work up gradually.
2. Don't bend, twist, squeeze, or yank his (or your own) genitals.
3. Never attach anything that can't be quickly and easily removed.
4. Genital bondage (a penis rope harness, for example) should never be attached to another object, especially a moveable one (like a door or a pet).
5. Never use any attachment where sudden movement (if the wearer gets bumped or falls) might give him an inadvert penis- or ball-ectomy. (For example, the dreaded "Humbler" is a locking testicle press whose wings rest *behind* the back of the thighs, keeping the wearer on all fours or hunched over. One wrong move and you can kiss your dreams of future kids goodbye. Though a lucrative career in eunuchry might be a possibility.)

For all these reasons, we think you should think of this as "cock and ball *play*" (as it's also known), since it's helpful for beginners to approach C & B attention as more playful than painful. For instance, rather than any of the more sinister items above, you may prefer a couples **love ring**, which is anything but torturous. Whatever you go for, please see its dedicated entry for specific safety information on that item.

## cock rings

Rings or straps made just for the penis and testicles. Traditionally, a cock ring is meant to strap around a man's penis and behind his balls so that the balls sit in front of the cock ring, though some men prefer to place the ring just around the base of the shaft. Some set-ups come with two rings, one for the whole package and one for just the shaft; others come with multiple rings that run along the shaft; still others have one ring for the whole package, another ring for the shaft, *and* a separate ring for the balls.

Because blood flows into the penis at its center and flows out through veins closer to the surface, the ring can restrict the outgoing supply without affecting the incoming. This can lead to harder, longer-lasting, and more sensitive erections, though some men will find that the ring *really* affects their sensitivity, causing them to come even sooner, thus overriding the longer-lasting benefit. If the ring is too tight and restricts the urethra, it can make ejaculation painful, or even impossible during orgasm, thus forcing the semen up into the bladder— what's known as retrograde ejaculation or injaculation. (Tantric sex devotees like Woody Harrelson do this on purpose, even without the cock rings, though we would NOT recommend it.) Even if it's sized just right, some guys won't notice any difference while wearing a cock ring…except for how *fabulous* their dick looks all dressed up.

While cock rings come in any number of non-threatening materials (like stretchy Cyberskin, jelly rubber, nylon, and silicone— we'd recommend the non-toxic and easily cleanable silicone), the materials of choice among the BDSM crowd are leather, rubber, aluminum, chrome, and steel. And while you can certainly buy them in pink or decorated with cute little animal faces, in the kink world the more it looks a medieval dungeon device, the better: think punk-rock metal studs, chains, ball-separating straps, **vibrators**, and hanging weights. It ain't called **cock & ball *torture*** for nothing.

That said, we don't think you should take the term literally. For newbies, that means no solid metal rings, unless you'd like to have one removed with bolt cutters at the emergency room. If you've sized it incorrectly, you won't be able to lose your erection, even when you're no longer in the mood. (That may sound like a dream now, but it's not.) So to be safe, go for a basic leather, pleather, or Neoprene cock ring with adjustable snaps, Velcro, **D-rings**, or a bolo-style closure. These kinds of rings are easy to don even if you're already hard, you can experiment with different levels of constriction, and they can be removed faster than you can say, "Is it supposed to be turning blue like this?"

If for some reason you think that "breaking the circle" is cheating, then try a rubber ring that can be easily stretched off with some **lube**. And if you decide to throw all caution to the wind and go metal? First, know that we think you're making a big mistake...huge! Second, follow JT Stockroom's instructions for sizing: measure the circumference around your erect penis and testicles (at the base, behind the scrotum), and then divide by 3.1 to get your absolute *minimum* ring diameter. Add a bit of **lube** to your bits, and before you get excited, pull your scrotal sack through first, followed by your testicles and then your penis (you'll probably have to do a little penile oragami to get it through). If you're having trouble removing it later, try icing your fella before heading to Urgent Care. And don't come crying to us.

For all you romantics, peaceniks, and yoga enthusiasts out there who find the above a bit too difficult to process, there are **love rings**—penile accessories that are a little more *giving*, a little less intimidating. The grip will likely be pretty light, especially if he wears it around the shaft only. The rings can feature little nubbins along the entire surface, which may gently stimulate her clitoris and/or vulva (just make sure you buy one that is **phthlate**-free). But even more exciting are the vibrating versions. We know: Vibrating clitoral stimulation during intercourse? Now, *that's* sex the way Mother Nature intended it! Try the Tor 2 or the remote-controlled Oden 2—they're waterproof, rechargeable, powerful, and made of body-safe silicone (both are pictured on the back of this book).

Whatever kind of ring you've got on, don't wear it for more than twenty minutes at a time—and less than that if it starts to feel uncomfortable. Better if the pain you're feeling is coming from your **top** and not your cock ring—at least until you get to know your penis better. A.k.a. **love ring**, penis ring. See also **ball stretcher**.

## collars

Literally: Just like Fido's, but for you. Metaphorically: A symbol of the **power** exchange between you and your partner. Fashionably: The kink version of the leather wrist bands all the rockers and wannabes wear. As with dog collars, some are studded black leather while others are hot pink and bedazzled (and some are literally dog collars, repurposed for kinky ends, though you're much safer off going with one designed for a human neck).

To avoid injury (or worse), you should always leave two fingers' width between neck and collar. And while many collars have **D-rings** attached for **leash** or **bondage** purposes, you should never *ever* restrain or hang someone by the

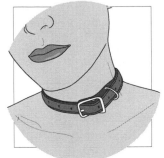

neck. (You'd be surprised...For as long as public pools have to remind bathers not to enter the water if they are experiencing diarrhea or have a communicable skin disease, advice ladies like us will continue to warn kinksters not to hang each other.) If you must walk your partner around to show them who's alpha, then make sure you lead by the front, to avoid pressure on the Adam's apple, etc.

For people heavily into the BDSM **scene**, a collar can take on the significance of a 1950s wedding band (a.k.a. ownership of property, see **collars [training]**). For others, it's simply a fetish **club** accessory or a bedside prop signifying who's **bottom** tonight. There are posture collars which keep the head up and restrict neck movement; actual neck braces for **medical** fantasies; and dramatic collars which creep up from under the chin and cover the mouth. As a general rule, newbies (that's you, Fluffy) should enjoy collars for their aesthetic rather than practical appeal. And don't ever *tie* something around your partner's neck to make a collar—stick with velcro and buckle fastenings that won't suddenly cinch their windpipe. Because there's nothing like an accidental choking to ruin a good bout of "Dog Whisperer" **role-playing**. For something playful and hip, check out the neoprene and velcro Speak No Evil Choker by PicoBong, available in black, hot pink, or blue. It's machine washable and "designed to stimulate a point where pressure meets pleasure." See also **cuffs** and **pony play**.

## collars, training

The class ring/varsity jacket/engagement ring of a budding **BDSM** relationship, given by a **dom** and accepted by their **sub**, sometimes as part of a collaring ceremony. Who says romance is dead? See also **slave**.

## communication

The cornerstone of any kinky **scene**. Because you can't just show up in a ski mask one night and hope that your new girlfriend has been secretly harboring a **rape fantasy**—something as heavy as that has to be figured out in advance. Lighter forms of kink—a **blindfold** or a pair of fuzzy **handcuffs**, say—can be negotiated on the fly, however, especially in a long-term relationship. (We like the simple, "I want to handcuff you tonight, Snookums," in your best **Christian Grey** sexy *murmur*.)

If you think you'd like to up the ante a bit (maybe you've been handcuffing each other since college and just attended your ten-year reunion together) but aren't sure where to start, try sharing your fantasies with each other during a **vanilla** sesh. In other words, use **dirty talk** to communicate. Take it in turns talking about something you'd like to try now, something you'd like to try eventually, or something you'd never ever want to try but are simply turned on by in your mind. The fact that you're having sex at the time will mean no awkward pauses (you can just fill them with moans); and if you're describing a story, there'll be less pressure for the fantasy to make narrative sense. Just a sentence or two here and there will get the point across.

If that doesn't give you any kinky ideas, browse a sex toy shop together (in person or online—see Appendix A for shopping advice), or invest in some **BDSM**-related erotica: The entire *Fifty Shades of Grey* oeuvre, *obviously*. But there's also the original *Fifty Shades of Grey* trilogy, Anne Rice's *The Claiming of Sleeping Beauty* series (turns out she doesn't just write vampire and Jesus novels), as well as anthologies like *Best Bondage Erotica*, *Best Fetish Erotica*, and *Sweet Life: Erotic Fantasies for Couples*. For a more how-to approach, try Violet Blue's *Ultimate Guide to Sexual Fantasy*. For a more popcorn-friendly activity, rent **Secretary**. Or, you know, you could always finish this book together. Hey, just an idea.

Some of you might be thinking that talking about sex this much is like dancing about architecture, or whatever it is that those hippies are always saying. But just because you have to plan for this kind of sex, doesn't mean it should be any less hot. Basically, you need to make the planning part of the fun, part of the foreplay: Once your imagination has been sparked, start exchanging dirty emails, texts, IMs, Gchat messages, and late-night phone calls about how the scene is going to go down (cutesy subject lines à la *Fifty Shades* entirely optional). Leave out books for each other with Post-Its marking the pages that caught your eye. Make a saucy to-do list and slyly show it to your partner under the table during drinks with friends. Surprise your partner with those props you've been ogling, instead of hoping they will read your mind and buy them for your birthday. The whole point of doing all this communicating ahead of time is so that you *can* lose yourself in the moment (instead of worrying, "Am I pressing too hard? Am I saying the right thing? Does this **gimp suit** make my butt look big?")

If the planning still feels duller than Excel spreadsheets or all that plot stuff between the sex scenes in *Fifty Shades*, then take consolation in this: The more you get into the kinky swing of things, the less communication a scene takes, and the more natural it feels. If you successfully negotiate a **spanking** scene, for example, and it turns out that you both love it more than *Cats*, then the next spanking scene will be a whole lot easier to set up. Eventually you'll get to know each other's kinky mood swings so well that you will be able to tell whether it's a good evening to suggest a bout of spanking. Basically, "communication" sounds clunky, awkward, and buzz-killing when we try to explain it in an entry like this, but on you, we think it'll work! A.k.a. negotiation (that's the "official" term for pre-scene communication). See also **aftercare**, **bondage safety**, **consent**, **dirty talk**, **safeword**, and **therapy**.

## consent

For those of you on the short bus (or on parole), consent is what makes the activities in this book legal. (Or at least, *more* legal: There are some pretty priggish sex **laws** on the books in many states, and there are some pretty priggish jackholes out there who like it like that. Yes, we're looking at you, Santorum. Your local **BDSM** organization should be able to tell you what's what—see Appendix B.) Consent should, therefore, come before anything else in this book, but we couldn't think of a word for consent that begins with the letter "A." A **bottom** is only a bottom if they consent to be a bottom—and they're not really a bottom unless their partner consents to be a **top**. (Because what are two bottoms going to do for fun—sit around blowing sunshine up each other's asses? "You are my all-knowing Master, I'm yours." "No, you're too wonderful to be anything but my god-like Mistress, how can I please you?" "No, how can *I* please *you*?"...) Sure, a scene may last for days, but it always begins with consent—and that consent may be withdrawn at any moment with the deployment of the **safeword**. See also **blanket consent**, **slave**, and **taken in hand**.

## contract

An agreement between a **dom** and a **sub** that covers the terms of a kinky relationship wherein the power play extends beyond a simple **scene** and is about ownership as well as control. There may be rules outlined about obedience, sleep, food, clothes, exercise, hygiene, and safety, to name a few, along with **hard limit**s or no-nos. For instance, **Christian**'s contract for **Anastasia** in *Fifty Shades of Grey* assured her there would be no fire play, **watersports**, **scat play**, **body modification**, **bloodplay**, **medical toys** or play, **breath control**, **e-stim**, bestiality or pedophilia (um, you—and about every serious kinkster alive—would think these last two items could have gone without saying). A sub may sign an actual contract, though it's not legally binding (thank you, 13th amendment). See the

**T.P.E.** entry for a complete description of full-time **D/s** relationships. See also **slave**, **taken in hand**.

## corsets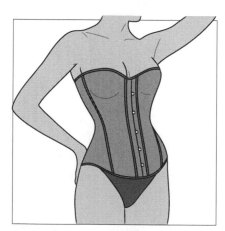

Tight-fitting, (mostly) female under-garments worn around the waist (and sometimes the bust and hips) to exaggerate curves. They lace up or hook together in the back, the sides, or the front. Some come with over-the-shoulder straps or garters, too. Corsets have been around for centuries, but those embraced by kink culture are usually those modeled after popular styles from the late 19th and early 20th centuries. Late Victorian era corsets, which usually ensconced the bosom, had elegant detailing, stiff structure, and an extreme hourglass shape. Edwardian era corsets usually began just under the bust, had a flat front and extended down past the hips, causing a forward-leaning posture, pushing the bust and bottom out, and thus creating the side silhouette of a full-figured "S." In those days, corsets were usually worn over a chemise and under a dress; modern fashion has embraced the corset as an acceptable outer-garment, either worn over a thin shirt as the upper part of a fancy gown worn to the Grammys, or alone, usually as a fuck-me/don't-fuck-with-me top.

The corset simultaneously represents female oppression and powerful female sexuality: Once a requirement for "proper" attire, the constricting and uncomfortable corset reflected a woman's refinement and good morals, while symbolizing her need for support; but with its exaggeration of the female figure, the corset also honors femininity, giving at least the modern wearer a sense of sexual strength. Its split personality makes it perfect for the dynamic **power plays** of **BDSM**: Are you a submissive Victorian lady tightly laced up in a corset who can hardly breathe, let alone move, who has broken the rules of polite society and is therefore deserving of corporal punishment? Or are you a strong, independent dominatrix who calls the shots (or even calls her own objectification) not unlike Madonna on any one of her international tours? As with **catsuits**, the best fitting corsets are custom-made.

*Extreme* corsetry involves "figure training," also known as "lacing": The corset is laced extremely snugly, and continually cinched ever tighter as it's worn over a long period of time, in order to actually create a severe hourglass figure in the person. It's body sculpting, or **body modification**, not unlike the Padaung women of eastern Burma who wear brass rings around their necks, the weight of which push their collarbones and ribcages down to create the appearance of really, really long necks.

For some of the coolest corsets around (and *the* most stylishly designed kink-related website in existence), visit LoveSickCorrectiveApparel.com. But if you just want to try one without making a huge financial investment, most sex toy shops have more affordable options. See also **body modification** and **hobble skirts**.

## costumes

If it's a uniform of some sort that's tight, revealing, and made of latex, there's a 99.99% chance it's a **fetish** outfit. However, you can certainly go for more realistic costumes by using things lying around the house (**D.I.Y.**-style), renting one from a non-fetish costume shop, or getting your hands on an authentic uniform (try eBay or industry supply shops). The idea is to get into character and find your **motivation** for a little **role-playing**, or at least for feeling like someone you're not: There's nothing like a naughty nurse's outfit to give you the confidence to finally poke your boyfriend with a lubed, **latex**-gloved, index finger. Other popular costumes (most of which come in handy latex versions) include: doctor, patient, priest, nun, military personnel, interrogator, vampire, Victorian, school marm, (Catholic) school girl/boy, cheerleader, governess, little kid/baby, police officer, Canadian mountie—basically anything that helps create or emphasize a certain sexual **power** dynamic. For something with a touch of class, check out the French Maid ensemble at LELO.com. And if you're feeling less than adventurous, know that wearing something just a little more sensuous than usual can help get you in the right mood for **play** (remember, **Ana** swapped her big T-shirts for some nice silk numbers). The Sussurra Intimate Apparel Collection fits this bill. See also **wigs**.

## couples rings

See **love rings**.

## C.P.R.

Cardiopulmonary resuscitation. Not to freak you out or anything, but if you're going to **top** or **dominate**, then you should probably know how to administer this emergency first aid procedure for reviving someone who has stopped breathing and is missing a pulse. But if you follow the safety advice in this book, avoid anything we label **edge play**, and think with your brain instead of your genitals, then you should never have to use C.P.R. And while we're at it, make sure your **safety kit** is fully stocked and within arm's reach. Better safe than sorry!

## crops, riding

Disciplinary devices for horses and "horses." However, even if you've never gotten on a real horse or gotten into **pony play**, you can enjoy the erotic benefits of this kind of rod. For one thing, it just looks good, and complements any outfit, whether you're wearing head-to-toe leather or just heels (okay, it *might* not work with Keds). You don't even have to wield it as an instrument of pain: If it lands on nary a bare buttock, the intimidating sound it makes as it slices through the air can nevertheless be threatening enough. Or simply use it as an extension of your hand, naughtily tracing their corners and curves—a constant reminder of how, at any minute, you *could* turn nasty. (Remember that disturbing scene from *Private Benjamin*...?) If you do indeed intend to turn nasty, some things to keep in mind:

1. Choose a crop that is 2 to 2.5 feet long with a triangular tip that's not too narrow.
2. You don't want the shaft *too* stiff, or *too* bendable, but just right: about 45 degrees of flexibility.
3. Crops are easy to control but they can give a biting sting, so start (and perhaps stay) soft. Many people like it simply as a gentle love-patting tool for frustrating the breasts and genitals, but remember the key word here is *pat*. Avoid any quick and heavy swings on these spots: Save those strokes for the fleshiest parts of the buttocks alone, and only if your little pony has requested

it. Reread the scene from the first **Fifty Shades** book, and do what Grey does ("This is not going to hurt. Do you understand?") with something like the Kookie Crop.

4. If you're afraid of leaving marks, you can get a crop with a silicone rather than leather tip for kinder, gentler beatings. For cute-as-a-button beatings (like birthday spankings), check out the leather and suede Just Desserts Cupcake Crop. Please see **flagellation** for more important safety info.

## cross-dressing

1) (*Sexual*) A transvestic **fetishism**. In other words, when a person (usually a hetero dude) dresses in the clothes typically associated with the opposite gender for sexual kicks (because it's naughty and/or humiliating). If you get your boyfriend to try on your thong one night when he's piss-pot drunk, it doesn't really count. If, however, you start to notice that all your best underwear is mysteriously disappearing from the wash along with those odd socks, and then you come home one day to find your boyfriend secretly admiring how good his ass looks in your "boy briefs" while he's got a raging boner—um, yeah, that counts. But don't go casting any stones: After all, *you're* the one wearing *boy* briefs because they make you feel sexy in the first place. Awwwww shit, bitch!

2) (*Not necessarily sexual*) Wearing clothing typically associated with another gender for any of the following reasons:
   a. You identify as that gender (though many transgendered folk would take exception to calling this "cross-dressing"—after all, they're just being themselves).
   b. You are making a political/sociological/fashion statement (19th-century French writer George Sand, a woman, dared to wear men's clothes not only as an act of rebellion highlighting the egregious female inequality of the time, but also as a way to gain access to the many places and experiences allowed only to men).
   c. You're simply more comfortable (it's way easier to ride a horse in slacks than a skirt).
   d. You're a drag queen or (less commonly) a drag king who exaggerates the "opposite" gender's typical style as a performative art (e.g. the huge sprayed hair, dramatic diva make-up, and to-die-for legs of Ru Paul).
   e. You just feel right in them, or perhaps you feel released from your strict gender shackles (e.g. the man who's happily married to his

female wife and simply likes to go to the movies with her while wearing her favorite DKNY dress and heels—we have a feeling we'd like this man).

3) (*Slang*) Urban dis for wearing two different brands or sports logos at once: "Excuse me, sir, but if I could call your attention to that cross-dressing maternal fornicator over yonder, you'll notice he is donning not only Tommy, but Bad Boy *as well*. How utterly gauche!"

## crotch rope

Rope tied around the groin area to put what is often called "delicious" pressure on the genitals and perhaps to assist in restraint. On women, the rope, which often begins in lengths around the waist, may be pulled in between the inner labia and/or around the outer labia; knots may be strategically placed over the clitoris; or fancy rope work can be done to further expose the clitoris. On men, the rope may be pulled around the penis and testicles or actually tied to them as a form of **cock and ball torture**. In all cases, the genital **bondage** my be part of a larger restraint system (like a body **harness**), or perhaps simply an anchor for two bound wrists. As with all bondage, especially *male* genital bondage, safety first! (See **bondage safety**.) Don't attach one end of the rope to his unit, the other to your hyperactive dog, and then play fetch. And avoid cutting off circulation—this is not an opportunity to give new meaning to the term *blue balls*. In fact, if you think this is something you might like to try out one lazy Sunday afternoon, we must insist you enlist the aid of one of the how-to books listed in the resources section in back (Appendix C). See also **Japanese rope bondage**,

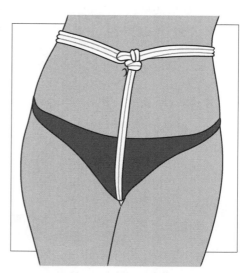

## cuddling

What you should always indulge in (twenty minutes minimum) after a good spanking or **sub-dom scene**. Hey, if **Christian Grey** can overcome his intimacy issues to do it, then so can you. Spooning works, too. See also **aftercare**.

## cuffs, ankle and wrist

If restraining someone by their wrists and ankles is the meat-and-potatoes of bondage, then **made-for-play** cuffs (sold at any sex toy store) are bondage's Hungry-Man frozen dinners: quick, easy, and surprisingly satisfying. Bondage cuffs are way safer than **handcuffs** and provide instant gratification—unlike **rope**, with its pain-in-the-ass learning curve. Most cuffs are made of either leather or nylon (for kinky vegans, e.g. Super Cuffs) and are often lined with faux fur, etc. (for comfort even during marathon seshes). And before you complain that faux fur is "not me" or "so last season," just *try* writhing around in a pair of police-issue handcuffs first. For real-world restraints that aren't a pain in the wrist, check out the surprisingly attractive institutional cuffs at MedicalToys.com. And for something a little more in line with the high-end *Fifty Shades* aesthetic, check out LELO's Etherea Silk Cuffs (on the back cover) and Sutra Chainlink Cuffs (on the front cover).

Bondage cuffs feature either buckles or Velcro (the former gives a stronger hold, the latter a quicker release and a sexy sound) and are fairly wide (at least two to three inches) to ward off the nerve damage that is a risk of traditional handcuffs. Speaking of risks: As with any form of bondage, the bottom should speak up as soon as he or she notices any numbness or tingling, and the top should allow for at least one finger's width between cuff and skin. And regular bondage cuffs should never be used for any kind of **suspension**—you need special equipment for that sort of advanced play (although you should *never* suspend someone from the wrists, no matter the gear). Bondage cuffs typically feature **D-rings** so that they can be tethered to each other, to bed posts, to chair legs, etc. And if you're still sleeping on your college futon? Most sex toy shops sell "Under the Bed" tethers that serve as makeshift bedposts. Another option is to attach the ankle or wrist cuffs to a **spreader bar**. For more self-contained bondage, just attach wrist to wrist and ankle to ankle. You can even attach bound wrists to bound ankles (either in front or back) for an instant **hogtie**! See also **bondage safety, collars, cuffs (grip), cuffs (rope), door jamb cuffs,** and **handcuffs.**

## cuffs, grip

A genius device, these leather wrist cuffs come with built-in handles so your **bottom** has something to grasp onto during the bondage. ("Get a grip, worm!") This reduces pressure on the wrists and helps prevent numbness (a few quick squeezes can get the blood flowing again). Plus, each grip cuff has two separate attachment points, meaning that even when the bottom lets go of the handle, the pull is distributed evenly. Great for standing bondage; not designed for **suspension play**.

## cuffs, rope

D.I.Y. ankle and wrist restraints you make with **rope**. The best place to start is wrist-to-wrist, with the palms facing each other. Lacing the fingers together will help create a natural gap between the wrists for breathing (or rather, circulation) room. Take about six feet of rope and center it over the two limbs you want to tie together. Wrap each end around both limbs several times (at least three or four), distributing the tension evenly over the skin and leaving a bit of room between the limbs so circulation does not get cut off (at least one and a half to two inches apart to allow for later cinching). When you've got only about a foot of rope left, twist the two ends around each other at a central point between the limbs (instead of on the side of one limb) to create an intersection with the rope. Then wrap those ends once or twice around the section of rope that's between the two limbs (you're now wrapping at a right angle to the initial binding, like a ribbon around a birthday present). Gently cinch the two ends to make everything evenly snug and tie them together with a square knot. (If there's enough space between the wrists, you can continue to wrap in opposite directions at right angles to the first set of coils until you run out of rope, and *then* tie the knot.) When you're finished, there should be enough room between skin and rope to easily slide a finger through. If you don't want your bottom nibbling their restraints, or you want them further restrained, use a longer length of rope (say, 10 to 12 feet) and then wrap the two long tails around the bed-post, -frame or -leg a few times and tie off using a bow **knot** if it's out of reach of your **bottom** (otherwise use a square **knot**). All of the above goes for ankles, too.

A popular Japanese technique is to tie the arms behind the back, with each hand extending toward the opposite elbow, creating a U shape with the arms. For this behind-the-back cuff, wrap the rope around the wrists. Since you won't be using the cinching method above, wrap a little more snugly, being extra careful to distribute tension evenly and still leaving a finger's width of room. Tie with a square **knot**. To help keep the hands up and out of the way of a spankable tush, use a longer piece of rope to begin with, and after you've tied the knot, separate the two dangling ends, pulling each end under one armpit, up and over the respective shoulder, and then back toward the nape of

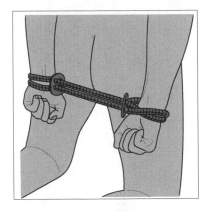

the neck to tie the ends together (never pull rope in front of the neck). Any rope that passes across the shoulders behind the neck for support is called a yoke **harness**. Someone wearing these kind of cuffs should never lie on their back, or they risk cutting off circulation.

If all of this sounds too labor intensive for you, you could just get a cheap pair of Love Rope Wrist Cuffs (pictured)—they're soft, adjustable, and remove all the guess work. But they can come loose and are easy to wiggle out of. Plus, there's no sense of accomplishment or pride in your own craftsmanship!

## cunt torture

Erotically **painful**, humiliating, **teasing**, decorative, and/or sensual attention paid to the female genitalia, in any number of ways, including **slapping**, flicking, waxing (**hair removal**), hot **waxing**, **icing**, **mentholating**, lightly whipping, **abrading**, or applying any of the following devices: **clamps**, **chastity belts**, **crotch ropes**, permanent piercings (as opposed to play **piercing**, which generally isn't done to the genitals), and **e-stim** electrodes. Most of this activity should be focused on the outer labia only, as the tissue of the clitoris and the inner labia is quite delicate and sensitive. And while the vulva is a tough cookie (especially compared to the delicate wafers that are the cock and balls), it can still crumble if you're not careful. As with any sexual "torture," it should be more figurative than literal, especially for beginners. You don't want to cut, burn, or otherwise **scar** this sacred space, you just want to tease the hell out of it and make it your **slave**. Also, never blow into her vagina (it can cause a fatal air embolism), never insert ice (it can damage delicate tissue) or **food** (it can cause an infection), and no poking around in there with anything that's been in her (or anyone else's) butt (again with the infection). A.k.a pussy torture.

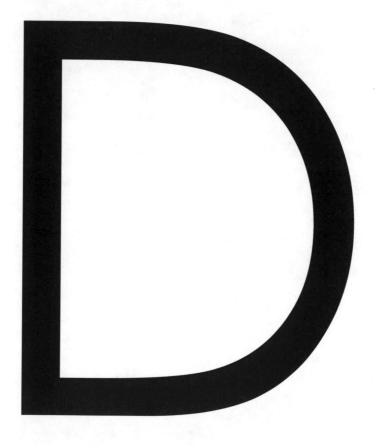

## daddy

Like a **master**, but more "nurturing"…more, you know, *paternal*. Daddies are typically gay men, though these days a lot of lesbians are getting in on the daddy game, too. Gay men in search of a daddy typically identify as "boy," while gay women i.s.o. the same may be either "boy" or "girl"—however, no actual age gap is required. Daddy play is not unheard of among straight players, though it's not nearly as common. And contrary to popular belief, serious baggage is not a prerequisite for het daddy-girl **role-playing**. On a final note, yelling out "Who's your daddy?" when you climax does not count as daddy play. A.k.a. **leather daddy**. See also **baby (adult)** and **mommy**.

## D.i.D. (damsel in distress)

A woman who has been "abducted" who is often bound, blindfolded, and/or gagged. In a **scene** or other erotic context, her clothes are usually strategically torn open over erogenous zones. In a non-erotic context—for example, as part of the plot of an action movie or thriller—it's just good luck for people who get off on D.i.D.s (see **didcaps** immediately below). While there are certainly plenty of people who enjoy **dudes in distress,** D.i.D.s are more often than not female.

## didcaps

Still or video captures ("caps") from movies or TV shows featuring a damsel in distress ("**D.i.D.**") or **dude in distress** who is gagged and/or bound, usually as

part of some non-sexual kidnapping plot, *not* as some kinky **BDSM** scenario. But hey, you gotta take it wherever you can get it: old episodes of *24, Beverly Hills 90210, Days of Our Lives*. Dude, if you think about it, the didcap is, in its own way, a figurative form of BDSM that takes the images out of context against their will (or original intent) and selfishly uses them as objects of sexual pleasure. So meta. Wanna hit?

## dick slap

Slapping someone in the face with your dick. A.k.a. pistol whipping. Not to be confused with genital **slapping**.

## dildos

A phallic-shaped object that can be worn (in a **harness**) or held and used to do things that penises are famous for, like penetrating a vagina, an anus, or even a mouth. A dildo doesn't vibrate or move unless *you* move it.

Most dildos have a flared base so they can be worn in **harnesses** or inserted into the butt without fear of getting lost up there. If a dildo *doesn't* have a flared base—like many **glass** dildos, for example—that means it's a handheld dildo and should not be used for **anal play** (lest it get lost up there). And then there are double dildos, which are exactly what they sound like: one end inserted in you (pick your orifice!) and the other end inserted in your partner (ditto). If you intend to employ your dildo solo, try one with a suction-cup base—just stick it to the shower wall and bend over to pick up your bar of soap and—oooh, *hello!* By the way, the majority of dildos these days don't look anything like actual penises, although you can still find ones that are "realistically veined" (that's an actual industry term). Glittery colorful totally unrealistic dildos reign supreme— which is a good thing, we think, because it reminds people that the dildo is not a stand-in for a penis: it's its own thing entirely.

Whatever kind of dildo you choose, however, make sure it's made from a body-safe material such as pure silicone, glass (seriously!), or stainless steel (e.g. LELO's Olga). Pure silicone is the most common because it's easy to clean, it retains body heat (so as not to feel like a speculum in there), it's durable, it doesn't get sticky or tacky, it's **phthalate** free, and it's nice and firm, while still having a bit of give.

Dildos aren't just for lesbians, by the way. A straight woman can bumfuck her boyfriend (or even—*gasp*—her husband!) with a dildo. A straight or gay man can use a dildo as a kind of wingman, while his own penis and hands are busy with other orifices or body parts, or after his own penis has, um, exhausted itself. And anyone can use a dildo during masturbation—some people like something to grip onto or something poking their G-spot while they get to their happy place. See also **harnesses**, **strap-ons**, and **vibrators**.

## dirty talk 🐾

The simplest way to add a dose of kink to your sex life, no props or **pinch-hitters** required! If you've never been particularly verbal in the sack, start slow: Moan a little louder, tell each other what to do next, narrate what you're doing and ask what it feels like, ask your partner what they want you to do next, etc. Dirty talk is basically just a description of sex, and the language you use is completely up to you. There's no need to cuss like a sailor (or a porn star), though some people actually relish the excuse to say "cock" or "cunt" out loud. And believe it or not, it is possible to conduct an entire hour of dirty talk without ever saying "pussy" once, if that word makes your skin crawl. Once you've got this down, you can graduate to story-telling…take it in turns narrating something that's not actually happening (a third in the bed, etc.—whatever floats your boat). And you don't need Demi Moore's husky tones or **Christian Grey**'s sultry **murmur** to pull this off—just slooooooww your daytime voice way the heck down and pause often for dramatic effect. (Besides, if you talk too quickly, you'll get to the end of the story before your partner's even close to their own happy ending!) Your voice may naturally get lower as you get more turned on, but if not, speaking softly and directly into your partner's ear may help you feel sexier. Whispering is fail-safe sexy—even if you're reciting the grocery list. If you've got dirty talker's block, try reading erotica aloud to each other instead (see **communication** for suggestions) or check out our friend Carol Queen's most excellent book *Exhibitionism for the Shy.*

Once you've become fluent in dirty talk (or at least the foreign language equivalent of being able to ask "Où est La Tour Eiffel?"), you can start breaking it out beyond the bedroom: Leave your partner a dirty voicemail during your lunchbreak, or start telling them a story over the phone during their evening commute home (but always practice safer sex—headsets please, people!). And hey, look—you're halfway to a phone sex sesh! The other half is the easy part: rubbing one out while you talk (another very good reason to own a headset…).

Finally, don't forget that we live in a multitasking world: Dirty talk works great over Gchat, text messages, Blackberries (hi Mr. Grey!), email, Post-Its in lunchbags, etc., too. And the shorter the form, the less you'll have to worry about narrative flow, not to mention pesky adjectives and conjunctions. If you're ever at a loss for how to kick off some high-tech dirty talk, take inspiration from the first line of Nicholson Baker's classic yuppie phone sex novel, *Vox*: "What are you wearing?" Make that: *Wot r u wearing?*

## discipline

Discipline is **bondage**'s B.F.F., at least as far as the **BDSM** acronym is concerned. That said, you might enjoy bondage for years without ever bringing any discipline into it (and vice versa, though for newbies, this is less common). As an umbrella term, discipline covers pretty much everything kink-related that you might do to a partner *besides* restraining them, from the physical (**whipping**,

**flogging**, inflicting **pain** or discomfort) to the psychological (**humiliation**, rule-making, giving orders, demanding **service**, **mindfucks**). Whatever form the discipline takes, and whatever the "reason" (punishment, training, behavior modification, disorientation, pure physical pleasure, pure physical torture, etc.), the general idea is the same: The **top** is creatively exerting the power that the **bottom** has handed over to him or her. The 19th century British Lord Acton once said that power corrupts and absolute power corrupts absolutely—but then he didn't know about **safewords**.

# D.I.Y. (do-it-yourself) 🖐

1) A homespun approach to BDSM. Kink is like fashion: You don't have to spend a lot of money or get only brand-name goods to be its **slave** (get it? slave to fashion/slave to a master…oh, forget it). Even **Christian Grey** shops for D.I.Y. supplies at the hardware store where Anastasia works, and he's a freakin' billionaire. Raid your closets, cabinets, and drawers and you'll find a veritable **BDSM** warehouse: A wooden spoon is a **cane**, a **spatula** or icing spreader is a **slapper**, clothespins are **clamps** (pairs of chopsticks bound by rubber bands at each end may be easier to adjust grip strength around nipples than stiff clothespins), a broomstick is a **spreader bar**, a ping pong paddle is a butt **paddle** (duh), salad tongs are medical forceps (for external use only!), a tie is a **blindfold**, a fork is a **Wartenberg wheel**, ice and hot tea and Ben Gay and soy candles are tools for **temperature play**, a large potato or big apple is a ball **gag** (i.e. nothing small enough to actually fit in the mouth and choke someone), **Saran Wrap** is **mummifying** tape, a hair brush or fine sandpaper can be **sensation play** accessories—the list goes on. (A household object that is repurposed for kink is said to be "pervertible.") If you like a little more craft in your kink, check out *The Better Built Bondage Book: A Complete Guide to Making Your Own Sex Toys, Furniture and BDSM Equipment* by Douglas Kent for dungeons on a dime—because the spanks are that much more satisfying on a portable **spanking** bench you made with your own two hands. If you're not exactly Bob Villa in a **gimp suit**, but money is an issue and the spatula just isn't doing it for you anymore, try the more beginner-friendly *Make Your Own Sex Toys* by Matt Pagett. See also **hardware store** and **zippers**.
2) **Bondage (self)**.

# do-me queen

An attention-hogging **bottom**. Within the BDSM **scene**, it's a pejorative term, because a do-me queen is only in it for what they can get out of the experience, and doesn't much care what kind of day their **top** is having. Being called a "do-me queen" at a BDSM **club** is like being called "Weiner Dog" on the playground. But for beginners or dabblers, such as long-term couples looking to spice things up, we see nothing wrong with coming home from a long, hard day at the office and wanting your partner to tie you up and ravish you while you just lie there and enjoy it, occasionally instructing your partner, "Pinch my nips harder, please." See also **bottoming, topping, topping from the bottom.**

## dom/domme

1) Short for dominant; the boss in a **domination** and **submission** kinky **scene**. While a dom could be either male or female, a domme is always female. A.k.a. **master, mistress.**
2) Short for **dominatrix**; someone who is paid to dominate a client in **BDSM** activities (sex is rarely part of the deal). Most working doms are female, as the client base in this profession is largely straight men; however, some male pro doms see gay male clients, and straight and gay women have been known to be paying customers of either. A.k.a. pro dom or pro domme.

## domination

While **bondage** and **discipline** occasionally have nights out without each other, domination and **submission** (or D/s) are entirely co-dependent (think Kim Kardashian and the paparazzi): D/s is essentially the psychological element of **BDSM**—the **power exchange** that takes place in just about all kinky **play**. A **dominant** (or dom) gets off on power—but first you have to find a submissive to give you that power (it's all about **consent**, remember?). A dom is always a **top**, though a top doesn't necessarily have to be a dom. D/s can manifest itself in pretty much any activity described in this book, from adult **babies** to **role-playing** to bondage to a good **spank**. See also **humiliation.**

## dominatrix

1) Most commonly, a woman who is paid to dominate a (typically male) client in **BDSM** activities. Sex is rarely part of the package, though **strap-ons** and **butt plugs** are not always out of the question. Other common dominatrix activities include **bondage, role-playing, humiliation,** and **flagellation.** Some feel that because the dominatrix caters to other people's fantasies (usually men's) rather than her own, her subs ultimately have the overall power in the relationship.

Then again, if a hot guy is going to pay a woman to let him wash her clothes, clean her bathroom, and scrub her kitchen floor, all while wearing a Speedo, and she's cool with it, can't we just call that even? A.k.a. pro dom or pro domme. See also **dom**, **domination**, **femdom**, and **nonsexual BDSM**.

2) *(Rare usage)* A female dominant, a.k.a. **mistress**.

## door jamb cuffs

A device for keeping your **bottom** in a standing position with their hands above their head. Two straps hook over the top of your door—like a coat hook—and are held in place when you close the door. **D-rings** on these straps allow you to attach your bottom's wrist **cuffs**—stick 'em up, cowboy! By the way, circulation issues are a particular concern when someone's arms are above their head in this manner (*you* try holding your hands up there for more than a minute) so the **top** should be extra attentive. The bottom's feet should be flat on the floor (this is decidedly *not* **suspension play**). And as with any form of bondage, never ever leave your door-jamb cuffed partner alone. For the most elegant door jamb cuffs we've come across, check out LELO's Boa Pleasure Ties—the ends are weighted with pearls, so when the ties are draped over a door that is then closed, the ties are prevented from slipping through. See also **bondage safety**.

## D-rings

Metal rings shaped like an uppercase "D," with the flat side often attached to various **fetish wear** and gear so that other restraints (**rope**, cord, straps, metal clips, etc.) can be looped through to bond certain body parts to other body parts or objects. For instance, D-rings on a pair of **cuffs** or **bondage mittens** could be fastened together with a metal clip or else fastened to two lengths of **chains** or rope tied tautly to two separate bedposts.

## drunk 🔨

What you don't want to be when fooling around with **BDSM** (aha, *now* you understand **Christian**'s booze rule!). If you're the **top**, you need to (a) have good judgment (whips and chains et al are potentially dangerous stuff) and (b) have quick reflexes (in case of an emergency). If you're the **bottom**, you need to (a) have all your pain and pleasure sensors fully operational, (b) remember your safeword, and (c) be able to say it coherently if need be. (A safeword slurred by a boozy bottom may sound like a moan of ecstasy to a tipsy top.) Serious kinksters tend to go completely teetotal, believing that the high of the experience is more than enough to get you through the night; we, however, will not frown upon one small glass of wine if it helps you get over the initial embarrassment of dressing up like a tarty nurse. Even Mr. Grey was down with that.

## D/s

**Domination** and **submission**, the cornerstone of **power plays**, and the "D" and "S" of **BDSM**. In case you have trouble remembering, the upper case "D" is the big daddy in charge of the pathetic little lower case "s."

## Duckie waterproof vibrator

A cute little yellow rubber ducky that doubles as a waterproof vibe. No wonder *Sesame Street*'s Ernie was obsessed with his! This battery-operated, super-quiet toy goes by different nicknames, depending on which store you visit—I Rub My Duckie is the original. If yellow is a little too conventional for your tastes, look for the **bondage** version complete with duckie **gimp suit**!

## dude in distress

A man who has been "abducted" who is often bound, blindfolded, and/or gagged. In a **scene** or other erotic context, his clothes (if he has any) may be strategically torn open over erogenous zones. In a non-erotic context—for example, as part of the plot of an action movie or thriller—it's just good luck for the people who get off on this kind of thing (see **didcaps**). While there are certainly plenty of people who enjoy a muscular man writhing against his restraints (think of professional dude-in-distress Daniel Craig in *Casino Royale, Girl with the Dragon Tattoo,* and *Skyfall*), more often than not abduction fantasies feature **damsels in distress**.

## dungeon

A **BDSM** room of one's own. A dungeon isn't always in the basement, and it won't necessarily have a medieval vibe, either; it's basically just a room set aside for BDSM play, and furnished with kinky accoutrements (**cuffs**, shackles, cages, stocks, a **bondage wheel**, a **St. Andrew's Cross**, kinky **furniture**, etc.). It might be a designated room in a fetish **club**, or it might be your guest room (sorry Mom, but we hear the local Best Western is lovely!). Or if you're a billionaire like

**Christian Grey**, then you simply outfit one of the twenty rooms in your apartment with luxury accessories, custom-made kink furniture, a top-of-the-line sound system, and dramatic mood lighting to create your own **Red Room of Pain**. Dungeon owners are often **pro doms** or **play party** hosts, but sometimes they're just really into BDSM. (Think of the dungeon as the kinky equivalent of getting a pool in your backyard.) DungeonDelights.com is a pleasantly nudity-free place to shop for shackles, cages, et al. If a dungeon is being used in a club or at a play party, at least one person (typically someone who's an old hand at BDSM and knows first aid) will be assigned to be **dungeon monitor**/master/mistress, a.k.a. DM. And you thought D&D dorks never got laid... A.k.a. play room.

## dungeon monitor

A kinky hall monitor who helps keep things **safe, sane, and consensual** at private **play parties** and fetish **clubs**. A.k.a. Screech in a **gimp suit**. See also **dungeons**.

**D**

"If it is the dirty element that gives pleasure to the act of lust, then the dirtier it is, the more pleasurable it is bound to be."

—Marquis de Sade

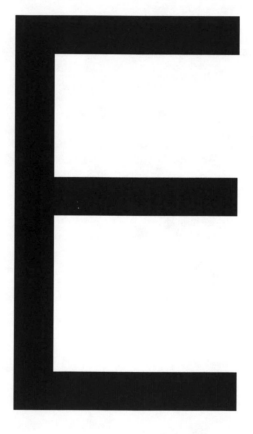

E

## eel

A squirmy little sucker who tries to break out of their restraints like some kinky David Blaine. But unlike David Blaine, eels usually fail to escape their chains *and* prove highly entertaining in the process.

## edge play

Incredibly risky **play** practices. Edge play is a subjective—and sometimes controversial—term in the BDSM **scene**. If you say something is edge play, you might mean any of the following: It's too risky for newbies; it's too risky, period; it's not **safe, sane and consensual**; you might die. Sometimes moral judgment is implied (by the speaker) or assumed (by their audience). When *we* use the term, we mean all the stuff that we can't, in good faith, recommend in this book, for a variety of reasons: We don't have the space to get into all the safety specifics; we don't have the space to get into all the heavy psychological implications; we don't think it's an activity you can learn safely on paper; our lawyers won't let us endorse it; you might die. No moral judgment is intended, though of course we can't stop you from reading that into it! We're certainly on the fuddy-duddy end of the spectrum, but actually, there are only two **BDSM** activities that we think you should never *ever* indulge in, no matter how many books you've read or how many seminars/**play parties**/**munches**/first-aid classes you've attended, and those are **breath control** and self-bondage (see **bondage** [**self**]). Many, but certainly not all, BDSM experts agree with us on this (**Christian Grey** has our back, we should note). Playing without a **safeword** is also pretty damn risky, but it's not quite as immediately life-threatening. As for the rest of our list—if any of the following activities take your fancy, don't think of the "edge play" handle as an embargo; rather, it simply means that you *must* engage in further research before jumping in: BDSM as **therapy**, **bloodplay**, **branding**, bullwhips, cutting, **e-stim**, **enemas**, **fisting**, *heavy* **humiliation**, **Japanese rope bondage**, long-term BDSM relationships or **T.P.E.s**, *heavy* **medical play**, play **piercing**, **scarification**, single-tail whips, **stretchers**, and **suspension** play. Other than that, play ball!

## empathy

The ability to take what you dish, to see things from the other side, to say you've walked a mile in your partner's 6-inch stilettos. Even if you determine you are a dominant at heart, you should know what it feels like to be spanked or paddled or tied up or whatever it is you want to do to your partner (remember, **Christian Grey** got his training as a sub). Being the recipient of a sensation will only make you a better provider (kind of like how shrinks are required to get therapy themselves). Besides, if you try it, you just might realize you like it! A.k.a. The Mikey Effect.

## enema

A procedure (or a device used for this procedure) in which liquid is inserted into the rectum using some kind of syringe, held for a short while (usually a few minutes), and then released (taking with it any "detritus" it encounters on the way). Enema kits can be bought from either your local drugstore or your little sex shop on the corner, which should give you a clue as to their broad-based

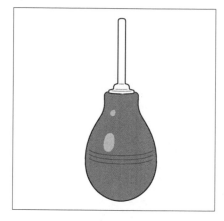

appeal. For some, an enema (a.k.a. anal douche) is a way to induce a particularly stubborn bowel movement; others simply enjoy the fresh-as-a-daisy-chain feeling that results from an anal spring cleaning. A little further down the kink scale, some people employ enemas to prep for heavy backdoor play, such as **fisting**. Move even further down that kink scale and you'll encounter people who consider enemas erotic in and of themselves—these folks are sometimes

called klismos, from klismaphilia (betcha that one didn't make it into the Spelling Bee). Maybe they're **role-playing** doctor-patient (there's only so many times you can take your sub's temperature…), or maybe they just like what it has to offer in pain (enemas cramp like a bitch), **humiliation**, and **submission** (in this context, most enema receivers tend to be subs).

You might also hear some people claim that you should use an enema before *any* kind of **anal play**, which makes us wonder about those people's bowel health and habits. In general, being "regular" (fiber, people!), going right before you play, and then sticking a soapy finger back there during a post-poop/pre-fuck shower should suffice. (Besides, using enemas too regularly can create a dependency, just like with laxatives.) Commercial enemas typically come with some kind of chemical solution, though you're better off just replacing that with warm water—anything other than water can cause irritation back there, making you more susceptible to HIV transmission. (In fact, some studies show that even water enemas can increase your risk, so always wrap up before enjoying the fruits of your labors: latex **gloves**, condoms, etc.) Some enema enthusiasts like to douche with any number of household products, claiming all sorts of restorative or euphoric effects: coffee, white wine, honey, catnip (seriously)… This is what we like to call **edge play**—in order words, beyond the scope of our book. (Try *Intimate Invasion: The Erotic Ins & Outs of Enema Play* by M.R. Strict if you *like* the idea of going beyond the scope of our book—it's out of print but you can find used copies on AbeBooks.com if you're *that* determined.)

We will say one thing, however: Douching with booze puts that stuff directly into your bloodstream immediately, and once alcohol is in your bloodstream, there's no going back (and no puking your way to some kind of sobriety). Which means, yes, it could kill you (call it public enema number one). So if your **dom** is tempting you with a little pinot grigio but insisting you take it anally, it's time to whip out your **safeword**. Just say no to under-ass drinking. See also **scat** and **watersports**.

## erotic asphyxiation

Intentionally strangling a partner—with your hands, a noose, or perhaps a full latex **hood** with gas mask—in an attempt to heighten their sexual pleasure by limiting the oxygen supply to their brain. Possible side effects include memory loss, windpipe rupture, brain damage, cardiac arrest, stroke, and, oh yeah, *death*. While this activity is *marginally* safer than its lonely cousin, **autoerotic asphyxiation** (at least there's someone around to dial 911), we cannot in good faith recommend you try this at home. We have no doubt the feeling fucking rocks, but then so does sex on meth (apparently). Losing consciousness, even for a matter of seconds, can lead to cardiac arrest, and there's no way to know for sure when someone's about to go under. And **C.P.R.** training is no safety net, either—the odds of even David Hasselhoff reviving someone that way are less than one in ten. Plus, if your partner happens to die, you could go to jail for it. Double whammy. It's one of the few practices that's banned at many SM **play parties**. Erotic asphyxiation might be considered the X-rated version of the classic playground "Fainting Game," wherein teens get "high" by strangling each other or hyperventilating their way into a blackout (a.k.a. "The Choking Game"). Some **BDSM** pros out there who are into "heavy" **scenes** will tell you that there's a safe way to practice erotic asphyxiation—if you insist, you should buy their books instead. We prefer the lite version ourselves: Go for a *psychological* rush (rather than the fuck-I'm-dying *physiological* rush) by squeezing or pressing on each other's necks *gently* during a rough-housing **sesh**, so long as the action is purely conceptual. (Or check out the Speak No Evil Choker we describe in the **collars** entry.) Call us wimps, but we like our "little deaths" to be non-literal. A.k.a. **breath control**, breath play, scarfing. See also **edge play**.

# e-stim

1) Getting hot and bothered by electricity—not in a crispy way, but in a kinky way. Small controlled electrical currents can be sent through the genital area, often in different patterns and at different levels, in order to stimulate nerve endings and cause involuntary muscular contractions (not necessarily orgasms, per se, but definitely sexy vibrations when delivered in the right context, whatever that may be for you). The resulting sensations can feel anywhere from tingly to throbbing to downright intense. For instance, many people use electrostimulation (as it's more formally known) as simply a step up from a vibrator, while those into **BDSM** use it as a novel way to ride that line between pleasure and **pain**. Now, before you get all excited about the idea of sticking your dick into a toaster, know this: Electricity can kill you. Hello, Death Row didn't use an *electric chair* for nothin'. Fooling around with electrosex (as it's also known) when you don't know what you're doing can result in burns, electrochemical changes in tissue, strains, sprains, fractures, muscle damage, blood clots, ventricular fibrillation, heart arrhythmia, cardiac arrest, and *death by electrocution*. It's **edge play** of the highest order. Which is not to say that you can't engage in e-stim safely; you just have to follow the rules of engagement *to the letter*:

1. Only use devices made specifically for use on the human body, that have a safe limit to their power. That means no cattle prods, no stereo equipment, no electric fences, no **D.I.Y.** shit with household currents, etc.

2. Many people use medical grade TENS units designed for pain management or Electro Muscle Stimulators (EMS) designed for physical therapy. But since they're not designed for genital use, they may not be able to offer the variety, intensity, and attachments of high-quality devices made specifically for erotic electrosex, like the digital ErosTek machines available at ErosTek.com. (E-stim aficionados recommend the ET-312 for beginners.)

3. Many people swear by ultraviolet wands—electrostatic devices which can cause sparks to jump from wand to body (like the zap you get when shuffling across the carpet in slippers or touching a metal door

handle in winter). While they look super cool in a darkened room, they give off heat, ozone, and UV rays that can be extremely dangerous to the body, so we definitely don't recommend them.

4. Don't be a cheap bastard: These are not products you want to scrimp on. Use these devices "below the belt" only. You want to avoid the head, neck, and especially anywhere near the heart (as tempting as it may be, your **nipples** will have to forgo the electrodes and just make do with some serious pinching).

5. You don't want to have a current cross anywhere near the heart: For instance, you've got an electrode on your Johnson, the power's turned on, then you pick up the other 'trode in your hand, and next thing you know you've got a current doing a drive-by near your heart on its way from your Johnson to your palm. Which brings us to safety point number…

6. Never handle electrodes when the power is turned on, i.e. turn off the power before attaching them to your partner's bod. And if you need to relocate them, turn off the power again.

7. Don't play with e-stim standing up: The shock can collapse you.

8. The rules of rollercoasters apply: Don't dabble in e-stim if you have any heart conditions, have a pacemaker or other electronic implant, suffer from epilepsy, or are pregnant. Duh.

9. *Do a hell of a lot more research on the topic than this dinky little entry can provide!* SmartStim.com, a free e-stim forum, is a good place to start.

   A.k.a. Frankenstein **fetish**.

2. (*Obscure*) Arousal from saucy emails or texts (e.g. sent from your significant other as foreplay), Internet porn, or the new bright and shiny Mac you just got from the Apple store that is so beautiful you wish you could fuck it.

## Eulenspiegel Society

See Appendix B: Surfing Suggestions.

## exes 🐾

The people you once got your kink on with. Safe activities for a "closure" meeting with an ex include: coffee, **communication**, **cuddling**, **dirty talk**, **vanilla** sex. Inadvisable activities for such a reunion include (but aren't limited to): **bondage**, **discipline**, **edge play**, **enemas**, **humiliation**, anything that requires a **safeword**.

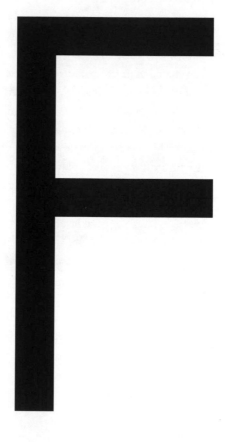

## femdom 🐾

1) **Domination** by a female, typically over a male. If femdom had a crest, it would most likely feature a **strap-on**, though really any form of female domination counts.
2) A female dominant, a.k.a. domina, **domme**, femdomme. A.k.a. **Mrs Robinson** (**Christian Grey**'s former domme and kink mentor).
3) A **dominatrix** who is paid to cater to men's fantasies.

## fetish

1) An inanimate object, item of clothing, substance, or body part that elicits sexual desire and arousal. Common objects of fetishistic attention include **leather**, **latex**, **rubber**, **fur**, high **heels**, **boots**, feet, hair, **corsets**, hosiery, uniforms, cowboy gear, schoolgirl attire, and shaved skin (see **hair removal**). Less common (but still popular enough to merit their own websites) fetishes include cigarettes (typically: women smoking), spandex ("I *really* love the '80s"), and balloons (we always knew there was something a little off about those clowns). The word fetish comes from an 18th century anthropological term used to describe the primitive religious practice of ascribing supernatural powers to certain objects. Freud theorized that men's fetishes were all about castration anxiety, and that women simply didn't have them. These days, people are more likely to chalk your fetish up to behavioral imprinting in childhood or conditioning during early self-love seshes. (Our friend Simon claims he has a shoe fetish because his cleaning lady always removed her sneakers before entering their house when he was but a lad…he would "keep them company" while she mopped.) Or maybe you just like the feel of pleather.
2) *(Falling out of fashion)* An inanimate object, item of clothing, substance, or body part that is *necessary* to achieve sexual arousal.
3) *(Coming into fashion)* Any sexual behavior or preference that is considered, by the speaker, to be beyond the pale: adult **babies**, **pony play**, **sploshing**, **wrestling**, etc. In this definition, fetish serves as a synonym for **kink** or **BDSM**, and could therefore refer to pretty much anything in this book.

## fetishism

The habitual use of a particular inanimate object, item of clothing, substance, or body part (i.e. a **fetish**) in order to achieve sexual arousal and satisfaction. The term "fetish" is often mistakenly used when referring to a fetishism (even by us), but the only people who'll correct you are nerds who spend more time studying semiotics than having sex.

## fetish wear

You know the old joke, "Are you into casual sex or should I dress up?" Many in the kink community would answer that question with a resounding, earnest "Yes!" Wearing fetish gear and clothing is basically dressing for kinky sex, or at least dressing for feeling sexy in a kinky way. In fact, unlike sex **clubs**, many fetish clubs are more about the outfits as an expression of the wearer's alternative sexuality or fantasies than they are about alternative sex actually being exchanged on the spot—they're basically big sex-themed costume balls. Fetish wear is also a way to express to passersby what you're into, like a "Hi My Kink Is" name tag: a head-to-toe **gimp suit** with a **leash** is kind of a dead give-away that you're a **submissive**. There's also an intricate colored hanky code which you can Google and memorize, but it's kind of old school, so don't be too surprised if you're the only one in the club who knows that the magenta snot rag in your left pocket means you like to have your armpits licked.

On the other hand, fetish wear can be a sexy secret: The **chastity belt** or **corset** you're wearing under your power suit can be a reminder to yourself of naughty things to come when you get home from the office.

But probably more than anything else, wearing fetish gear is dressing for success: When it comes to **role-playing** and **power plays** and BDSM **scenes**, the right outfit can help you **suspend your disbelief**. In other words, clothes make the man-slave. When you're wearing your six-inch, buckled-up shitkickers you *will* feel powerful like a proper **dominatrix** should; when you're wearing your posture **collar** you *will* feel owned liked a pet; and when you're wearing your little French maid **costume** you *will* feel like bending over to do some light dusting, "accidentally" exposing your frilly-bottomed panties. Many people find they have a certain affinity, or **fetishism**, for a particular material—**latex**, **rubber**, **PVC**, **leather**, Spandex—or a particular item of clothing—waist cincher, **boot**, stiletto, **mask**… Whatever your fancy, there's a website, a store, and a support group for it (see Appendices A & B). But if you haven't quite found your medium, and a custom-made **catsuit** or bare-assed chaps seem a bit premature for you, then a **wig** or a **body stocking** or even just a pair of **leather** pants can be high-impact, low-commitment fetish accessories. Or try high-end erotic boutiques for items whose high prices won't make you feel so cheap and dirty. Otherwise, check out these online retailers for help snazzing up your wardrobe: VersatileCorsets.com; Baroness.com and Syren.com for all things latex; HipsAndCurves.com for plus size numbers; Northbound.com for everything leather (and the only hot hetero-seeming male model we found during our online BDSM travels); Lip-Service.com if you lean more toward goth, punk or rock; TheVeganSexShop.com for vegan fetish gear; and the kink section of IrreverentShirts.com for totally un-PC tees. See also **cross-dressing**.

## Fifty Shades of Grey

The first in a trilogy of erotic novels by E.L. James (the next two are *Fifty Shades Darker* and *Fifty Shades Freed*). The series—which began as online *Twilight* fan fiction—focuses on the kinky power-play relationship between billionaire-with-baggage **Christian Grey** and virginal college grad **Anastasia Steele**. In between all the very steamy—and effective—sex scenes are a lot of unbelievable plot twists and bad, repetitive, imprecise writing. But that hasn't stopped more than 40 million copies (and counting) from being sold worldwide. In fact, it set the record for fastest selling paperback of all time, beating even the Harry Potter oeuvre! As a result, *Fifty Shades* made it acceptable for morning shows to discuss **spanking** and **safewords**, and for women who never considered sex toys before to start investing in their pleasure. What Oprah did for books, E.L. James has done for **vaginal beads**. If you want to know any more than this, just call your mother-in-law—we're pretty sure her book club is reading it right now.

## Fifty Shames of Earl Grey

The first book-length parody of **Fifty Shades of Grey**. Written by "Fanny Merkin" (a.k.a. Andrew Shaffer, author of *Great Philosophers Who Failed at Love)*, *Fifty Shames* makes fun of the original's sex scenes, the brand-name dropping, the writing, the **murmuring**, the meandering inner monologues, and most especially Anastasia's various inner voices. Earl Grey's awesome deep dark secret is that he's not nearly as kinky as he thinks he is. He wants to **spank** Anna Steal and she's kind of like, "That's it?" His other dark secrets are equally shameful: He rocks out to Nickelback albums, he has a man-crush on Tom Cruise, and he thinks that Italian food doesn't get any better than the Olive Garden. Oh yeah, and the kind of **role-playing** games he likes involve wizard hoods and sorcery, and the only **dungeons** he's familiar with are the kind that come with dragons. Other pitch-perfect details (which you'll probably only appreciate if you've slogged through at least one of the original books) include the following:

- When Anna Steal first shows up to interview Early Grey, the receptionist hands her a security badge that reads VIRGIN. And when Anna approaches the elevators, she says, "We don't have elevators in Portland. This will be my first elevator ride. How do they work, exactly?"
- Anna has an "inner guidette" who speaks with a thick Jersey accent. "I can tell it's her," Anna muses, "because when she talks inside my head there's this weird echoey sound."
- HOLY MOTHER EFFING SPARKLY VAMPIRES IS HE HOT.
- She feels a jolt of electricity when they shake hands... because he's a prankster with a joy-buzzer in his hand.
- She writes an essay for her ethics class (via quill pen and candlelight!) on the legalities of fan fiction.
- He buys her Snooki's book.
- He runs "his finger over my most sensitive spot like it's a MacBook trackpad."
- He pulls a white dove out of her "sex." Seriously. You'll have to read the book to find out what happens to the dove when it hits the ceiling fan. It could be a metaphor, Anna realizes.

Other parodies include the dude-centric *Coupla Shades of Taupe*, and *Fifty Shades of Louisa May*, an imagined memoir from 19th-century feminist writer Louisa May Alcott about transcendental sex.

## finger toys

Diminutive, wearable **vibrators** that turn your fingers into miniature sex machines. One of the only complaints we ever hear about vibrators is that they can make you feel a bit distant from the whole orgasm process. And how many guys, on first being introduced to their girlfriend's **Rabbit Vibrator**, have pouted and said, "Well, I don't see why you need *me* around." Sure, you could hand over the control panel or buy a **remote control toy**, but that doesn't change the fact that when you're using a vibrator, your own hand can't really *feel* what you're doing.

But what if you could let your fingers do the walking, like the good folks at the Yellow Pages used to say? What if your fingers could vibrate at approximately the same frequency as a **Rabbit**? Enter—cue the singing angels—finger toys!

A finger toy, sometime called a finger extension, is basically a finger-size vibrator covered in a soft sheath that straps onto your own finger. **Lube** it up, turn it on, and carry on doing whatever you would usually do with your hands during sex—handwork for her, hand job for him, perineum **massage** for either, etc. (Note: Finger toys are for *external* use only.) You can strap the toy onto the fingertip side for direct application, or you can swing it around to the knuckle side so it's your own vibrating finger that's touching down on your own or your partner's genitals. Either way, you'll get much more subtlety and range of motion than you do with a regular ol' **vibrator**—it's like someone replaced one of your fingers with a vibrating prosthetic. And who could possibly feel trumped by their own prosthetic digit?

Finger toys are quiet and inconspicuous, which makes them great for couple play. The original finger toy is the Fukuoku 9000, though other manufacturers are starting to get in on the game—we prefer the silicone Ipo Finger Vibe. For more versatility, check out PicoBong's Koa Ring, which can be worn around fingers *or* penises and dildos.

## fisting

Inserting a *very* well **lubed** hand into your partner's vagina or rectum. Yep, the whole freakin' hand. But enthusiasts don't go barging into their favorite orifices with a left hook. Instead, they cup their hand like they're trying to squeeze off a tight bracelet—it automatically curls into a fist as it gets inside. Fisting is not for everyone—in fact, it's not even *possible* for everyone—but those who get into it (hi **Christian Grey**) claim it's a pretty mind-bending experience (fans of Lee Press-On Nails need not apply). We're going to have to go ahead and tag this as **edge play**, seeing as we can't possibly get into all the safety aspects here. For further reading (essential if you want to give fisting a chance), check out the "Going Deep" chapter in our sex manual *The Big Bang*, plus *A Hand in the Bush: The Fine Art of Vaginal Fisting* by Deborah Addington (out of print but used copies are available at AbeBooks.com), and *Trust, the Hand Book: A Guide to the Sensual and Spiritual Art of Handballing* by Bert Herrman (talk about finding your niche). By the way, some people would classify *all* **anal** play—and not just fisting—as kinky. We think that attitude is so '80s. A.k.a. fist-fucking, handballing. See also **anal play** and **enemas**.

# flagellation, erotic 🐾

Getting hit, or hitting, with a hand, **pillowcase**, **paddle**, **slapper**, **cane**, **riding crop**, **whip**, or **flogger** in order to arouse (or intensify arousal), punish, reward, **massage**, cause **pain**, release endorphins, or simply get that fresh, kinky feeling. If you really want to become a master flagellator, you should do two things: A) Watch a master flagellator in action, and B) *get* a master flagellation. (Hey, **empathy** goes a long way.) Always practice on inanimate objects before you move on to live meat.

When you do, remember to stretch beforehand and wait at least fifteen minutes after you eat before you go whipping. Place your whipping boy or girl in a comfortable position so they can relax and won't get hurt if they faint or collapse, e.g. lying across your lap (good for spanking), kneeling on all fours on a bed, or lying face down on a bed (put a pillow under their chest so they don't have to turn their head to breathe). They can graduate to stand-up positions once you've carefully developed your craft with extensive practice and research *beyond this book* (see Appendices B and C). Bondage is a good idea to keep the whippee in place and, thus, your aim intact—plus it just feels good (unless they're nervous first-time types who'd feel more comfortable retaining the ability to get up and walk out the door).

A good rule of thumb for beginners is to hit *only* the lower buttocks; the upper back (not the spine or neck!); or the front, sides and backs of the thighs. The more fat or muscle on these spots, the better (as much as you'd probably like to whip the shit out of Nicole Richie, she's not a good candidate). Hit any other areas and you risk doing serious (if not fatal) damage to joints, tendons, bones, fragile bits (like ears, eyes, balls), and internal organs (especially those around the midsection). Be particularly careful to avoid the delicate tailbone when working the tush. If you're a flagellation virgin (either giving or receiving), limit your first few rounds to a short **spanking** or light whipping with a **pillowcase**: With your hand you get much more control over where and how hard you hit, not to mention biofeedback (if your hand can't take it, then your partner probably can't either); with a pillowcase, you have an opportunity to work on your stroke and aim without the threat of serious injury should you miscalculate. Even if you've graduated to more advanced tools like a cane or crop, it's good to warm up first with something lighter, like hand spanks.

Whatever your weaponry, start slowly and softly, gradually working your way into heavier hits if your **bottom** requests it (each body area you hit requires this warm-up). You're going for redness ("I aim for pink," as **Christian Grey** tells

**Anastasia Steele**) and, at the most, welts and bruises that will heal quickly without any scarring—you're *not* going for open wounds. Don't hit the same little spot over and over—that's like annoying, piston-esque intercourse. Many people enjoy a rhythmic, repetitive, and thus sensual working that can go on for an hour (it takes at least a quarter of that time for the whippee's runner's high to kick in). Others like more variation in their blows, both in terms of intensity, sensations (thudding vs. stinging), and the tools they are delivered with. Just make sure the bottom is keeping up with the whacking and isn't getting overwhelmed: Ideally, you want them begging for more, not screaming for mercy (well, at least not screaming for mercy and really *meaning* it—see **safeword**). So **communicate**. And alternate or combine the lashing with some sexual stimulation—or at least dangle that sexual stim like a carrot they'll get at the end of the sesh. Finally, and most importantly, **cuddle**. See each tool's specific entry for more **safety** info.

## floggers

The pom pom of the **BDSM** world. ("Give me a W! Give me an H! Give me an I! Give me a P!") A popular flagellation tool, a flogger consists of a fairly stout handle and several "tails" of equal length (from one- to three-feet long) made of **leather**, suede, nylon, pleather, **rubber**, or even ribbon. Depending on the number of tails, their length, their material, and whether they have knots or beads at their ends, the sensation a flogger provides can be anywhere from soft to holy-fucking-shit.

Beginners should go with a well-made, small, light-impact flogger: This kind will evoke more giggles than actual cries of pain. Avoid heavy-leather, braided, beaded, or knotted tails in the beginning. As with most BDSM equipment, you don't want to scrimp: A cheaply made flogger won't be balanced correctly (making it harder and heavier to wield), its tails won't land in the same spot (what you want), and/or the edges of the tails will be sharp (what you *don't* want). Try companies that specialize in making floggers, like Bare Leatherworks—with their Midsize Cowhide Flogger, the handle feels great, you can give your partner a good whack without it hurting them, *and* it makes your victim's butt jiggle, too! For the kind of posh flogger you might find in the **Red Room of Pain**, there's LELO's Sensua Suede Whip (pictured on the back of this book in purple, but available in red!).

To make sure you've got good aim, practice on inanimate objects first. Work on your different strokes: twirling, backhand, infinity symbol. Don't graduate to animate objects—that have of course given you their consent—until you've got the eye and aim of a national darts champion. The ends of the tails should be hitting only the safe zones: lower buttocks, thighs, and upper back (not the spine or neck!). As a beginner, it's a good idea to protect areas you don't want to hit with clothing, a towel, blanket, or pillow, just in case you accidentally let the tails "wrap" around the body beyond these safe zones—the epitome of poor form. (Another good reason to have your bottom lying down if you're a beginner.) See **flagellation** for more important safety info. A.k.a. **cats**. Mini-floggers for **genitorture** are called flails, pussywhips (ha!), or ballwhips.

## florentine flogging

You know the term double-**fisting**? No, we're not talking about putting each hand up a different special friend's butt at the same time (man, what kind of book do you think this is?!). We mean when you've got a beer in both hands. Well, florentine flogging is the same thing, except instead of beer, you're holding two **floggers**. And instead of chugging, you're administering a rhythmic **flagellation**, not unlike a fire twirler or that crazy nunchucks guy on YouTube. (Let's hope you're more coordinated than the latter.)

## food play 🐾

Everything from wet and messy **sploshing,** to blind taste tests à la *9 1/2 Weeks,* to being forced to eat out of a dog bowl, to **Christian Grey**'s cutsie mama-bird impression with the white wine. If you're really going to *play* with your food (in the sexual sense of the word), then please read up on the safety guidelines in the **sploshing** entry first.

## foot fetishism 🐾

Getting turned on by the feet (duh). Usually someone else's. It's mostly a guy thing (famous fetishists include Casanova, Goethe, Thomas Hardy, and Elvis).

Feet are a funny thing: Not since Victorian times have people felt the need to cover them up for the sake of propriety—and yet admitting that you are a "foot person" (as opposed to, say, a breast or ass person) is akin to wearing a "Hi, I'm

Kinky" t-shirt. And sure, for some people, their foot **fetish** is an all-consuming kinky passion and a necessary component to any sexual activity. And for others, their overwhelming interest in feet is a source of shame and terror that they can't control (read the brilliant book *The Other Side of Desire* by Daniel Bergner for a moving case study on one such guy).

But the foot is an erogenous zone and there's no reason why you can't enjoy it, fetish or not. The feet abound in nerve endings! And considering the amount of money some people—especially women—spend on shoes (and the amount of pain they suffer to wear them), it would be downright wrong *not* to treat the feet as sexual objects. **Boots** and **high heels** are a key component to fetish or kinky attire, but bare feet can be worshipped, too: toe-sucking, licking, tickling, suckling, **massaging**, etc. And don't forget the foot-job (a.k.a. *really* dirty footsie)!

By the way, seven-inch platform latex boots won't necessarily leave your feet in prime shape for a little worship. Unless you or your partner are into the **humiliation** aspect of toe cheese, we recommend a shower or foot soak, a pumice scrub, and a little foot lotion.

## forced orgasm

When a **top** makes a **bottom** climax, whether they like it or not (**consensually** speaking, of course). In the spectrum of "punishments," it ranks right under "I'm not going to ground you, because I'm sure the guilt you must feel is far worse."

## frogtie

A form of **bondage** wherein the **bottom** is bound into a crouched, frog-like position—their ankles are tied to their thighs, and their wrists might be attached to either side. For shits and giggles, gently put a frogtied partner onto their back and watch them squirm like Ralphie's little brother in *A Christmas Story*. See also **hogtie**.

## fucking machines

If "Battle Bots" on Comedy Central had been X-rated, this is what you would have gotten: crude (in every sense of the word), oversized contraptions whose motors turn rotational force into the thrusting movement of a shaft with a **dildo** on the end of it. These bastard children of the Industrial Revolution can be used for both vaginal and **anal** stimulation and, in the context of kink, on someone who's tied up. Unfortunately, the piston-heavy sex machines—like the Antique

Intruder, the Drilldo, and the Fuck Rogers—look about as likely to get a person off as an inebriated frat boy jackhammering away like he's in a race to the cervix or colon. Downloadable videos (for a price) of women getting it on with these **vibrators** gone wrong are available at, you guessed it, FuckingMachines.com. Or, if you want to purchase your very own metal boyfriend, visit MyLoveMachine.com. A.k.a. orgasmos ex machina.

## fuck-me boots

See **boots**.

## fur

The outerwear of Thumper and friends, used for erotic **sensation play**. Fur may be the focus of a **fetish**, as was the case with the Austrian author and **masochist** Leopold Ritter von Sacher-Masoch (see **history of kink**) *and* his main character in the 1870 novel *Venus in Furs*—both got off on being degraded by dominant women wearing fur. Fluffy **massage** gloves are used at holistic spas and Tantra sex clinics as relaxation therapy and sensuality enhancers. Many like the contrast of soft, delicate fur with more brutal sensations, like that of a cold, hard **paddle**: A tickling love pat with something fuzzy can be particularly soothing to the butt cheeks after a good whacking; or kill two birds with one stone by delivering a **spanking** *with* the glove on. Minkglove.com sells a variety of real fur gloves, chokers, eye masks, and even nipple warmers. But wouldn't you prefer faux-fur cuffs, so you can limit your abuse to the human animals that can actually give you their **consent**? See also **furries**, **leather vegan**, **plushies**, and **vegan gear**.

## furniture 

Anything kinky that you get on (or in, or under...). Kinky furniture is usually referred to as **dungeon** furniture, and much of it is elaborate enough that you'd probably need a dungeon to store it in (though a **queening stool** could make a lovely planter during **BDSM** downtime).

Dungeon furniture includes stocks and pillories (those medieval wooden frames that trap your head/hands/feet while you receive your due punishment), **swings**, **slings**, surgical tables, bondage racks, **bondage wheels**, cages, **St. Andrew's Crosses** (like the one in the middle of the **Red Room of Pain**), butterfly chairs (featuring two horizontal planks on a pivot so the person's legs can be secured and then spread), inversion tables (bondage tables on a pivot so that a person can bound and then inclined, rotated upright, or turned upside-down), and bondage benches, **spanking benches** (like the red leather number **Christian** bends **Anastasia** over at the end of the first *Fifty Shades*), horses, stands, or beds (basically custom-designed pieces with hooks to attach to your **cuffs** so that you are forced to stand/sit/kneel/lie, etc., like the one in the middle of **Christian**'s playroom). For erotic furniture that you can actually keep under your bed, try a small foam "Black Label" **Liberator wedge** with restraints.

Looking to outfit your own dungeon? Check out Sonny Black's uber swanky "as seen on MTV" merchandise at SaxonDungeonFurniture.com, Metalbound.com, or VeryAlternativeFurniture.co.uk. Or for something a little more subtle, affordable, and D.I.Y., you can download free plans for incognito pieces at FoxyFurniture.com...your neighbors will have no idea they just hung their hat on your bondage stand, or they're perched on your spanking bench while nibbling on that deviled egg (just be a good neighbor and use disinfecting wipes, please).

## furries

A community of people who share a common interest in the anthropomorphism of animals. Oh, and they like to dress up in fuzzy, full-body animal costumes. In fact, furries are fond of attending furry conventions dressed as the animal they most identify with (a.k.a. their "fursona"). As a general rule, these folks have more in common with rabid soap opera fans and Barbie collectors than they do with any of the types identified in this book. However, some furries take their hobby into the bedroom: They're called "furverts" (we *wish* we could take credit for that awesome pun, but it's an "official" term). God bless the Internet for helping these people find each other. Often confused with **plushies** (there is a fair amount of overlap between two, both in activities and members). See also **animalism** and **pony play**.

## gags, mouth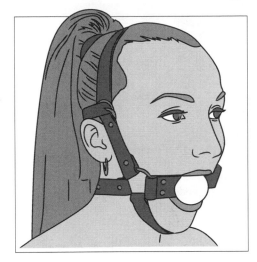

A form of face **bondage**, usually created by sticking a **made-for-play** device in the mouth, obstructing speech. A hallmark of abduction fantasies, gags can increase a **top**'s sense of control or a **bottom**'s sense of helplessness by removing the latter's ability to communicate in the conventional verbal way, transforming them into a sort of pet that can whimper, follow commands, communicate with its eyes, and wag its "tail"—without ever giving lip back!

Gags can also add to a bottom's **humiliation**: When you can't close your mouth, you can't easily swallow your saliva, which can result in serious drool dripping down your chin...um, *embarrassing*. Gags are serious **BDSM** biz, so please read the next entry on **gag safety** after going through the following categories of mouth pieces:

*cloth (or cleave) gags:* An appropriately-sized piece of cloth (perhaps twisted like you would a wet towel to snap someone's ass), the middle of which is placed in the mouth and the ends of which are tied together behind the head. You can also tie a knot in the middle of a scarf or bandana, place that in the mouth, and tie the ends 'round back. If the gag-ee will be lying on their back, tie the ends together a bit to one side so they don't have to lie on a lump...unless of course discomfort is your goal.

*ball gags:* A (usually rubber) ball which fits behind the teeth and is attached on either side to a behind-the-neck adjustable strap or a full head harness. The classic red ball gag was made famous (and practically mainstream) in the "bring out the **gimp**" scene of 1994's *Pulp Fiction*. For something without that classic rubbery taste (yum), try one made of medical grade silicone—it'll be longer lasting, easier to clean, less toxic, and way better tasting. For a more hippie look, try a rope ball gag. And for the sweet-tooth in your life, there's the Jawbreaker Gag, made with real candy! (We suppose giving your submissive a cavity is one creative way to inflict pain.)

*O-ring gags:* Open rings (made of plastic, rubber-coated metal, or leather-wrapped metal) which force the wearer's mouth open and are secured with a behind-the-neck strap, making the wearer particularly exposed and vulnerable. However, most of these rings aren't large enough for penile penetration. (Don't even try, lest you end up with a complex about your penis size.)

*medical or dental retractors:* Most often actual dental tools made of stainless steel and designed to keep the mouth agape for oral examination or surgery. Most don't come with straps to secure in place on uppity **eels**, so you may have to add your own. Open wide! And don't say we didn't warn you when you get a boner in the dentist's chair during your next visit. (See also **medical toys**.)

*penis (or pecker) gags:* Gags with insertable mouth pieces usually in the shape of a penis head, held in place by straps (i.e. "Put *that* in your pipehole and suck on it!"). Many come with permanent or detachable **dildos** protruding from the mouthpiece for hands-free penetrative service. Because love is a two-way street.

*inflatable (or pump) gags:* Rubber balls, penis heads, ovals, or other shapes which can be inflated to a "just right" size by a bulb pump connected via a tube. Most come without a strap.

*bit gags (pony bits):* A (usually rubber) horse-style bit with metal loops (think silver hoop earrings) on either side which attach to a behind-the-neck strap or a full head harness. Usually employed by those into **pony play**.

*doggie bone gags:* Same idea as the pony gag, but the bit is in the shape of a rubber doggie bone for those whose fantasies are more Lassie-driven than Black Stallion–inspired (see **animalism**).

*fishhook gags:* Remember as a kid how you'd hook a finger on either side of your mouth to make a silly face at someone? Same thing here, except there are actual hooks on either end of an adjustable behind-the-neck strap.

*attachment gags:* These gags can be bought with various attachments so your **submissive** can serve you a cocktail on a small tray, scrub your boots with a shoe brush, do a little light dusting with a feather duster, offer an ash tray to your party guests, and, let's not forget, fuck you with a big black dildo—all with their hands tied behind their back!

*funnel gags:* A kinky and—let's be honest—pretty fucking disturbing version of the beer bong. Except instead of beer... Hey, **Y.K.I.O.K.,I.J.N.M.K.** See also **watersports**.

*figurative gags:* The kinder, gentler gag, but no less powerful if you're in the right **subspace**. The top simply threatens to punish you if you make a peep (punishment could be anything from a whipping to a time-out in the closet to an unplugging of the electric vibrator currently being applied to your naughty bits). This is the only gag Miss Steele consents to in *Fifty Shades*—but then again, we did find ourselves wishing she'd shut up on more than one occasion. For a bit more physicality, a hand over the mouth (but not the nose) while the top whispers sweet threats in your ear will do quite nicely, too. See also **bondage (verbal)**.

## gag safety

When you're messing around with someone's air passageways, you *must* be incredibly careful. Please adhere to the following safety regulations:

1. Never stuff anything loose in the mouth, otherwise the item could get stuck in the throat and cause suffocation. Not even wadded up panties (tempting, we know). Whatever is placed in the mouth must not be able to make it to the throat and should be inextricably anchored to an external strap or harness.

2. Yes, they're called gags, but don't take it literally: Nothing should be placed so far back in the mouth as to trigger the gag reflex. Start off with something that simply keeps the mouth open (e.g. a small, typical ball gag or an O-ring) rather than something that goes *inside* the mouth, because it doesn't take much for that reflex to kick in.

3. Bigger doesn't equal better when it comes to gags. You want something that fits the person's mouth well, not something that strains the jaw, cuts off passageways completely, or triggers the gag reflex (all possibilities with an inflatable gag).

4. Similarly, don't keep a gag in for longer than an hour or two, lest it cause sprains or damage to the muscles, tendons, ligaments, or joints of the jaw.

5. Don't be **drunk**. As the gagger, you need to have good judgment and quick reflexes in case of an emergency. As the gag-ee, you don't want to pass out or, worse, throw up in your mouth.

6. The gag should be easy for the top to remove quickly in case of an

emergency. So stay away from gags with locks. And if you've tied a cloth gag in a super tight knot, have the **medical scissors** at the ready to cut it off.

7. *Never* leave someone alone when they're gagged.

8. Don't use tape for gags: It's hard to remove, gets stuck in hair, and can take off skin like a Band-Aid from Hell.

9. Since the gag-ee won't be able to utter their usual **safeword**, you need to determine a safeword signal ahead of time: Either dropping something they're carrying in their hand (not great if you're in the dark) or a very specific noise pattern (like three Morse code grunts) that you're sure they can make with the gag in place.

10. When you're with someone for the first time or even just trying something for the first time (like **flogging**), it's good for the bottom to be able to communicate freely. So in these instances, *don't* use a gag.

11. Use dental retractors with extreme caution because they can be ratcheted up too wide or chip teeth.

12. If you're sick, don't agree to be gagged (in fact, what are you doing getting tied up? You should be in bed with a blanket and some hot soup). You can't risk your nose clogging up or your stomach regurgitating its contents into a dead end.

13. If you can, get a gag made of non-toxic materials, like pure silicone. A gag made of jelly rubber that stinks may be seeping toxins. They don't make kids' or pets' chew toys out of that material anymore. Doesn't your piece-of-shit **slave** deserve the same consideration?

## genitorture

Short for "genital torture," which includes **cock-and-ball torture** and **cunt torture**. Ah, good times…good times.

## gimp suits

Kinky onesies made out of **leather**, pleather, **rubber**, **PVC**, etc., and typically worn by a (usually male) **submissive**. Some have attached hoods, while others are combined with a bondage **hood** or **mask**. Made famous by the 1994 Quentin Tarantino movie *Pulp Fiction*; made sexy by FX's 2011

TV show, "American Horror Story." Please note: Saying "Bring out the gimp" at a kink **club** will not go over as well as you might imagine.

## gloves

1) Medical **latex** hand gloves that help protect against STDs, allow for smoother entry into orifices, and are the perfect accessory for your doctor/patient **role-playing**.

2) Fancy **fetish wear** for the hands and arms. The gloves are usually opera-length, either super-shiny latex or laced-up leather, and a solid color (black is by far the most popular choice). Perfect for festive occasions like fetish balls or breaking in a new **slave**. See also **armbinders** and **bondage mittens**.

## grope boxes

Like those magicians' boxes that the lovely assistant climbs into, except instead of holes for wiggling hands and feet there are holes for easy access to erogenous zones. A staple at **play parties**, the grope box usually prevents its captive from resisting fondling from passersby or even seeing who is doing the fondling.

## hair removal

Shaving, waxing, depilating, or lasering off hair is often a part of **vanilla** sex prep for many people, but this activity can have a distinctively kinky quality when done by one partner to another, or when one partner dictates the hair removal, i.e. "I want you to have this removed" (à la **Christian Grey** in *Fifty Shades*); "I want *you* to shave *me*" (said by a lazy **dom**); or "I'm going to shave off all your body hair, including your eyebrows, as a symbol of my total control over you" (said by kind of a jerk).

Body hair (which includes, but is not limited to, pubic hair) may be removed for any number of reasons: to create a different skin **sensation** (for either the newly bare person or the one touching them); to achieve maximum total nudity; to get better access (a cock ring pulling on pubic hair can be a pain you don't want); to get a better visual (you can see where to put the clamps); to create a different aesthetic (e.g. one of cleanliness or neatness); to infantalize (see adult **babies** and **age play**); to foster intimacy and trust (*You're getting near my family jewels with a razor?!*), or to **humiliate** (what better way for a woman to prove her devotion to her master than by going for a full Kojak?).

## handcuffs

What you might be restrained with in a cop car, at a bachelorette party, or in bed. Usage of the typical metal kind is reserved for truly advanced players, because what you'll soon discover is that handcuffs aren't actually built for comfort (shocker, we know). Metal cuffs can cause nerve, soft tissue, or bone damage; the cheap kind tighten under pressure; and most kinds come with teeny-tiny keys that can easily go missing. (*Mr. Whiskers, what did you eat now...?*) For safer, easier, more comfortable (but still sexy) bondage that can be worn all night, go with made-for-play **cuffs** instead, available at your corner sex shop. That said, we will admit that handcuffs have a certain C.S.I. charm to them, so if you insist, bear the following in mind:

1. Believe it or not, standard police issue handcuffs are safer than some cheapie novelty versions, because the former are double-locking, which means they don't get tighter

once on. Sex shops are starting to catch on, and the most responsible outlets typically sell only the double-locking kind.

2. Don't use handcuffs if you want or expect your "prisoner" to struggle against them—they're more appropriate for situations in which looks matter more than purpose.
3. Keep the handcuffs loose (the wrists should be able to move freely).
4. Don't put any weight on the handcuffs, e.g. no lying back on handcuffed wrists or hooking the cuffs high overhead so the wearer's wrists are strained.
5. See also **bondage safety**.

## hardware store 🐾

A one-stop shopping center for all your **BDSM** needs. Who needs specialty sex shops when you can find everything at your friendly neighborhood True Value at half the cost? Even **Christian I-Fly-My-Own-Helicopter Grey** does it, and he could afford freakin' diamond-encrusted BDSM gear if he wanted. (And how *convenient* if your potential sub just happens to work at the hardware store—oh, the foreplay possibilities!)

Of course, you've got to have a bit of a **D.I.Y.**-streak, but if you're willing to put in the extra elbow grease (or should we say Crisco?), you can completely decorate your dungeon or playroom with the following: welded-link chains with "quick links" to aid in adjusting chain lengths; two-by-fours, tubing, and rods of wood, metal, or plastic to create **spreader bars**; duct tape for **bondage** (over material only please, to avoid pulling off hair and skin); keyed locks (safer than combo locks which may take too long to undo in an emergency sitch); single- or double-ended snap hooks, snap shackles (or "**panic snaps**"), and carabiners for securing **D-rings** to other things; eyebolts (not flimsy screw eyes) to anchor chain ends; block and tackle devices for **suspension**; and miles of natural filament **rope** for bondage masterpieces. But please, whatever you do, don't buy **cable ties** as wrist and ankle restraints like kink "expert" **Christian Grey** does in the first book of *Fifty Shades*—not only is that bush league, it's dangerous.

If your hardware store doesn't have the high quality and durable materials you're looking for, try boating or outdoor adventure stores.

## harnesses, body and chest

1) (*Pre-made*) Typically made of **leather**, **latex**, or **rubber**, a **bondage** harness is a series of straps that buckle around the body to aid in kinky play—though many people simply wear harnesses out to their local fetish **club** as a kinky

accessory. Full body harnesses have a strap which passes between the legs (men's harnesses are usually anchored by a **cock ring** at this point); smaller harnesses encompass just the breasts, shoulders, and back (women's harnesses may incorporate some breast bondage—see **bondage [breast]**); even smaller ones are made for just the head. A harness can serve as a bondage platform, because it offers so many different places to attach other restraints and **cuffs**. All of a sudden your **sub** is just covered in **D-rings**! But you can't use just any old harness for **suspension play**—you'll need a specially designed suspension harness for that. A.k.a. bondage harness.

2) (*Rope*) Some bondage enthusiasts take great pride in fashioning their own **D.I.Y.** body harnesses out of rope. They can get pretty ornate and complicated (see **Japanese rope bondage**), but any kink newbie can make the following chest harness—it's (relatively) simple, works on all shapes and sizes (possibly even on man boobs), and looks and feels great:

Double (or fold over) around 30 feet of rope so that the cut ends are aligned and there's a folded loop at the other end (that's called a "Lark's Head"). Place the Lark's Head in the middle of your partner's back, between their shoulder blades. (If their hands are tied in front and they will be lying on their back at any time, position the Lark's Head slightly off to one side of the spine.) With your partner's upper arms against their sides, wrap around the chest (including the arms) above the breasts back to the Lark's Head. Pass the two ends of rope to the center of the back and pass them through the Lark's Head, and then wrap in the opposite direction below the breasts to the back and pass the two ends through the Lark's Head again. From here you have two options:

A) To create a *yoke* chest harness (good for both flatlands or mountains), bring both ends under one armpit (below the chest wrappings), up and over that respective shoulder, behind the back of the neck, in front of the opposite shoulder and under that armpit (below the wrappings) back to the Lark's Head; separate the ends and pull one through the Lark's Head, then tie a square **knot**.

B) To create a bikini harness (mountains, or at least hills, are required), pull the two ends up and over one shoulder, down between the breasts, under the horizontal wrap below the breasts, back up and over the opposite shoulder, back down to the Lark's Heads, then tie a square knot. For another simple chest harness that includes the hands, see **cuffs (rope)**.

## harnesses, strap-on

Built to hold a **dildo** in place, for hands-free **strap-on** fucking.

## headphones/ear plugs 🔖

Ear plugs aren't just for construction workers and insomniacs, and noise-canceling headphones aren't just for prissy cubicle workers. Controlling your partner's soundtrack (or lack of one) takes **sensory deprivation** to a whole new level, especially when combined with a **blindfold**. If white noise is too nerdy for you, make a booty mix on your **MP3 player** and have your partner listen to it through headphones—**Christian Grey** was fond of the kind of classical music serial killers like to do their scalping to (all of which is available on "Fifty Shades of Grey: The Classical Album" via iTunes). Headphones and earplugs deprive your partner of aural clues and distractions, insulating them from sounds like your breathing, the smack of a **paddle** hitting their skin, the dog barking, etc. They can only speak when spoken to, and they can only be spoken to when you choose to lean in real close and lift their headphones. This all helps your partner focus—exactly what that prissy cubicle worker is going for, too, except the object of focus in this case is not what's happening on a spreadsheet but, rather, what's happening on a bed sheet.

## heels, high 🔖

You don't necessarily have to be a shoe fetishist to enjoy the look, feel...hell, even the *smell* of high-heeled shoes. They're sexualized by our society wherever you look: Women and drag queens obsess over them, strippers and porn stars are practically *required* to wear them, and Freudians get off on their phallic symbolism. The stiletto—named for the long, thin, stiletto dagger—is totally impractical for walking, which automatically makes it *très sexee*! You can't really do anything in them *but* fuck...or at least look pretty. They create the illusion of longer legs, (further) feminize the wearer by creating that dainty tippy-toe look and forcing the butt and boobs out, and make him or her supermodel-tall. On the mainstream, overpriced fashion fetish end of the spectrum are the Louboutins and Jimmy Choos featured in *Fifty Shades* (an erotic novel which also operates as a guide to product placement); on the foot fetish end of the spectrum are the popular platform pumps with three or more inches under the ball of the foot and six (or more!) inches of pure, spiky heel.  Which begs the questions: The higher the heel, the better the BDSM? Or could it be overcompensation for a short whip? See also **boots** and **feet**.

## history of kink (abridged) 🔖

Despite what your grandmother might think, kink is not something that was invented around the same time as boomboxes and thongs, just to piss her off. In fact, all the way back in the 4th century (or thereabouts), the *Kama Sutra* was practically a kinky how-to manual (Biting? Check. **Slapping?** Check. **Body modification?** Check). Do you think all those medieval religious ascetics wearing hair shirts and self-**flagellating** were just having ecstatic visions? How about ecstatic orgasms?! And what of Alexander Pushkin's *Secret Journal* from the early 1800s, which recounts tales of anonymous **masked** group **anal play**?

But then the Victorian era brought with it a kink backlash, when even the legs of roast chickens and pianos were deemed obscene. In 1886, an Austro-German psychiatrist named Richard von Krafft-Ebing published *Psychopathia Sexualis*, coining the terms **sadism** (after **Marquis de Sade**) and **masochism** (after Leopold Ritter von Sacher-Masoch, author of *Venus in **Furs***), and finding both activities to be severely depraved. Plenty of other Dead White Men weighed in on the matter (Freud among them), and the consensus seemed to be that pretty much *anything* that wasn't related to procreation was considered pervy. And as for **SM**-ers? They were suspected to be violent criminals or sociopaths in the making.

Then the '50s gave us Kinsey, god bless his pervy little heart. His research found that 20 percent of the men and 12 percent of the women he studied were aroused by **SM** stories. Unfortunately, this finding got him in big trouble with the American Medical Association, and it wasn't until the '70s that kink was seriously studied again—and was found to have no link to sociopathological behavior. The '70s also ushered in SM support groups like the **Eulenspiegel Society** (in New York) and the **Society of Janus** (in San Francisco), as well as a more public image for the leather subculture (see **leather**, def. #2), and the publication of the first books about the **scene**.

But kink was still considered to be largely a gay thing—or, when hets *were* involved, distinctly misogynistic. In fact, as recently as 1980, the National Organization for Women passed a resolution denouncing SM (in their defense, they did give a generous two thumbs up to gay rights in the same year). It was around this time that the term **BDSM** began to gain currency, too: SM was the original term, derived from Krafft-Ebing's clinical terms; later the leather community switched to "B&D" as a way of setting themselves apart from the disapproving docs; eventually the two were combined and used by both dissers and devotees alike.

And then along came the Internets, which turned out to be the best thing that happened to kink since the *Kama Sutra* (or the worst, if you were part of the Family Research Council *or* one of the stalwart members of the old school leather scene who liked their community exclusive, discreet, and inaccessible to plebes). Kinky networking—the foundation of today's scene—was suddenly available to anyone with a modem, and kinksters across the globe started sharing **safety** tips, **fetish** suppliers, **munch** invites, club recommendations, lingo, rules— even **slaves**. And kinky gear was suddenly available to people who lived on farms in Iowa (or people too shy to visit their local leather store).

Finally, of course, there was the *Fifty Shades of Grey* trilogy, which introduced items like **butt plugs** and **nipple clamps** to soccer moms, middle-aged book club attendees, and mother-in-laws across the country—indeed, across the *world*. We're pretty sure it was the first time that a book topping the *New York Times* bestseller list featured a scene with a **spreader bar**. While the series promoted the myth that most BDSM enthusiasts are products of childhood abuse (**Christian Grey**'s "crack whore" mom let her johns use his four-year-old body as a human ashtray), it also gave many women across the country permission to indulge their darker fantasies without abandoning their penchant for romance.

That all said, you'll still hear plenty of people today declare that kink is immoral or pathological or anti-feminist or "largely a gay thing" (and we'd bet that at least one of them keeps a **gimp** in the basement). And you'll hear plenty more people declare that kink is just plain weird (and we bet a good chunk of *them* can't have sex with the lights on). Then again, what fun is a taboo if there's nobody left to disapprove of it? See also **BDSM**, **kink**, and **law (the)**.

## Hitachi Magic Wand

It's the Cadillac of **vibrators**, the best seller, the MVP, the box office sure thing, that '70s toy. The Hitachi is marketed as a muscle massager. It makes sense; after all, electric body massagers work by bringing blood to the area, which is—hey!— exactly what happens when you get turned on. (You might also hear back massagers referred to as **wands** in the biz...and in *Fifty Shades of Grey*.) And because the Hitachi was designed to be a workhorse, it can last for decades— unlike those crappy novelty items designed to last for the duration of a bachelorette party. (The Wahl Massager is similarly marketed and has a similar, saucy dual purpose.)

The Hitachi has a foam head covered in soft acrylic, about the size of a tennis ball, and a foot-long white plastic handle (so no arm cramps!). It's definitely not as cute as a **Rabbit Vibe** or as elegant as a Smart Wand—in fact, it's rather medical looking (see the **wands** entry for more information on how these newer wand vibrators are reinventing the concept for the 21st century, in everything from design to portability). But that might work for your doctor-patient fantasy. And if you've got a nosy housekeeper or a dog who likes to drag inappropriate "presents" into the living room whenever your mother-in-law is over for tea, its clinical facade might be a good thing. Its size and heft also make it a great intimidation device to use on a tied-up luvva—slap it into the palm of your hand like a Good Fella would a baseball bat, except instead of violence, you're threatening them with mind-blowing ecstasy.

The Hitachi is a plug-in device (unlike Smart Wands, which are cordless and rechargeable), and it's an outie **vibrator** only—but it can be turned into an innie toy with one of the specially designed attachments. (While the Hitachi is available in many mainstream outlets, the accessories are mostly just sold at sex shops.) You'll probably want to turn up some background music to muffle its sound, which you may find reminiscent of a birthing cow. That's because it's so powerful. In fact, if your partner's wielding this wand, you might end up begging them to temper its strong vibrations by keeping clothes, a blanket, or a pillow between you and the bulbous head, or by limiting its contact to areas *near* erogenous zones (like the thighs) and just letting the vibes radiate out. Whether your partner honors your request will depend on how obedient you've been lately. See also **wands**.

## hobble skirts

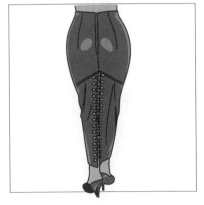

Very early 20th century high fashion items that were cinched tight around the ankles, forcing women to mince like geishas, fall down steps, and trip when crossing streets on their way to the voting booth. Oh wait, that's right—the 19th amendment was still up for debate back then. Though the fashion industry continues to torture the female body (come on...*thongs*?!), the hobble skirt, at least, has been retired to the world of **fetish wear**. More commonly constructed out of **leather**, **PVC**, or **latex** these days, it's considered a form of wearable **bondage**—perfect for that women's suffrage fantasy you've been working on. See also **clothing** and **fetish**.

## hogtie

Securing all four limbs together, as one might a, well, hog. Not to be confused with a **frogtie**. Can be used as a verb ("Finish your broccoli or I'll hogtie you tonight"), a noun ("Nice hogtie, dude"), or an adjective ("Can I take a message? She's hogtied right now"). While farm animals can be hogtied in front only, the most common **BDSM** hogtie pose is for the **bottom** to lie on his or her front with ankles and wrists attached to each other behind the back (kneeling is also possible). Fancy-pants kinky types know how to hogtie with **rope**; newbies (that's you, sunshine) should check out the beginner hogtie cuff sets at kinky outlets. These kits comprise four **cuffs** and a little hogtie ring that lets you hook the cuffs at a central point. (The cuffs can also be used on their own if you're not in a hogtying mood…because let's face it, sometimes you feel like a pig, sometimes you don't.)

What you then do with your hogtied friend is none of our business. However, we should warn you of the following:

1. Hogtying should be a short-term operation—those contortions put a lot of pressure on the joints, and can make breathing labored. As with most BDSM practices, if you're a beginner you should be on the receiving end for only a few minutes and work your way up, depending on your physical condition— but even experienced players probably wouldn't want to hold that pose for much longer than 30 minutes, 60 tops (tip: the front hogtie is a lot more manageable than the behind-the-back one).
2. Never lie on top of hogtied limbs.
3. Never involve the neck in the hogtie (a.k.a. a pretzel hogtie). That's how the mafia weed out their undesirables—'nuff said?
4. Never hogtie with **handcuffs** or thin cord—thick rope (ideally over gloves) or cuffs only, please.

5. Hogtying can be combined with **suspension play**. We're not going to go there, and neither should you without *a lot* more research (see **edge play** and Appendices B and C).

6. If you Google "hogtie," you'll find a lot of pics of sad-eyed calves amidst all the hot bondage tips, which may inadvertently turn you into a **leather vegan** (which wouldn't be the worst thing in the world).

7. See **bondage safety**.

## hoods

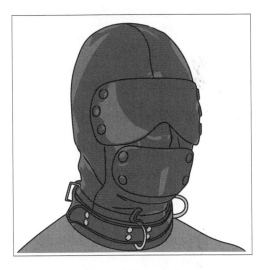

They're like sweatshirt hoodies with the two strings pulled so tight there's just a little hole left through which to breathe— except the **BDSM** version is much less "cute." Made for **sensory deprivation** of the **bottom**, hoods come in almost infinite styles: **gimp** hoods with zipper mouths; **leather** ones with laces or buckles; skin-tight **latex** ones with nose-, mouth- and/or eye-holes; form-fitting Spandex ones without any holes (the material's thin enough to breath through); colored ones with detachable **blindfolds**, mouth **gags** and/or protruding **dildos**; even inflatable **rubber** ones which blow up into perfectly round orbs—because nothing's sexier than your best impression of the Bic man.

## houseboy

A live-in **bottom** whose roles may include chef, maid, handyman, and flunky. But this houseboy doesn't just don a frilly apron and then stand there looking pretty. Nope, he (or, rarely, she) actually mops the floors, answers the door, calls Dominos, and scrubs the period stains/skid marks out of his **top**'s tighty-whities. Sex may or may not be part of the package. Signs that your friend's "butler" may be compensated in kink rather than cash: A) He wears a collar; B) When he bends over you catch a glimpse of his leather thong; C) He calls your friend **Daddy**; D) He can't clean for shit. A.k.a. housegirl, house slave. See also **service kink**, **slaves**, **taken in hand**, **24/7**, and **T.P.E.**

## human furniture

A form of utility **D/s**. IKEA's great for affordable interior decorating, but all that Swedish blonde wood doesn't exactly have a high kink factor. Sometimes you just want a living, breathing, bound person to kick back, relax, and put your feet upon.

A gifted human furniture maker can, with extreme **bondage** techniques, and equipment, transform their partner into a working ottoman, office chair, standing lamp, chandelier, coat rack, lawn sprinkler...with a warped imagination, the possibilities are endless. Of course, these pieces are only temporary—your nightstand will eventually have to get up and go to the bathroom. Visit HouseOfGord.com for a veritable online catalogue. A.k.a. forniphilia, kInkEA, Jennifer's Convertible.

## humiliation

Causing your partner to feel embarrassed, humiliated, degraded, ridiculed, and/or shamed—in other words, a total **mindfuck**. And yes, this can be a **consensual** thing: Some people (typically **subs**, natch) get off on being humiliated, while others (typically **doms**, duh) get off on doing the humiliating. While humiliation *can* occur via physical acts (face-**slapping**, spitting, coming on the face, **watersports**, **scat**, adult baby play (see **baby [adult]**), **chastity devices**, "forced" **enemas**, "forced" **cross-dressing**, even **forced orgasms**), it is largely a head game (*I control you and I'm going to punish you whether you like it or not, toad!*). It's also one of the hardest **BDSM** activities to negotiate in advance (see **communication**), because the definition of humiliation is such a personal thing. Thus things can easily go awry. You might agree in advance to be verbally abused, imagining that your partner will call you a whore, a wench, a slave, etc....only to have them tell you that you're fat/your breasts are saggy/your penis is too small. Some people actually enjoy having their appearance disparaged in this way during humiliation play—but if they don't? Good luck rebuilding your relationship from the emotional wreckage. Hence, we feel that heavy humiliation should be classified as **edge play**. (It's much easier to unbuckle someone's cuffs than it is to take back the phrase, "You're so ugly, you make blind kids cry.") But if you know each other very well (and if the one taking all the crap is of a strong constitution) then humiliation can be a powerful thing to explore within the bedroom.

If you're trepidatious about verbal abuse, try **Christian Grey**'s more touchy-feely approach to humiliation. Have your partner kneel in front of you in the outfit of your choice or in no clothes at all. Forbid them from looking at you directly or speaking to you unless spoken to. Make them request permission to orgasm. Or go for a softer embarrassment—whispering something dirty to your partner in public so only they can hear, or coaching your partner through some **dirty talk** (*Tell me again what you want me to do to you? I won't do it unless you say it out loud...*) when you know it makes them squirm and blush.

By the way, some people like to achieve humiliation via public ridicule, i.e. by taking their **scene** beyond the bedroom. If by "public" you mean your local fetish club, then ridicule away—people entering such a space are implicitly agreeing to be passive participators in other people's play (You down with O.P.P.? Yeah you know me! Other People's *Play*, geddit? Are we the only ones who remember "Yo! MTV Raps"?). But if by "public" you mean the local Starbucks... don't you think people deserve to enjoy their ridiculously overpriced mocha latte in peace? See **scene** (def. #1) for more of our particularly strong feelings on this matter.

## humiliatrix

A **dominatrix** who specializes in **humiliation**. Never let it be said that the kink community is lacking for portmanteaus!

## ice

One end of the **temperature-play** continuum (hot candle **wax** being the other). Cheap, readily accessible, non-staining, and just baby-step kinky, one cold cube —traced down someone's back on a hot summer's day, or strategically placed on a lazy nipple, or sucked on right before an oral administration—can make an otherwise ordinary sesh extra hot (er, cool). You can even make sensual aromatic ice cubes with an ice tray and some water enriched with essential oils. Just be sure to keep the actual ice on the outside of the bod and away from delicate internal linings. See also **sensation play**.

## Japanese rope bondage

Extremely complicated (but rather fetching) form of **rope** bondage that dates back to medieval times. The main difference between Japanese **bondage** and regular rope bondage is that the former, if done right, is supposed to provide a constant erotic **massage** (kind of like shiatsu) in addition to the restraining factor. Plus, Japanese bondage tends to be more ornate and decorative than plain old Western bondage—it's typically applied in layers and can take hours to complete. That said, many bondage junkies who've never studied the Eastern art also enjoy rope bondage as much for the look and feel of the rope as for the fact of it. And many Japanese tie-tricks have been incorporated into today's **BDSM** bondage practices.

One common Japanese technique is asymmetric bondage, which is just what it sounds like: The **bottom** is put in a slightly asymmetric position (e.g. just one leg is bound), which can screw with your balance *and* your head (you know how infuriating it is when someone massages your right shoulder but forgets your left…?).

It wouldn't be very Eastern of us to attempt to cram a how-to description into this entry (nor would it be particularly safe); instead, if you'd like to read more, check out *The Seductive Art of Japanese Bondage* by Midori, recently back in print by popular demand, or *Shibari You Can Use: Japanese Rope Bondage and Erotic Macrame* by Lee "Bridgett" Harrington. And visit CompleteShibari.com for some beginner tutorials. See also **bondage safety**.

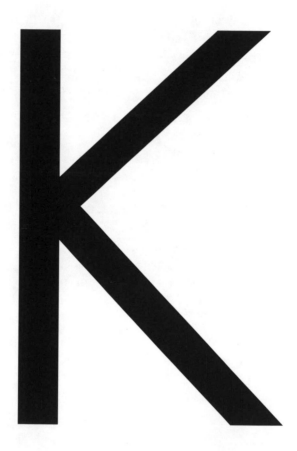

## kink 🐈

1) Any sex or erotic play off the beaten path. This has less to do with fucking in the woods near a hiking trail (though that could count, too) and more to do with **BDSM** or **fetishes**—in fact, the word "kink" has come to serve as a friendly synonym for both those things. The opposite of **vanilla** sex. A.k.a. kinky fuckery (à la *Fifty Shades*), pistachio sex (or, if you're a Ben & Jerry's fan, Chunky Monkey sex). See also our Introduction to this book.

2) *(Archaic)* Deviant sex. It's a pejorative definition which implies that those who do things a little differently in bed are touched in the head. But that meaning has gone out of favor with progressives—because if something is **safe, sane, and consensual**, then it's fair play. *Unconventional* is the preferred adjective. (Of course, if Bill O'Reilly engages in it, it's automatically, unequivocally, and unarguably *deviant*.)

3) Any sexual act that you are not into personally.

## kits, kinky

No idea where to start? A kink kit is a great way to dip your toes in kinky waters —and the better packaged ones can make great gifts for partners who have expressed interest in spicing things up (or who can't tear themselves away from *Fifty Shades of Grey*). Most sex shops offer *Fifty Shades*-related kink kits, as well as various other kinky kits for beginners. These kits typically include kink-lite items like **cuffs** and **blindfolds**. But our favorite kits of all are LELO's Pleasure Sets: Gorgeously packaged like all LELO products, the "Dare Me" set comes with black **vaginal balls** (called Luna Beads Noir), black silky cuffs, and a black suede flogger (oh so *Fifty Shades*!). And the "Indulge Me" set features a purple silky blindfold, a purple feather teaser, and a pink Noa wearable couples **vibrator** (worn by the woman during intercourse). Many of these items are pictured on the back cover of this book. Both kits come with a faux-leather presentation box, a satin storage pouch, and a stylish card for sharing fantasies with your partner. See also **Bend Over Beginner**.

## knots

You might think the Boy Scouts would be a great resource for bondage knots and tying techniques. Plus, they've got that whole uniform thing going on. (Can you say "hot"?!) But scouting knots are meant to go around tree trunks and tent steaks, *not* around human limbs. Rock climbers don't use the same knots as sailors, fisherman don't use the same knots as cowboys, and grown perverts shouldn't use the same knots as eleven-year-old happy campers. So drop the scouting manual and get yourself Jay Wiseman's *Erotic Bondage Handbook*. Once you've boned up on proper bondage techniques with *EBH*, you can certainly use scouting handbooks to help clarify the particular knots outlined by Wiseman. And if you're looking for some more advanced techniques, visit KinkyRopes.com.

Here are the few knots you'll need to know in order to accomplish the techniques described in rope **cuffs**, chest **harness**, and **bondage (object)**. Use them exactly as instructed: Don't go applying them willy nilly or they won't work properly or—more importantly—safely.

1. GRANNY KNOT: This is the knot you'd automatically tie if someone handed you two pieces of rope and just said, "Tie a knot." You twist the right end over and around the left; the end that started on the right should now be in your left hand and vice versa. Now repeat that same tie to create the granny knot. It has a tendency to come undone in certain situations, so should only be used as directed (for instance, don't use this to secure two rope tails around an object, like a bedpost). See **bondage (object)**.

2. SQUARE KNOT: To make this knot, also called a reef knot, you twist the right end over and around the left; the end that started on the right should now be in your left hand and vice versa. Take the end that's now in your left hand and twist it over and around the right; you should end up with a symmetrical loop inside a loop. Good for rope cuffs and securing them to a post that's within reach of the bottom's hands (since simply tugging on one tail won't release it). See **bondage (object)**.

3. BOW KNOT: When tying one end of rope to an object that's out of the bottom's reach, it's handy to use a knot that will come undone with a quick pull of one tail, in case of an emergency, say. Simply wrap each of the tails of the rope around the post at least one time each. (Unlike with wrapping limbs, it's okay—actually it's preferred—if these wraps overlap each other, as pressure put upon them will secure them.) Then simply tie with a bow knot, the kind you use to bow your shoelaces (i.e. the first half of either the granny or square knot, and then the bow bit).

"I'm all for bringing back the birch,
but only between consenting adults."

—Gore Vidal

## latex

A fairly thin, form-fitting, highly glossy **rubber** material, available in many bright solid colors, that's used to make much **fetish wear**. Think: Britney's red catsuit in the "Oops!...I Did It Again" video. **Fetishized** for its tight, almost **bondage**-y fit, its rubbery smell, and its body consciousness (your cellulite might get smoothed out a bit, but if you're smuggling raisins, everyone will see). Getting into it may be a bitch, so you might need a little **lube** to help things along (hey, scuba divers need lube, too, it's nothing to be ashamed of). Be careful not to rip the latex, because without its integrity, it's nothing (plus, you can't really take it to your tailor for repair). Keep it shinier than a pubescent teenager's nose by polishing with a water-based or silicone **lubricant** (available at all sex toy stores).

## latex gloves

See **gloves**.

## latex, liquid

Paint-on **fetish wear**, for when a regular old skin-tight latex **catsuit** just isn't thin enough, revealing enough, or kinky enough. Do a test patch first to make sure you're not allergic. If things look good, paint on a few coats with a foam brush, foam roller, or air brush to get an even look, waiting a few minutes between each coat for it to dry. As it dries, it will shrink, creating a really snug fit. The latex is breathable, so you can cover a lot of ground. But don't get it in hair, eyes, or orifices. In fact, you should use it only on skin that's free of hair or that has only very fine, very short fuzz; like duct tape, it'll take the hair with it when you peel it off. Not to be confused with chocolate paint kits from your local sex toy shop: Liquid latex is *not* edible.

## law, the

An institution that is not always clear on the role of **consent** in kinky play.

In 2009 a woman in the South Central U.S. temporarily lost custody of her children after her own parents discovered her involvement with the local **BDSM** and swing communities and took to the courts to challenge her fitness as a parent —they claimed abuse and neglect. The woman contacted the National Coalition for Sexual Freedom (NCSfreedom.org), an activist group that advocates for BDSM rights, and they helped her win back custody.

And back in 2000, two cops broke into a warehouse in Attleboro,

Massachusetts, and came upon a private BDSM party in progress. While they would later claim they were looking for stolen guitars, they ended up arresting the party host and one guest and confiscating many guests' fancy BDSM gear. The guest was charged with assault (for wielding a wooden spoon) while the host —whose Palm Pilot and guest list were confiscated along with his gear—was arraigned on thirteen charges, including operating a prostitution ring and possession of an item of "self abuse" (a **vibrator**). The prosecution was working with the "**consent** is not a defense to assault" legal precedent. The episode was dubbed "Paddleboro," and the local kink community rallied around the so-called criminals and raised tens of thousands of dollars for their legal defense fund, again with the help of the National Coalition for Sexual Freedom. Eventually all charges were dropped, but not before the party host and guest became household names in their rather conservative New England town.

Kinksters in *old* England have not fared quite so well: In that country, consensual BDSM is illegal if it results in an injury that is "more than transient or trifling." In 1991, sixteen British gay men were convicted of serious assault in a police investigation codenamed Operation Spanner, despite the fact that all sixteen men told the police they were participating in consensual BDSM activities. (The court even convicted a **bottom** for aiding and abetting in his own assault!) The British High Court, the House of Lords, and the European Court all rejected their appeals, and the men were jailed.

Wherever you live, the best defense of all is not getting caught, obviously —so if you've got thin walls, save the piercing screams for those nights when you're indulging in purely **vanilla** activities. And remember that the heavier the BDSM play, the more sober you should be—because consent will also not hold up as a defense if your "victim" is judged to be lacking the capacity to consent (see also **drunk**). Finally, if you're going to be undertaking any activities which may leave a mark, make sure you're fully qualified to be wielding that **whip** (etc.), and consult your local BDSM organization, the NCSF, or the National Leather Association (NLA-i.com) to find out what the law has to stay about kink in your neck of the woods.

## leashes

Usually made of a length of **rope**, **leather**, nylon, or **chain**, they transform **collars** from aesthetic prop/**fetish** fashion accessory to something more utilitarian. They're a common sight at fetish clubs, if you enjoy making it clear to the other club-goers who's the boss of you. The number one rule of leashes is this: *Always* *lead by the front*—you don't want to put *any* pressure on the Adam's apple, windpipe, etc. If you really like to tug on the leash, then you're better off attaching it to a body **harness** instead. The number two rule is, if you want to lead your leashed **sub** to a **food** bowl, find out ahead of time if they're a dog person or a cat person.

## leather

1) (*Noun*) Common **fetish** material in the kink world (along with **latex, rubber, fur,** and **PVC**). So common, in fact, that even kinksters who don't fetishize tanned animal hides often wear it just to announce their kink factor. Pretty much any **BDSM** accessory can be found in a leather version (usually black), including, but not limited to: chaps, **cock rings, crops, cuffs, gags, floggers, harnesses, paddles,** saddles, **spreader bars,** vests, **whips,** and **furniture.** In fact, we bet somewhere out there you'll find an adult **baby** in a man-sized black leather diaper.

2) (*Adjective*) Of or relating to **BDSM**, dating back to the uber-macho gay male leather-biker-BDSM culture (think Tom of Finland) that was an offshoot of the post-WWII biker gang culture. It's a long story, but basically, if you send a bunch of horny young men off to a foreign country and keep them away from women and make them wear military garb and teach them about **discipline,** at least a handful of them are going to come back realizing that they're gay and kinky and like to wear leather. These so-called **leathermen** were known as the Old Guard and had a complex hierarchy and strict rules about dress and behavior; they also networked as if their life depended on it (and actually, back then, maybe it did), hanging out in leather bars (basically gay biker bars, and just as scary as hetero biker bars to outsiders). But as BDSM was co-opted by lesbians and breeders, so too went the leather culture—and these days, "leather" is pretty much just a synonym for "kinky" or "BDSM." For some people, the word's macho overtones linger, but that view is far from universal —hence a "leather dyke" might not be nearly the outlaw you imagine her to be. See also **you're with me, Leather.**

## leatherette

Imitation leather, a.k.a. "pleather" in less polite circles. Popular among the **vegan** kink crowd (a.k.a. **leather vegans**) and, we're assuming, PETA spokesboobs Pamela Anderson.

## leatherman

A gay man who is into leather and/or **BDSM**. See **leather** (def. #2). There's no rule that says a straight man can't be into leather and BDSM, but he's not usually referred to as a leatherman—just "dreamy."

## leather virgin

1) A person in the **BDSM** scene who does not have sexual intercourse. See also **non-sexual BDSM**.
2) A person who is new to the BDSM world ("So, this is your first **fetish** ball? How about an inaugural **spanking**?") or a certain BDSM experience (i.e. "**suspension** virgin" or "**flogging** virgin"). Treat them as you would any virgin: Be respectful, go slowly, build up intensity gradually, and **cuddle** for at least an hour afterwards. See also **leather** (def. #2).

## leather vegan

A person who enjoys kinky sex without the aid of **BDSM** or **bondage** accoutrements made of animal by-products: namely **leather**, suede, **fur** and any meat or dairy used during **sploshing**. For more, see **vegan gear**.

## leatherwoman

A woman who is into leather and/or **BDSM**. See **leather** (def. #2).

## LELO

LELO is a high-end sex toy company based in Sweden whose products make us swoon. All LELO toys are manufactured in-house, come in a gift box with a satin storage pouch, are quieter than a mouse but oh so powerful, and have a one-year warranty (and the ones that buzz are all rechargeable and feature LED indicators). A few of their designs are award winners, including the Tiani, which won the coveted Red Dot Award for Product Design in 2012. Yes, LELO takes your pleasure seriously—so if you're going to invest in one good sex accessory, then let it be a LELO. And if you know your partner would be pleased with something saucier than a pair of socks, look no further: Not only does LELO offer personal massagers and couples rings, they have **massage oils**, gift boxes, and an intimate apparel line for women and men (pictured on the front & back cover). LELO items are available at 10,000 stores worldwide and at LELO.com.

## Liberator wedges

Variously sized foam wedges and ramps—as seen in *Meet the Fockers*—that slide under butts, backs, pelvises, heads, etc., to facilitate greater comfort (or better G-spot/prostate/clitoral access) in a wide variety of positions. We particularly like their Black Label edition—it features the same convenient shapes, but every piece is black (the original Liberators were a less kinky red and blue) and has tethers for bondage cuffs—perfect for those marathon **spanking** sessions!

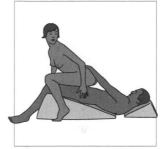

## lifestyle

1) (*Noun*) **BDSM** activities and the kink community, as in, "I'm new to the lifestyle: What is the proper etiquette for **boot**-licking?"
2) (*Adjective*) **T.P.E.**, as in, "They're total lifestyle **D/s**-ers: He's not even allowed to touch the remote."

## limit, hard

A hard limit is something you just won't do—it's off the table, no *ifs, ands* or *butts* about it. In *Fifty Shades of Grey*, **Christian**'s hard limits included fire play, **watersports**, **scat play**, **body modification**, **bloodplay**, **medical toys** or play, **breath control**, and **e-stim**. **Anastasia** insisted on adding **fisting** to that list (perhaps she had a bad experience with hand puppets as a child). Whatever your no-no's, they should be explicitly discussed and agreed upon with your partner beforehand.  Because there's nothing worse than getting whipped with a *leather* **flogger** when you're **vegan**.

## limit, requirement/must

A requirement limit, also sometimes called a must limit, is something you insist upon happening during a scene, in order for you to be happy and feel satisfied. E.g.: "If we're gonna do this thing, I'm gonna need you to go ahead and kick me in the balls, or else I'm outta here."

## limit, soft

A soft limit is something you think you'd probably really rather not do, but could possibly be persuaded to try under the right circumstances, with the right modifications or limitations, and/or with the right person. **Anastasia** initially thought **anal play** would be a hard limit for her, but Mr. Romantic really wanted to *claim her ass* and so she agreed to it being a soft limit; one stainless steel butt plug later and she was a convert! **Christian** initially didn't want to allow Anastasia to have a mind and will of her own, but one wedding, two kids, three near-death experiences, and 569 sex scenes later and he eventually came around. Which just goes to show: Don't knock something 'til you try it.

## limit, time

A set amount of time for your kinky endeavors. A good idea for newbies, especially when dabbling with specific activities like **bondage** or **clamping**, which could result in bad **pain** or injury if done for too long. Not only can **BDSM** be physically grueling, it can be psychologically intense, too: power, vulnerability, suspense...these are all heavy emotions that you need to take a break from while you go get a snack and watch a little *Daily Show*.

## love rings

A kinder, gentler **cock ring** intended for couples, often made of soft, giving material (ideally body-safe silicone) with a protrusion (usually one that vibrates) at the top of the ring which lines up with a woman's clitoris when the man wears it during heterosexual intercourse. Perfect for newbies who may find the **leather** or metal jobbies a little too hardcore for their tastes. Depending on the model, the stretchy ring will either fit around his penis and behind his balls so that they all sit in front of the accessory, or it will just fit around the base of his shaft, like a little belt. Their intended effect is harder, longer-lasting, and more sensitive erections. Of course, penises are as unique as snowflakes, like Grandma always said, so some men will find that the ring *really* affects their sensitivity, causing them to climax even sooner, thus overriding the longer-lasting benefit. Others won't notice much difference at all—but, still, it's always nice to accessorize. LELO has some tasteful (and waterproof!) rechargeable couples rings: the Tor 2 and the Oden 2 (pictured on the back cover of this book). These sensual rings don't require the kind of safety reviews the more pain-inducing instruments do, but it wouldn't hurt you (no pun intended) to read the rules outlined in the **cock rings** and **cock and ball torture** entries anyway.

## lubricants or lubes

A liquid or gel that mimics—indeed, improves upon—the body's natural genital lubrication resulting from arousal that makes sex acts, especially handwork and penetration, easier and more pleasurable. **Anastasia Steele** was consistently naturally "ready" for **Christian**, but things don't always work so *smoothly* in real life. Sure, some women gush at the brush of an elbow, but others produce only a drop or two even during the best sex of their life. Plus, dehydration, the time of the month, medications, age, and a hangover are just a few factors that may diminish a woman's own geyser.

Simply whipping out the lube during plan old **vanilla** sex can certainly spice things up. But for many kinky activities, it's a necessity: **anal play**, **fisting**, marathon sessions, etc. Spit may seem dirty, but it just won't do the job (no matter what you might have seen in *Brokeback Mountain*). Whatever you're doing, lube allows for more intense and more varied stimulation all over, while helping prevent over-sensitivity. It's great for quickies, when there's no foreplay buildup. And adding lube to the outside of a condom means it's less likely to break, while adding a drop of lube *inside* a condom will improve his latex experience, too.

Most sex toy shops offer lube sampler packs, which is a good place to start, since there are many types to choose from. They fall into three basic categories:

1. WATER-BASED: One of the most popular types of lubes, these can be used with latex condoms, dams, diaphragms, and any kind of toy. They wash off easily with water (which means, obviously, they're not waterproof). Try Astroglide (very thin and natural feeling), Liquid Silk (a great My First Lube), Maximus (long lasting, so popular for anal play), and the elegantly packaged Personal Moisturizer by LELO. Some water-based lubes are "warming" lubes, which means they warm up with friction—some ladies swear by these muff warmers, while others claim it's all gimmick. K-Y's Warming Jelly is available *everywhere*, but we prefer Sliquid Organic Sensation (it's glycerin- and paraben-free). There are also flavored lubes—try one without glycerin, since sugars can lead to infection.

2. SILICONE: Also popular, these feel and work just like oil—i.e., they're waterproof (bring on the shower nozzle!), a little goes a long way, and they're longer lasting than water-based lubes because they don't absorb into the body (which means you may have to use soap to remove them completely). But, *unlike* oil, silicone-based lubes *are* safe to use on latex condoms and dams. However, there's one very important rule about silicone lubes: *Do not use silicone lubes on toys made from silicone*—it can cause a chemical reaction and destroy your toy.

3. OIL-BASED: These are usually household products like baby oil, olive oil, hand lotion, and Crisco, and are best saved for man handjobs only, because *oil-based lubes cannot be used with latex products* (the lube degrades condoms, dams, diaphragms, etc.). Also, oil-based lubes are not particularly compatible with vaginas, either, because oil has a tendency to hang around, which makes it a very hardy lube, but also a very likely culprit in urinary tract infections in women.

Once you've settled on a favorite—or a few favorites—you can invest in a full bottle with a pump dispenser, which allows for one-handed reapplication, meaning reapplication is less likely to disrupt the flow of events. See also **menthols**.

"Thou art to me a delicious torment."

—Ralph Waldo Emerson

## made-for-play

Specifically designed for kinky purposes (as opposed to, say, medical, domestic, or crime-enforcement purposes).

## Marquis de Sade

Patron saint of **sadism** (the proclivity was named for him by a very disapproving Austro-German psychiatrist—see **history of kink**). De Sade was a French aristocrat who wrote numerous scandalous works—many of them while in prison, where he served time for being a perv—including the novel he is most famous for, *Justine*. His trademark subject was violent sex that was neither **safe, sane, nor consensual**. Nothing wrong with that in fiction, of course…unless you happen to be writing in the eighteenth friggin' century. De Sade's reputation is complicated somewhat by the rumors that his taste for the nonconsensual extended to his personal life. Still, he's given sex-positive people over the centuries a lot of good quotes to work with, e.g. "Sex is as important as eating or drinking and we ought to allow the one appetite to be satisfied with as little restraint or false modesty as the other." See also **Story of O**.

## masks

**Fetish wear** for the face (probably what conservatives would consider a gateway accessory to more hardcore **hoods**). Most masks just frame the eyes rather than the entire face, and may be made of leather or chrome and decorated with feathers or studs. Others assist in **role-playing** scenarios, especially those of the **animalism** variety (remember the piggy scene in *Bitter Moon*?). Still others go the whole nine, e.g. a full-on, military-style gas mask. Whatever the style, masks help protect identities and hide first- or second-hand embarrassment when attending an *Eyes Wide Shut*-style orgy.

## masochism

The "M" of **SM** and **BDSM**: Getting your rocks off on physical—and, less commonly, emotional—pain and abuse. (By some definitions, pain is a masochist's *requirement* for sexual gratification.) In 1886, an Austro-German psychiatrist named Richard von Krafft-Ebing published *Psychopathia Sexualis*, coining the term masochism after Leopold Ritter von Sacher-Masoch, author of *Venus in Furs*: Both Masoch and his main character got off on being abused by dominant women.

Contrary to popular belief, you don't have to feel like your life is worthless and everything is meaningless to befriend erotic pain. While masochism has been associated with mental illness in the past, it's widely considered fair play these days, so long as it's **safe, sane, and consensual**. Some people theorize that masochists are genetically predisposed to enjoy pain, while others think masochists are made (and not necessarily born), whether through early childhood "imprinting" or a series of life experiences. Just as you can be a submissive who's not interested in pain, you can be a masochist who's not interested in **submission**. And accidentally slamming your finger in a car door won't automatically and instantaneously evoke explosive multiple orgasms: The pain must be delivered and received in an erotic context. See the **pain** entry for reasons why this works for some people.

And, if you have a strong stomach, check out the 1997 documentary, *Sick: The Life and Death of Bob Flanagan*—the cystsic fibrosis sufferer, performance artist, and infamous "SuperMasochist" who did (or let his wife do) unconscionable things to his body, all while maintaining a (some might say) sick sense of humor. He once provocatively declared, "Christ was the most famous masochist." See also **sadism**.

## massage (oils)

A rubdown is a great form of foreplay, easily kinked up with some simple wrist **cuffs** and some deliberate **teasing**. And massage oil is a great gateway drug for the world of sex toys, if either you or your partner is feeling shy: Massage oil is affordable, sensual rather than shocking, and readily available. Keep in mind: Oils are incompatible with latex condoms, and not great for vaginal health either, so, for the "special" portion of your massage, you should always switch to a safe, ideally organic **lube** made specifically for the genitals. But for the body, any kind of oil will do.

At beauty outlets at the mall, you can buy plain oil (e.g., organic soy oil) and flavor it with your own favorite essential oil. (Though if you go with patchouli, we don't want to know about it.) There are warming oils that heat up as you blow on them, cooling menthols, and also edible, flavored lotions (though *edible* and *tasty* are usually two entirely different concepts). We like LELO's Flickering Touch Massage Oil (pictured on the back cover)—it comes in three *actually* sensual fragrances (i.e. no cherry or strawberry!) and contains 24K gold flakes to leave your skin glowing afterward. For more details, see **wax (hot)**.

## master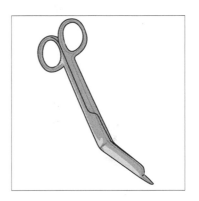

1) Another term for **dom**.
2) What you might call your dom, a.k.a. **daddy** or **sir**.
3) A (typically male) slave owner, either for a **scene** or for an entire relationship (see **slave** entry for full explanation).

See also **mistress**.

## medical scissors

The most important item in any bondage **safety kit**: The blunt ends protect your partner's delicate bits while you free them from that **knot** that simply can't be unknotted, thanks to twenty minutes of ecstatic writhing that pulled it tight. A.k.a. paramedic, bandage, or EMT scissors or shears.

## medical toys & fantasies

Patient-doctor or patient-nurse play—often, though not always, as a subset of **domination** and **submission**. (*Bend over so I can take your temperature...*) Playing doctor can be as simple as **role-playing** a scenario where one partner lies back obediently while the other "examines" the "patient" or gives a sponge bath and perhaps asks a series of increasingly inappropriate questions. But sometimes —as you may have accidentally discovered last time you dressed as a nurse or an escaped psych patient for Halloween—it's a little easier to get into that headspace if you have a few props.

Many kinky outlets stock actual medical paraphernalia, which can be surprisingly cheap (*latex gloves: $4.99 for a box of 50; clear plastic speculum: $6; getting fucked by your OB/GYN: priceless*). Just be sure to **lube** up that speculum before taking it anywhere (and if it's metal, you should warm it up slightly with some hot—*not* scalding—water). Other fun toys to carry around in your black bag include: **Wartenberg pinwheels**, medical forceps (think: nipples, labia, tongue, and, if you're nasty, scrotal sac); institutional padded **cuffs**; anal dilators (all the better to **lube** you with…just don't stretch beyond your partner's comfort level); kegelcisors (to test your patient's internal "grip"); and **enemas**. Oh, nurse! More aesthetic props include: clipboard, glasses, stethoscope, scrubs, white uniform. Warning: If you buy your nurse outfit from a sex toy shop, chances are it will expose approximately 97 percent more flesh than your average RN's duds, and will most likely be constructed out of vinyl or **latex**.

And then there's the **edge play** aspect of medical role-playing —in other words, techniques and "toys" that you really shouldn't be experimenting with unless you've had bona fide medical training (a few discipline sessions with your "doctor" doesn't count): catheters (his and hers); needles (see play **piercing**); **cutting**; and something called "urethral sounding" (inserting rods into the urethra). Remember, just because something—a sounding kit, say—is sold in a sex toy shop, doesn't mean it's safe for you to get jiggy with. We wouldn't let McDreamy, McSteamy, or Major McHottie from "Grey's Anatomy" come within ten feet of us with those things—and neither should you.

If you want to put together a kinky doctor's kit, visit MedicalToys.com: Speculums, catheters, enemas, black **PVC** "Nasty Nurse" uniforms, plus a bunch of other stuff we're too squeamish to mention, but all presented in the best possible taste. Their "Ask the Doctor" and "Ask the Nurse" columns are friendly and down-to-earth, their safety information is extensive and wicked smaht, their customer service is excellent, and they give mad props to real-life nurses.

## menthols

The hot sauce of kinky sex: balms, creams, and/or liquids which, unlike the McDLT, combine both the cool and the hot to create a tasty sensation on the skin as a form of **temperature-** or **sensation play**. We're talking Icy Hot, Tom's of Maine Cinnamon Toothpaste, Hall's Mentholyptus cough drops, Vicks VapoRub, curiously strong mints, etc.

But before you go slathering a big ol' scoop of Tiger Balm on your crotch, please understand that this is seriously strong stuff, to be used in only the *smallest* of doses, and *not* internally or on broken skin. We wouldn't even use them on your erotic **mucous membranes**, unless the products are edible—but even then you've got to be *more* cautious, since the menthol will pack a greater punch there than it will on your thicker skin elsewhere. (Do we need to tell you not to put it in the eyes?) Just to beat off a dead horse: Menthols are not to be used as lubrication for penetrative sex—besides, they're usually made of oils which will degrade **latex** condoms.

Test a smidge on yourself first before you go offering Ben Gay rub-downs all over town. Make sure you're a stone's throw from a water source and a bar of pure vegetable soap, in case of menthol miscalculation. And remember, that stone's throw will seem like a football field if the mentholated can't be unbound quickly. We'd recommend starting with a single Tic Tac Bold (or your mint of choice): Suck on it for a few seconds, then suck on a body part for a few seconds, then wait and see how the recipient feels—you're going for sensation that enhances rather than distracts from the pleasure (unless you're dealing with a real **masochist**). Build up gradually, but remember that most menthols take some time to really kick in, and may last longer than your allotted diddling time.

If you're working with stronger, inedible menthols, you might consider applying them—to, say, the nipples—with latex **gloves** so your fingertips don't get "burnt." (The nipples will get hot, of course, but that's the point! Burning nipples = erotic pain; burning fingertips = distracting and annoying, especially if you're meant to be the torturer, not the tortured, tonight!)

## mindfuck

1) (*Sensual*) An experience intentionally created by a **top** which blows the **bottom**'s mind because their body is trying to reconcile two contrasting **sensations**. For instance, being fellated while being **flogged** can feel like Republicans paying Hillary Clinton a sincere compliment. *Whaaaaat?* A.k.a. contrapolar stimulation.

2) (*Impish*) A damned-if-you-do-damned-if-you-don't situation mischievously created by a top for their bottom. For example, the top may tie the bottom up in such a way as to make walking impossible and then ask them to go get the mail. A.k.a. **mistress/master** game.

3) (*Sinister*) A situation created by a top which intentionally makes the bottom feel confused, scared, **humiliated**, surprised, or psychologically devastated

because their mind and/or body is trying to reconcile an expectation with a contrasting experience. For example, the top makes the bottom think they are about to be (or are being) broken up with/**raped** by a stranger/killed/etc., even though that's not the case. It's a form of **edge play** we cannot condone for beginners, and are not even sure is that cool for advanced players. Can you say post-traumatic stress disorder? A.k.a. head game, some fucked-up shit.

4) Being turned on by the sex scenes in *Fifty Shades of Grey* despite the mind-numbingly awful writing and the constant, annoying interruptions by **Anastasia's** cart-wheeling, back-flipping, gum-chewing Inner Goddess and her arch enemy, the arm-crossing, foot-tapping, eye-rolling Subconscious.

## mistress

1) Another term for **dom** or **domme**.
2) What you might call your dom, a.k.a. **ma'am, Mrs. Robinson**.
3) A female slave-owner, either for a **scene** or for an entire relationship (see **slave** entry for full explanation).

See also **master**.

## mommy

1) Like a **mistress**, but more "nurturing"…more, you know, *maternal*. Mommies are not nearly as common as their **daddy** counterparts, and are mostly seen in the context of adult **babies**. (who'd a thunk it—even among **leather** mommies and daddies, it's the woman who gets stuck changing the diapers.)
2) The only person we *don't* want reading this book.

## motivation

Something that pretentious actors need to have explained to them (by their director or writer) in order to understand why their character is behaving a certain way, rather than just accepting that they'd do that—as in, *What's my motivation?* A patient director may tell said pretentious actor, "Your mother used to abuse you, therefore you don't trust women and it's hard for you to accept love, which is why you would say this mean thing to your lover. Though you may adore her and want to be nice, you push her away as a form of protection—that's your motivation for treating the woman you love like shit." When a pretentious **role-playing** *sub* asks to have their motivation explained, their **dom** is likely to reply, "Because I said so."

## MP3 players 🐾

When Mac Geniuses want to practice **sensory deprivation**, their iPods and a pair of **headphones** are the first tools they reach for. After all, music in ear buds helps drown out the world around you and lets you focus on the pleasure at hand. If you're looking for suggestions for your kinky booty music, all the classical tunes featured in E.L. James's erotic trilogy are available on the *Fifty Shades of Grey* Soundtrack via iTunes (and for the record, we were calling the iPod a sex toy years before **Christian Grey** appeared on the scene). If those instrumental songs are too old-school, cliche, and/or creepy, try Nine Inch Nails, Muse, Radiohead, The Brazilian Girls, Massive Attack, Marilyn Manson, Prince, Peaches, The Cure, or Kings of Leon. (If you discover an even better band for your kinky soundtrack, let us know at EMandLO.com and we'll publish a list!)

## Mrs. Robinson 🐾

The nickname **Anastasia Steele** gives to **Christian Grey**'s erstwhile **domme**, Elena Lincoln, in *Fifty Shades of Grey*. It references the classic 1967 movie *The Graduate*, in which recent college grad Benjamin Braddock (Dustin Hoffman) is aggressively seduced by the manipulative and controlling wife (Ann Bancroft) of his father's business partner. In *Fifty Shades*, we learn that years ago Elena Lincoln took a delinquent, teenage Christian Grey under her wing...and under her whip. While their sexual relationship is long over and he's gone from submissive to full-on dominant by the time he meets Ana, Elena still retains some hold over Christian—and Ana sure as hell doesn't approve. Melodrama ensues.

## mucous membranes, erotic

The labia, the clitoris, the anus, the urethral opening, and the tip of the penis.

## mummification

Wrapping the body from head (or neck) to toe in Ace bandages, muslin, **Saran Wrap**, **bondage tape**, latex bondage strips, a **body bag**, a **sleepsack**, a **vacuum bed**, or a **straitjacket**-pants set, as a form of full-immobility **bondage** and/or **sensory deprivation**. The effect can be peaceful, like a big full-body hug from God; it can be frustrating, especially if your naughty bits are being tormented and teased over or through the material; or it can be maddening, if, say, you're *seemingly* left alone in the dark with only your thoughts and the inability to scratch your nose. Mummification should not be taken as lightly as a day at the beach (although burying someone in the sand from the neck down could certainly work, too); you've got to follow some important safety guidelines:

1. Beginners, make sure your mummy's mouth is an unobstructed air passageway: Some experienced players leave only the nose open, but you want your captive to be able to breathe/**communicate**/ say their **safeword**.
2. Their chest shouldn't be wrapped so tightly that they can't expand their lungs to breathe easily.
3. Don't cut off circulation anywhere, either.
4. Make sure your bottom is lying down or safely secured to the encasing's **D-rings** with stabilizing chains (at least by the time you get to securing their legs together), otherwise they might lose their balance and go boom.
5. If you're cocooning your inchworm in materials that will cause them to sweat (like Saran Wrap or latex), you need to make sure they stay hydrated and don't overheat.
6. If they're going to be wrapped until their next bathroom break (no more than 15 minutes for first timers, though), you should add padding between knees and ankles and under pressure points for extra comfort.
7. Don't *really* leave your boundee alone: Be sure you can see and hear them at all times.
8. Keep your **medical scissors** handy so you can release them quickly.
9. Once unraveled, be ready to warm them up with a blanket.
10. Finally, if they're up for it, take full advantage of their newfound respect for movement and sensation.

Read **bondage safety** and **Saran Wrap** for more safety tips. A.k.a. cocooning.


## munch

A **BDSM** networking event—it's the kink world's golf game. A munch (think meet + lunch) typically takes place in a low-key locale like a bar or restaurant, and **vanilla** attire (think khakis not chaps) is the norm. It's essentially a kinky kaffeeklatsch—people share advice on **clubs**, toys, **fetish** shops, etc. Munches are decidedly not sex parties and they're not meant to be pick-up spots either, though you wouldn't be the first to "network" your way to a new **slave**. The first munch was held at a burger joint in (where else?) San Francisco in the early '90s and was known as a "burger munch." It was organized (how else?) online.

Gatherings are still mostly coordinated online, though these days the Big Macs are optional. To find a munch near you, check out the kink community site, FetLife.com

## murmur

The only acceptable way to communicate in *Fifty Shades of Grey*, whether you're discussing **vaginal balls** or what to eat for breakfast. *Not* a requirement for kinky sex.

## muzzles

Face bondage devices intended to restrict the wearer's ability to speak and make them feel more like the pathetic dog they are. Not unlike actual animal muzzles, they're usually made of leather and held in place with a full head harness, which may come with a **collar** or **leash**. There are even muzzles to satisfy your Hannibal Lecter fantasy from the "Oh, and Senator, love your suit" scene in *Silence of the Lambs*. (We must, however, insist that you not actually eat people.)

See also **animalism** and **gags**.

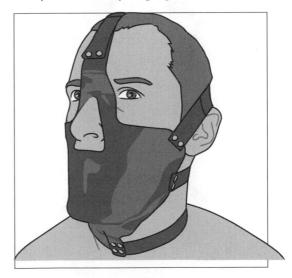

## nipple clamps

See **clamps** and **nipple play/torture**.

## nipple play/torture 🐾

Pinching, twisting, biting (without breaking skin), flicking, **clamping**, sucking, suckling, suctioning, hot **waxing**, icing, **mentholating**, **pumping**, **teasing**, or otherwise tormenting the teats (either his or hers). While the nipples are built to take a beating (*hello*, there's nothing more torturous than *breastfeeding*), you never want to break skin, cut them, or clamp them so long and hard they fall off. And while some people's nipples are the gateway to ecstasy, other people's nips are the doors of Hell.

Assuming you're working with the former species: When applying any kind of pressure, avoid the *very* tips of the nips—grab just beyond the tips to keep the **pain** pleasant and bearable. If you're working with clothespins (see **clamps**), it's better to apply them parallel to the body, rather than sticking straight out (unless the clothespins are really light and the nips in question are impossibly perky).

If you want something a little more stylish or **made-for-play**, there are about a-million-and-one kinds of nip equip available: **pumps** for creating T.H.O.s (titty hard ons); rubber rings for maintaining said T.H.O.s; non-piercing shields and jewelry for adornment (à la Janet Jackson); **clamps** with chains which connect to a **collar**, a **gag**, a clitoral clamp, **a cock ring**, or each other; clamps with weights, bells, or even mini vibrating devices. For now, we'd avoid the clover-style clamps, which actually get tighter when you tug on them: not great if their chain accidentally gets caught on someone's braces. Go for adjustable clamps so you can start off with an erotic niggling sensation rather than hardcore pain. See **clamps** for more important safety information. See also **nipple suction cups**.

## nipple suction cups

The lazy person's alternative to nipple **pumps**. These are small, often clear, tubular suction cups that bring blood to the surface quickly, increasing sensitivity much like a nipple **clamp** does. They're easier, cheaper, and less intimidating than pumps and fancy clamps, and the sensation when they're removed is much less violent than when removing clamps. By the way, if you happen to have a snake bite kit handy, you can use its venom-extracting suction cups for the same saucy result. A.k.a. nipple suckers, nipple sucklers.

## no

A word that doesn't necessarily mean no, if—*and only if*—you're playing with a **safeword** (one that has been negotiated and agreed upon by all parties before any sexual encounter commences). So next time you're in a BDSM **club** and hear someone cry out, "No more! I can't take it! Please stop! Bad touch!" think twice before swooping in to rescue that "victim." Awkward! If you're truly concerned, notify the designated **dungeon master** rather than risk interrupting a **scene** in progress.

## non-sexual BDSM

Kink without the happy ending. If you get deep into the **scene** (see def. #2 of that entry), you'll discover that kink does not necessarily mean kinky sex. Some people **play** together without ever getting off (because the **whips**, **rope**, **pain**, etc., are their own erotic end), while others choose mutual masturbation as their climax. And some kinky couples in long-term relationships may have non-sexual play partners on the side (*See you later honey, I'm off to meet the slave for a mocha with extra whip!*). You have to be a pretty evolved kinkster to be capable of separating **BDSM** from sex in this way. For kinky dabblers, BDSM is a way to spice up foreplay and sex, and thus "non-sexual BDSM" would be an oxymoron. Then again, there are plenty of folks out there (we're looking at you, red states) who'd claim that consensual violence is an oxymoron, too! See also **dominatrix**.

## nose hooks

Pairs of small, blunt hooks which are inserted into the nostrils and attached, via strap, to the back of a head harness, turning the wearer into one of the Little Piggies, the Crypt Keeper, or a victim of rhinoplasty malpractice. A.k.a. nostril strap. See also **humiliation**.

"Don't worry,
it only seems kinky the first time."

—Unknown

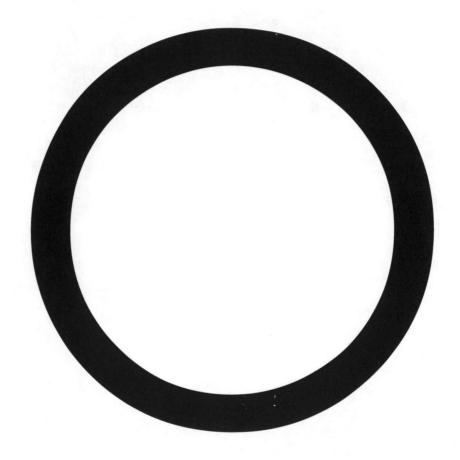

## online personals

How to meet your kinkmate. Whether you're a lifestyler (see def. #2 of **lifestyle**) who wants to avoid one of those "when someone you love is kinky" talks on the second date, or just a **bondage** fanatic looking for someone to practice on, **BDSM**-related online personals are one way to go (especially if you live a very long tractor ride from the nearest kinky **club**). Most "adult" dating sites, such as AdultFriendFinder.com, will let you search for kinky ads only. Or, if you want to get *really* specific in your search, try FetLife.com, Bondage.com, or Alt.com (see Appendix B for website info), where you can search the personal ads by every fetish described in this book *and more* (Denim, anyone? Lactation, perhaps?). As with any online personals, but especially in the world of kink, you should "date" with care: Always tell a friend where you'll be and when you'll be home; always meet in public first (you can get down to the naked **wax** play later); remember that no matter how hot and heavy the emails were leading up to the occasion, you owe your date nothing except half an hour and a cup of coffee (even if you're a **sub**!); and never *ever* let a stranger tie you up or gag you. For more great advice, check out *The Kinky Girl's Guide to Dating* by Luna Grey.

## O.T.K.

Over the knee. See **spanking**.

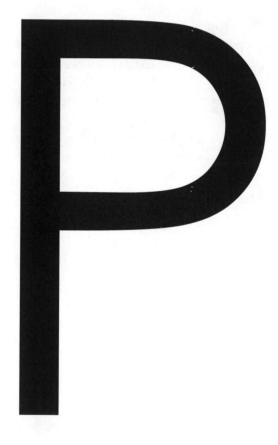

## paddles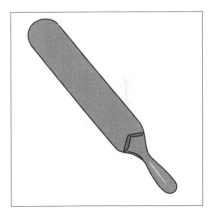

A heavier, hardier stand-in for your hand during spanking administrations. Great for wimpy tops who don't want to hurt their precious palms. Often employed in **role-playing** scenarios featuring sadistic priest/Catholic school student, or sadistic fraternity brother/frosh pledge, or sadistic father/delinquent kid, or sadistic drill sergeant/undisciplined recruit, in which the one getting hit is usually instructed to shout, "Please sir, may I have another?" after each whack. You don't want to get stuck up the River Kink without a paddle, so find one in a material and size that's right for you: a heart-shaped plastic one, a velvety rubber one, a one-of-a-kind hand-made artisanal wooden one, or even a real ping-pong paddle (if **D.I.Y.** is the way you roll). Some whackers come with holes to lessen wind resistance and thus increase impact. The wider the paddle, the bigger its thud; the narrower the paddle, the greater its sting (see also **slappers**). Number one rule of paddling: Keep the tool precisely targeted on the lower, fleshier parts of the buttocks only (away from the tailbone). If they don't have any fleshy parts to their tush, put down the paddle and make them a fucking sandwich. Avoid instruments with rough edges or hard corners. And realize that a paddle whack of the same force as a hand spank hurts a lot more. Please see both the **flagellation** and **spanking** entries for more important safety information.

## pain

You know "Hurts So Good" by John Cougar (Mellencamp)? Yeah, we hate that song too, but you gotta admit the lyrics make a good point: "Sometimes love don't feel like it should." When you're really turned on, pain can feel a lot like pleasure. Ever wake up the next morning with dark purple fingerprint bruises on your outer thighs and have *no idea* when that happened the night before? You don't have to get a **Marquis de Sade**–style ass-kicking or a punishing spanking from a Christian Grey–type to get a kick out of pain—sometimes a nibble on the nipple, one single well-timed **spank**, or a little hair-pulling is all it takes (or all *you* can take) to heighten the sexual tension.

But pain can also be more than a side dish: Sometimes it can be the main entrée. Pain triggers the autonomic nervous system, which produces endorphins (opiate-like chemicals in your body) and increases your heart rate, breathing, and blood pressure—all of which is a lot like sex. This endorphin rush, also known as runner's high, can make the pain feel less like discomfort and more like intense, euphoric sensation. We could go into more, excruciating detail—but we think E.L. James already did. If it wasn't clear before: *This* is why people like to get tied up and **flogged** for an hour. Add to this the eroticism of the **power** dynamic involved in a pain exchange, the intimacy engendered by the trust necessary for such an exchange, and the sexy vulnerability (or even **humiliation**) of being **whipped** while naked, and it's no wonder some people (admittedly, the lucky few) can actually orgasm from erotic pain alone.

Remember, the key word here is "erotic": Getting kicked in the nuts (see **tamakeri**) or punched in the face is neither sexy nor safe. There's good pain and then there's bad pain: You're only interested in the former. And you get it by strictly following the safety guidelines for all of the methods and equipment described in this book. If good pain starts to feel like bad pain, stop immediately. Beginners shouldn't get greedy: One kind of erotic pain at a time. (It's either nipple **clamps** or a flogging, but not both.) Breathing steadily, making some noise, and relaxing your muscles will also help you better appreciate how pleasure and pain, like love and hate, are two sides of the same coin.

Then again, pain in any form, even a lightly pinched nipple, may not interest you at all: You can be into submission and only ever want soft and fuzzy touches; you can be into spanking and never want to try anything more *sharp*. But if you do, make sure you've got a responsible, well-informed partner who'll treat you wrong in all the right ways, which includes lots of **aftercare**: Namely, rubbing on some **arnica cream**, fixing you a cup of tea, and giving you a good **cuddle** afterwards.

## painslut

A person who just can't get enough of pleasure through pain, and will go to great lengths to get it. Some say it's synonymous with an unashamed masochist. Others say this is different from masochism, which is about the pain, in and of itself, and not about the endorphin-fueled, almost sexual pleasure that comes from some pain, which in their opinion is what the painslut is all about.

## panic snaps

Small metal devices used to connect two **ropes** or **chains** that can be easily released even if your 250-pound **bottom** is bearing down on those ropes or chains and screaming their **safeword**. Essential for **suspension play**; handy for any kind of **bondage**.

## penis rings

See **love rings** (if you're nice), **cock rings** (if you're naughty).

## phthalates

Potentially carcinogenic substance found in many plastic products—especially cheap sex toys. Phthalates help make plastic soft and flexible, so the substance is particularly common in jelly toys. Basically, if your toy has that new car smell, you probably don't want to put in inside you. And always check the packaging! A "phthalates-free" promise is what you're looking for—in fact, responsible sex toy manufacturers and outlets won't even sell products with phthalates in them these days. But this is an entirely self-regulated move, and you can't always rely on the goodness of folks. If you wouldn't let your baby chew on it, then don't insert it where the sun don't shine either.

## piercing, play

Temporary piercing as part of a kinky **scene**, where the idea is to get off on the experience, rather than suffer through the pain for the end result. Needles are inserted into various parts of the body (at a tangent so that both ends of the needle are exposed) and then removed at the end of the scene so that the piercing heals over. The sensation can cause a huge endorphin high (see **pain**) and might even lead to orgasm (if you can believe it). It could also lead to, oh, HIV, to name a random blood-borne disease. And it's not just a matter of using brand new, sterile hypodermic needles and swabbing with alcohol—do us a favor and Google "needlestick injuries" if you need convincing. Needless to say, this kind of piercing is **edge play** and thus we cannot even come close to endorsing it. For further reading, check out *Play Piercing* by Deborah Addington, published by the kink specialists at Greenery Press. A.k.a. needle play, recreational acupuncture.

## pillowcases 🔨

As recommended in Jay Wiseman's *SM 101*, a pillowcase makes a great "my first whip" for beginners. Gives you all the fun of **flagellation** without any of the dangers (like accidental death)! Also handy to weep into on those nights when you just can't stand **Christian Grey's** cold, steely gaze any longer.

## pinch-hitter

A temporary third party in the bedroom.

## play 🪃

1) (*Noun*) Any kind of sexual activity between two (or more) people that all participants consider fun, whether it be experimenting with a little **bullet** vibrator or enjoying a black-leather **strap-on** with an 8-inch **dildo**.

2) (*Noun*) **BDSM** activities engaged in during a **scene**: *What kind of play are you interested in: **cock and ball torture**, **slave** training, domestic **discipline**, diaper dominance…?*

3) (*Verb*) Engaging in BDSM activities, usually with another person (or several people): *I love playing with Bobby because he's such an obedient slave: He'll clip my toenails with his teeth whenever I ask him, without question or hesitation.*

## play parties

Private **BDSM** gatherings where people participate in **scenes** (as opposed to fetish **clubs**, which are open to the public, or **munches**, which are **play**-free BDSM gatherings). Play party hosts are the Martha Stewarts of the kink world: They provide dungeon **furniture**, safer sex supplies, snacks, and the house rules.

Each play party will have its own code of etiquette regarding issues such as attendance (e.g. single men have to be accompanied by a woman, or all plus-ones have to be cleared with the host), attire (**fetish wear** only, perhaps), **safewords** (always required, but some parties have a universal safeword, such as "red" or "safeword"), benchwarmers (some hosts may like all attendees to be joiners, while others may enjoy the tension that inexperienced onlookers bring to a scene), **edge play** (very few private parties are down with **breath control**; some may allow activities such as **blood play** only if cleared with the host first, or in a designated area only, etc.), nudity (there may be a nudity zone, or a nudity-free zone, or full nudity may be frowned upon due to local regulations), penetrative sex (often disallowed due to local "house of disrepute" laws, etc.), and discretion (wear a coat to cover your fetish gear until inside, etc). In general, a play party's house rules will be very similar to the accepted etiquette at a BDSM **club** (no touching without asking, etc.), but the host's own policies always trump whatever you might consider to be the "done thing" among kinky types.

Your best shot at getting invited to a private play party is to seek out a local **munch**—most hosts like to vet new players over coffee and cake before inviting them over for some light **paddling**. See also **law (the)**.

## plushies

People who take a rather, shall we say, *adult* interest in stuffed animals. They don't necessarily want to *be* furry animals (like **furries**), they just want to fuck little stuffed ones (or at least fuck *with* them). However, plushies who also identify as **furries** like to dress up as those stuffed animals, too.

## pony play

One of the most popular forms of **animalism**, complete with its own subculture and events calendar. There was even once a full color print magazine, *Equus Eroticus* (it's online only now, though back issues are available for purchase— get your Xmas shopping done early!).

While pony play is certainly erotic, with its power exchanges and nudity (ponies don't usually wear anything but their equipment), there isn't a whole lot of actual sex, except perhaps between a pony girl and a pony boy (i.e. a stud) for breeding fantasies. (A trainer wouldn't fuck their pony because that would be a form of bestiality, which is not what pony play is about. See **animalism**.)

As for the gear, you can certainly trot around in the privacy of your own living room one evening with just some long ribbon for reins, but many pony players enjoy the accoutrements as much as the acting: horse "tack" or harnesses, bridles, bits, saddles, belts or **butt plugs** with horsehair tails, blinders, hoof gloves and hoof **boots**… And that's just the stuff for the pony! The trainer may have riding pants, riding boots, riding **crops** (rarely used for whippings in this crowd), and grooming supplies.

You can be a Black Stallion, a Budweiser Clydesdale, a Sea Biscuit, or your own breed…say, an Ocean Cookie. And you might have different responsibilities: Cart ponies draw small, lightweight wagons with their trainer at the reins; riding ponies are outfitted with saddles for carrying their masters on their shoulders or backs; and show ponies are trained for style and grace in mimicking actual horse movements, gaits, and, yes, neighing. It can be backbreaking work, walking around on all fours and taking people on pony rides, so good health and good form are required of both pony and trainer (e.g. if riding a pony on all fours, the responsible trainer will use their own legs to carry some of their weight). It's not considered cheating in the pony world to stand upright, as long as you don't use your hands or speak. Pony girls and pony boys may be fed sugar cubes or carrots as rewards, eat dinner out of a feeding bag, or sleep in a hay-filled stable.

Don't have your own barn? Equestrian retreats for pony players provide the opportunity. If you still don't get it, watch the sweetly earnest introductory movie on The-Stampede.com. Okay, you still might not get it after watching this, but points for trying. See also **furries** and **plushies**.

## power play/power exchange

The unifying theme running through the entries in this book; the glue that holds **BDSM** together; the creamy center of all kink. If good sex is about a mutual give and take, then good kinky sex is about deliberately manipulating that give and take together (i.e. **consensually**) in order to create psychological and/or physical drama.

Typically, one person—referred to as the **top**, or the **dom**—agrees to take control (and thus most of the responsibility for everyone's physical and emotional **safety**) while the other person—referred to as the **bottom**, or the **sub** —trustfully agrees to relinquish it. This is the definition of the **D/s** of BDSM, or **domination** and **submission**.

But power play spills over into other areas of BDSM: For example, in **SM** situations, the top is *in charge* of inflicting erotic **pain** on the bottom, and in **B&D** scenarios, the top takes the reins (and in some cases *literally* picks up the reins—see **pony play**) when it comes to binding or **disciplining** the bottom. Even though this creates the illusion of an unequal or unfair erotic relationship, ideally *both* parties get off on their respective roles, each of which actually—and in the top's case, ironically—puts the pleasure of the other first and foremost.

While this power exchange is often set up for a finite period of **time** (a **scene**), it can go on indefinitely, not just in an erotic context but in all aspects of mundane daily life, which we guess somehow makes even doing the laundry ('cause your top told you to) erotic. This is known as a *total* power exchange, or **T.P.E.** See also **slave** and **taken in hand**.

## pro dom

See **dom/domme** and **dominatrix**.

## pumps (penis, nipple, & clitoris)

Appropriately sized devices that draw blood to the penis, nipples, or clit. With ordinary arousal, blood flows into these parts, causing them to become engorged and stiff (more obviously so in the case of the penis). A pump, on the other hand, forces the maximum amount of blood in, creating an erection/engorged clit/ upright nipples on demand. Many people like the feeling of suction—it's like a very localized **vacuum bed**! It makes everything even more sensitive to touch, too—perfect for **teasing** your bottom while they're bound to the bed. And if you're prone to less-than-fully-inflated erect body parts, a pump will probably make you look, or at least feel, bigger (of particular interest to penis owners, we have noticed). Of course, this lasts only as long as the erection itself—once your pumped part has deflated, you'll be left with the same old penis/nip/clit, except it might be a little tender and maybe even bruised.

Though bruising might sound like a good thing in the context of **BDSM**, we wouldn't recommend aiming for that: If you pump for too long or too often or too vigorously, the pump might cause burst capillaries, tissue damage, or ligament damage. (And no bottom deserves that.) Some gentlemen also report that they find it, er, *harder* to ejaculate with a pumped-up stiffie. So stick to a 10 to 15 minute limit. Start slowly and pace yourself. These devices work by creating a vacuum around your bits—lubing up first will help seal this vacuum; so will removing any area hair.

Finally, don't use a pump, even for novelty purposes—ready for the fine print?—if you bleed easily, have a blood-clotting disorder, are diabetic, suffer from any peripheral vascular disease, are nursing, or take anticoagulants, aspirin, or any other blood-thinning medication. If something feels funny afterwards, swallow your pride and tell your doc what you did. See also **nipple suction cups**.

## PVC

Short for polyvinyl chloride, a synthetic plastic used to make **bondage tape** and **fetish wear**. Looks like shiny patent leather, but works for **leather vegans** and cheap bastards. If the look of it doesn't get you all hot and bothered, wearing it might, since it's not a very breathable material: Be prepared to sweat your balls off. See also **latex** and **rubber**.

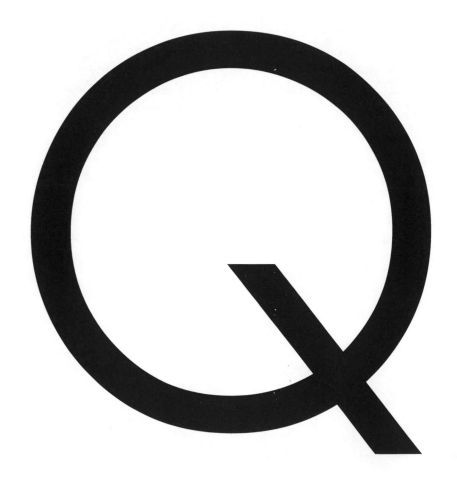

## queening stools

Low stools with a hole in the seat to aid in the old "sit on my face" game, often employed in **domination/submission** activities. A variation on the theme is a smotherbox (see illustration), which looks like a kid's potty training toilet: One hole on the top of the box is for the **top's** naughty bits and one hole on the side of the box is for the **bottom's** head, in order to gain oral access to said naughty bits. Say goodbye to inconvenient leg cramps and a performance-diminishing squashed nose!

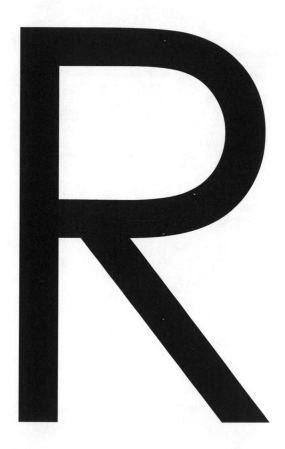

## Rabbit vibrators

Probably the most widely recognized dual-action vibe in the world, thanks in large part to the *Sex and the City* episode in which prudish Charlotte gets so addicted to her battery-powered, floppy-eared companion that her friends stage a vibrator intervention. The original Rabbit vibrator is made in Japan by a company called Vibratex and features a swirling shaft, undulating pearls inside the base for stimulation of the vaginal opening, and an external rabbit whose ears flutter against the clitoris. You can vary both the vibration intensity and swirling speed.

Because the Rabbit is such a legendary sex toy, however, cheap knockoffs are widespread. So if you're going to invest in a hoppy friend, make sure you buy a quality version. Vibratex makes a **phthalate**-free Rabbit which we highly recommend. For the woman who doesn't need or particularly want her sex toy to feature an adorable animal face, try the silicone Kaya Rabbit by PicoBong. And for a sophisticated, deluxe experience—again without the adorable (or would that be creepy?) animal face—you can't go wrong with LELO's dual-action Ina 2 vibrator (pictured on the back cover).

## rape fantasy

1) The bread and butter of the entire romance novel genre, though they usually refer to it as a "ravishing," or a "**ravishment fantasy**." A.k.a. the bodice-ripper.
2) Something many many women and men, but especially straight women, masturbate to (it's right up there with the "exploring lesbianism-lite with Angelina Jolie" fantasy). And it's far from the new kid on the block—all the way back in 1973 (when the babyboomers were the ones doing the masturbating), Nancy Friday had an entire chapter dedicated to this kind of fantasy—called "Don't Just Stand There, Force Me!"—in her best-selling classic of real women's sexual thoughts, *My Secret Garden*.

   For the record: Fantasizing about rape doesn't mean you actually want to rape or be raped (it doesn't even mean you actually want to act out the fantasy—see def. #3), it doesn't make you a bad feminist, and it doesn't mean you need **therapy**. (Can a bazillion healthy, happy, well-adjusted romance-novel readers be wrong? See def. #1.) It doesn't necessarily mean that you have latent guilty feelings associated with sex, either. In fact, recent research found that women who frequently fantasize about being overpowered are more likely to have positive attitudes about sex, to have higher self-esteem, and to entertain fantasies about forcing a man to have sex.

But even if you do have feelings of guilt associated with sexual desire or activity, leftover perhaps from an uber-conservative upbringing or a particularly stern religious leader from your youth, then that's okay, too. Many rape survivors even have these types of fantasies, since they can be **therapeutic**. After all, even though you're imagining being sexually **dominated**, you ultimately have total control. Which is why we use the term *ravishment fantasy* (see the entry immediately below) instead of *rape fantasy*: No one who enjoys these kinds of fantasies actually wants to be raped in the real world; instead, they have a specific scenario of sexual domination in their mind which, again, they control and can manipulate. In this make-believe world you can be wanted so badly by someone who is blinded by their lust for you that all of your sexual responsibility—indeed your shame—is removed. The appeal of that is certainly understandable, whether we're talking about someone who's been sexually assaulted or someone who's *never* been sexually assaulted, someone who is sexually liberated or someone who's a bit sexually repressed.

What it boils down to is this: Fantasizing about this stuff while rubbing one out simply means you get off on the notion of overpowering or being overpowered. So if you enjoy the occasional masked intruder fantasy, then just enjoy it. Don't deny yourself the pleasure of a very common fantasy to fit some politically correct notion of what's mentally tasteful or appropriate. That's the great thing about fantasies—they can be absolutely inappropriate! But if, on the other hand, you feel these fantasies are negatively impacting your life, your relationship, and your self-worth, then it's time to seek some professional help: Visit AASECT.org and see Kink Aware Professionals in the Surfing Suggestions list, Appendix B.

3) A pretend **scene** between two consenting adults, most commonly a man "raping" or ravishing his female partner. And for those of you who cry out, "That's so fucked up, dude!" or "That woman's got more issues than *Reader's Digest!*" may we refer you to definition #2, as well as to the notion of **consent**. A domination fantasy can be accomplished as simply as with a pair of **cuffs**— though it should be noted that not every woman who wants to be tied up has a rape fantasy.

In heavier, *previously-negotiated* scenes, which should always involve a **safeword**, a man may "surprise" his partner at home and force himself on her —the specifics are up to the two of you (forced blowjob, **bondage**, mouth **gag**, etc.), but again, all should be agreed upon in advance. Often a couple will discuss this kind of fantasy and then agree to wait a few weeks or months (or more) before acting it out, at a time and date of the man's choosing—thereby bringing back an element of surprise. The more intense the scene will be, the more prior **communication** it requires.

Heaviest of all is when an attached kinkster has their partner—or an unattached kinkster has their friends in the **BDSM** community—arrange a "rape" scene to be perpetrated by someone the "victim" has never met before —the idea being that the person gives their permission to be "raped" at any time by the person of their partner's or their friends' choosing, and may or may not know that it was only a scene until after the fact. This is way out there (a.k.a. **edge play**) and not all that common, either—probably due to the likelihood that it could end in arrest, a nasty pepper spray, or at the very least a black eye.

Most of the time, though, scenes like this take place between two people in a committed, loving relationship who trust each other completely. That said, you should still be forewarned that it can be quite a **mindfuck** to see what one's loving, committed partner looks like as a rapist (not to mention how screwed in the head that loving, committed partner might feel after "raping" his loved one). Rape fantasies certainly lack the levity that is often associated with other **role-playing**.

## ravishment fantasy

This is our preferred term for **rape fantasy**. Unfortunately, "rape fantasy" is entrenched in the vocabulary of human sexuality, enjoying widespread and accepted use, especially in the **BDSM** world, where many things are enjoyed that aren't pretty or P.C (or even *because* they aren't pretty or P.C.). Some people find the term "ravishment" too soft and romantic or just plain inaccurate for their particular fantasy (for example, we don't think romance paperbacks feature a lot of ball **gags** or beatings). And these people certainly don't want their fantasies sanitized by the likes of two fairly prudish sex writers. For all these reasons, we've kept the *rape fantasy* entry above as the main area for the description of these types of fantasies.

The last thing we want to do is prescribe rules for people's fantasy lives. After all, the sex you have in your own head is the one time you get to break all the rules—rules of law, rules of morality, of monogamy, of hygiene, of gravity... So if you want to fantasize about the kind of rape that would be more fitting on an episode of *Law & Order: Special Victims Unit* than in a romance novel, then go right ahead. And if, in the privacy of your own bedroom, you want to call it a rape fantasy, then go right ahead with that, too.

But it's important to keep in mind that *no one actually wants to experience rape*, rape they have absolutely no control over, in the real world. And it's important to consider the potential consequences of word choice when you're talking about these kinds of fantasies *outside* the bedroom. We suspect using the term "rape" in a fantasy context only helps keep our culture from taking the crime of rape as seriously as it should—especially rape in the context of a committed relationship (where a victim might be told that the fantasy simply got out of hand). Sure, "ravishment fantasy" might sound a bit too purple-prose for your tastes, but if it helps preserve—or, in some cases, return—the rights of actual rape victims in the real world, we're sure you can suck it up.

## Red Room of Pain 🍷

**Anastasia**'s nickname for **Christian Grey**'s high-end play room/**dungeon** in *Fifty Shades of Grey*. Dark burgundy walls; varnished wood floor; soft, ambient lighting; a mahogany chest of small drawers; a large chesterfield couch; a stout six-foot-long table with intricately carved legs and two matching stools underneath; an oxblood leather padded bench; a rack of **canes**; a display of **paddles**, **whips**, riding **crops**, and **floggers**; **ropes**, **chains**, and shackles hanging from an expansive iron grid suspended from the ceiling; a **St. Andrew's Cross** made of polished mahogany; an ornately carved rococo four-poster, bigger-than-a-king bed made of red leather with chains, cuffs, and red satin pillows. You know, just your standard IKEA furnishings. A.k.a. playroom, **dungeon**.

## remote control toys

**Vibrators** that you control with a remote, duh! Sometimes the remote is detached and sometimes it's on a wire that simply stretches to the other side of the bed. (But trust us, when you're waiting for the next buzz in your happy place and your partner has the remote, the other side of the king-size can feel an awfully long way away!) The quintessential remote control accessory is the vibrating panty or thong, with a little pouch over the clitoris for inserting a cordless miniature **vibrator**. The activation range on these is usually around 12 to 25 feet, so a sadistic partner might be able to make a sandwich in the kitchen while keeping you "entertained." On the other end of the spectrum, some remote control toys can be operated via a cellphone, which means your control freak partner can diddle you from the other side of the *country*. And if you find yourself single and wanting to cede control, some remote toys can even be activated by nearby noise...*hello*, bus driver! Two of our favorite remote control toys are the classy (and waterproof!) bullet-style Lyla 2, and the Club Vibe 2.OH, which responds to music while resting in your undies, hugging your curves. And most sex toy shops sell panties with pockets for remote-controlled mini vibes, if you want to kick it old school.

## resistance play

A "catch me if you can" game played in an erotic context—the idea being, "If you catch me, you can have me." In other words, a form of **role-playing** in which one person struggles against the advances of another. This can include **wrestling**, **tickling**, abduction and/or **rape/ravishment fantasies**, or simply trying to **eel** out of your **ropes**. A.k.a. taming of the shrew.

## restraints

**Bondage** devices, including **cuffs**, **handcuffs**, and **rope**, among others.

## reverse prayer position

A bondage position where your hands are bound, palm-to-palm, behind your back, between your shoulder blades, so you look like Linda Blair praying to Satan. Maintain this tough form of **endurance bondage** for too long, and you too will feel like spitting up split pea soup. For advanced players and yoga enthusiasts only, please. See also **armbinders**.

## riding crops

See **crops (riding)**.

## role fatigue

When you just can't be bothered to eat your dinner out of a dog bowl on the floor while naked and covered in grease anymore.

## role-play

Why do we like to watch Hollywood blockbusters, read trashy novels, catch the big Sunday game, or download Internet porn? Because we like to live vicariously through others! Like the Love Boat, it's exciting and new.

Well, role-playing is like that, except the thrills are experienced *first-hand*. It's make believe for grown-ups…really pervy grown-ups. The beauty of pretending to be someone you're not in a safe, predetermined, sexual scenario is that you get a break from being your own bad self. In other words, if you're kind, giving, shy, and timid in your daily life, then role-playing gives you permission to be cruel, selfish, confident, and bold in your private life (at least for the duration of a **scene**). If you're a strong, powerful, independent feminist, then role-playing gives you an excuse to be a weak, vulnerable, sexual doormat for a change. If you're normally a rational, civilized human being with a decent job, then role-playing can make you a four-legged creature who doesn't have to worry about 401K plans, polite small talk, or constricting clothes (see **animalism** and **pony play**). You can get all of the benefits of being bad, with none of the soul-fattening guilt!

Role-playing might also give some helpful context to your **power plays**: If it feels weird to **spank** a grown man, then pretending he's a naughty boy who needs to be taught a lesson might make things feel more *believable*. **Costumes** and props might help you get into character as well: An authentic-looking police uniform can make frisking come more naturally to you. Even a simple **wig** could be enough to make you feel uncharacteristically saucy. If you're still unconvinced, use Halloween or your next costume ball to test the sexual benefits of role-playing: Wear something a little out of character that makes you feel sexy and use it as an excuse to act a little differently—no one will think you're weird, they'll simply think you're committing to the costume. When you get home with your partner, keep the costume on and stay in character while you start making out. The kickass sex will practically happen by itself.

Admittedly, role-playing definitely requires some **suspension of disbelief** (especially when it's *not* Halloween), but so do Hollywood blockbusters, trashy novels, and watching the big Sunday game as if it really mattered.

## rope 🐾

A cheap, versatile, and readily available **restraint** for **BDSM** play. You can certainly hop on over to the **hardware store** for some basic rope (hey, it was good enough for **Christian Grey**), but it's worth the time (and, in some cases, the money) to get higher quality materials: poly-blend bondage rope from kinky retailers, nylon boating line from boating stores, the nylon tubular webbing and accessory cord sold at climbing stores, magician's ropes made of 100% cotton (including the core) from magic stores, and twisted rope made of soft flax or rugged promilla fibers available at rope specialists (e.g. KinkyRopes.com)—*all* are washable and easy to work with.

Ropes made from synthetic fibers are very smooth on the skin, long lasting, and easy to loosen, though you might find it tricky getting knots to stick; keep their ends from unraveling by carefully melting them with a candle flame. (Save the candle for hot **wax** play later.) Natural fibers like the kind Christian bought at Ana's store feel and look more rugged, are pliant, and knot tightly (though sometimes too tightly, making them difficult to undo); keep the ends from fraying by dipping in glue or nail polish, or wrapping with duct tape, twine, or rubber bands.

Many **bottoms** like the comfort of nylon rope, even though it can stretch out and loosen during wear; some like the tell-tale pattern twisted rope can leave on the skin; and others (especially Japanese rope bondage enthusiasts) prefer the rough texture and grassy smell of hemp (TwistedMonk.com sells hemp bondage rope).

Whichever material you go with, get about 50 to 100 feet so you can cut it into several shorter pieces, varying from about 10 to 30 feet; shorter lengths are good for tying ankles and wrists, and longer lengths work well for chest harnesses. The thicker the rope, the less likely it is to cause circulation problems: Beginners, stick with something between 3/8 of an inch and 1 1/2 inches in diameter. As you accumulate mad skillz, you can go down to 1/4 inch thick.

In addition to following all the rules of **bondage safety**, remember to distribute the tension over a wide area to avoid too much concentrated strain on muscles or joints at a single point: Use *several* coils, a.k.a. "wraps," of rope spread evenly over an area, keeping room between rope and skin. One wrap is never enough; three to six wraps should be fine; too many and you won't be able keep them from bunching up or overlapping (a no-no). You should always leave a finger's width of space between skin and rope. A single turn of rope around *all* the wraps (running perpendicular to them) can comfortably and safely provide a snugger fit while maintaining this finger's width of space. When untying (or even tying), make sure you don't carelessly whip the ends of rope around and accidentally hit your bottom in the face.

For more in-depth safety and technique info, check out Jay Wiseman's *The Erotic Bondage Handbook* or, for more advanced players, *The Seductive Art of Japanese Bondage* by Midori. And for more instruction in our book on specific ways to use rope, see also **crotch rope, cuffs (rope),** and **harnesses (body and chest)**.

## rubber

A popular material for **fetish wear**. While **latex** is a form of rubber and the two words are often used interchangeably, sometimes the term "rubber" refers to a thicker, more matte version of the material: the kind used for Wellington **boots**. Those with a fetish for rubber, latex, **PVC**, and the like are ingeniously called "rubberists." The International Association of Rubberists (Rubberist.net) is a free educational online support group with the church-like tag line "You are not alone."

"I have fallen to my knees unable to rise, what kind of trap is this?
What kind of chains has tied my hands and feet?
It is so strange, so wonderful this helplessness of mine."

—Rumi

## sadism 🐾

The "S" of **SM** and **BDSM**: Deriving sexual pleasure from inflicting physical—and, less commonly, emotional—pain and abuse on a willing recipient. In 1886, an Austro-German psychiatrist named Richard von Krafft-Ebing published *Psychopathia Sexualis*, coining the term **sadism** (after **Marquis de Sade**). While a **masochist** can happily exist without a sadist in their life (that's what masturbation is for…masturbating with sandpaper, that is), a sadist *needs* a willing masochist: After all, any self-respecting sadist's pleasure is dependent on the knowledge that the recipient of their erotic "torture" is truly enjoying it. (Getting off on an accidental five-car pileup is not what we're talking about here.) When **Anastasia** asked **Christian** if he was a sadist, he replied "I'm a **dominant**." We're guessing Anastasia's ass would call that splitting hairs.

## safe, sane, & consensual (SS&C) 🐾

A **BDSM** motto that emerged in the '80s (along with shoulder pads, A-ha, and political correctness) to distinguish kinky play from the kind of sadomasochism found in the classic shrink handbook *Diagnostic and Statistical Manual of Mental Disorders*. "Safe" means taking care to avoid (unintentional) injury, playing within the limits of your expertise and experience, and using common sense (e.g. never letting a complete stranger or a vengeful **ex** tie you up). "Sane" refers to your frame of mind, i.e. don't play when you're **drunk**, high, sad, mad, or otherwise incapable of operating heavy machinery. And "consensual" means that all involved parties agreed to the activity (and no one was stumbling drunk when they gave said **consent**—see **law [the]**).

But never let it be said that the BDSM **community** is lacking for drama—even this catchy little safety mantra has caused some controversy. Apparently some people like to throw the phrase around as an accusation, as in, "That scene is *so* not safe, sane, & consensual." Thus, some kinksters—particularly those who have been accused of flouting the motto—prefer the term Risk Aware Consensual Kick, or RACK (because what's a motto without a catchy acronym?). RACK supposedly embraces **edge play** and no-**safeword** play—some people consider it a synonym for "safe, sane, & consensual," while others believe it to be a motto that allows for behavior that would never be condoned by a "SS&C" policy. Ah, kids. See also **history of kink** and **safety**.

## safety 🐾

While **consent** keeps us out of jail, safety keeps us out of the emergency room (or the morgue). Remember, it's all fun and games until someone loses a testicle. See also **bondage safety, C.P.R., gag safety, medical scissors, safety kit, safeword, safe, sane, & consensual**, and the many *many* safety guidelines described within all the specific technique entries (e.g **e-stim play** and **flogging**). Also, remember never to use a **vibrator** on unexplained calf pain! (Because if, god forbid, a blood clot is causing this pain, the vibrator could dislodge it.)

## safety kit

All the tools you'll need if your **scene** goes wrong. For the activities we endorse for beginners in this book, that pretty much just means **medical scissors,** extra keys for any locking device you're playing with, and safer sex supplies like condoms and dental dams. **Edge play** activities require more complicated safety kits (bolt cutters, sterile bandages, your shrink's home phone number, etc.) that are beyond the scope of this book.

## safeword

A pre-agreed-upon word that means "game over" (or at least, "time out") during a kinky **scene**, so that "no" doesn't have to mean **no**—in other words, the **BDSM** equivalent of crying uncle. Because in the world of kink, the word no is one of the sexiest tools at your disposal—why spoil the fun by making it actually do its job? A safeword means you can beg and moan all you want, you can cry for your **mommy**, you can yell "Stop it, Bitch Tits," you can whisper, "You're hurting me, Pookie," but your partner's going to keep on going—and you'll like it, damn it. A safeword should be something you would never actually yell during sex—like, say, "Grey Poupon," or "snakes on a plane." Some people (including **Christian Grey**) use the traffic light system, where "yellow" means "Could you ease off there a little buddy?" and "red" means "Stop everything right now." And we should mention that safewords aren't just for **bottoms**—the top might invoke it to mean, "Woah, serious **mindfuck**, I need to break for a Mountain Dew."

By the way, if your scene involves some kind of mouth **gag**, then you'll need a non-verbal safeword: Give your "victim" something to hold onto that they can drop to the floor as a means of crying uncle. But if you're in the dark and might not be able to see them "drop the ball," determining a noise pattern they can make with gagged grunts or foot stamping is a good idea (don't play music so loud that you won't be able to hear it). Even when there's no gag involved, a non-verbal safeword is never a bad idea—sometimes it can be kind of hard to muster that safeword when you've been floating in **subspace** for half an hour. Perhaps a quick handsqueeze from the **top** during an intense session with a table tennis **paddle** means, "Hanging in there?" and two quick squeezes back from the bottom means, "Yup."

Of course, not all kinky scenes require a safeword. For example, if you've been married for ten years and have got that whole **communication** thing down, then it's pretty safe to say that you could experiment with ankle and wrist **cuffs** or a little **spanking** without a full-on **scene** negotiation or **safeword**. We we'd like to think that in long-term committed relationships, people know each other well enough to be able to tell the difference between an ecstatic "no" and a panic-stricken or pissed off "seriously, no." That said, the more intense the **play** gets or the less you know each other, the harder it is to tell the difference—so if in doubt, pick a safeword.

At the other end of the dungeon, you'll find people who intentionally play without safewords to be more edgy (see **edge play**)—this is also known as consensual nonconsensuality, metaconsent, or "being edgy." (These people probably use RACK rather than SS&C as their safety motto—see **safe, sane, & consensual**.) In this kind of play, the top makes all the calls for the duration of the scene, no matter how many times the bottom says "red" or "safeword" or "seriously, dude." If we owned a **dungeon**, we'd make edge players like this take their **ball-stretchers** and go home. See also **blanket consent** and **slave**.

## Saint Andrew's Cross

A piece of bondage **furniture**, named for the X-shaped cross that Saint Andrew was allegedly crucified on, featuring restraining points at the wrists, ankles, and sometimes the waist—a **bottom** is strapped in and then sensually teased or **whipped** or **flogged** or just plain fucked. A Saint Andrew's Cross might be affixed to a wall, as in **Christian**'s **Red Room of Pain**, or it could be free-standing, making it essentially a **bondage wheel** without the wheelie part. If your own "St. Andrew" should faint on one of these free-standing ones, it'll be difficult (if not dangerous) to get them down;

plus these crosses can be very unstable—so serious **dungeon** masters only, please. A.k.a. saltire cross, X-cross, or X-frame cross.

## Saran Wrap

A cheap, **D.I.Y.** material for binding and **mummification**. Plus, it's see-through! (If you've never seen *Fried Green Tomatoes* with Kathy Bates, don't.) Don't use Saran Wrap as a wrist or ankle **cuff**, unless you use a lot of it and evenly distribute it over a large area (more like lower-arm or lower-leg cuffs to avoid the Saran Wrap biting into the skin). Or make your own pair of **bondage mittens**.

If you want to go head to toe, buy at least five rolls so you don't run out in the middle (major **BDSM** bummer). Start by wrapping the arms and legs independently, the chest (go from shoulder down across chest, under pit, straight across back, under pit, up and over opposite shoulder, down across back, under pit, straight across chest, etc., a few times) and then around the torso and tush, working the arms in at the sides. By placing cotton balls over the nips and maxi pads over the genitals, you can cut holes in those spots without risk of cutting skin, then pull out the stuffing, and voilà: Convenient diddling access! If you don't have a trusty assistant to make sure your mummy doesn't fall over before you're done, don't wrap the legs together or wrap the head until you've safely laid them down where you want them (since you don't want them losing their balance and falling). As you wrap, try to keep the sheet as wide as possible; avoid wrapping too tightly and cutting off circulation or making breathing difficult (especially around the neck and chest); and make sure you leave the mouth and nose open (or at the very least, the mouth—though we'd consider mouth-only to be **edge play**) so they can breath easily, **communicate**, and say their **safeword** if need be.

You can use generic brand plastic wrap, but it just won't stick as well. Duct tape can be added *on top* of the cling film for extra security, just be sure no tape comes in contact with bare skin (always a no-no). Sarah Wrap is hot: not just in a Paris Hilton-hot way, but in a temperature-hot way as well. Make sure your mummy doesn't overheat and keep them hydrated. Before your butterfly emerges from their cocoon, have a blanket at the ready, because once all that sweat hits the air they're gonna get chilly (remember 8th grade science: Evaporation is a cooling process). While it can certainly be neat to unravel them like Gwynnie in *Shakespeare in Love* when you're done, it's always good to have your **medical scissors** handy for quick escapes. Please don't reuse for sandwiches. If you follow all these rules as well as those in **mummification** and **bondage safety**, you'll never wrap up leftovers again without blushing.

S

# scarification

**Bloodplay** or **branding** that leaves a permanent mark in a pre-approved design —and anything that has the word "permanent" in it is automatically **edge play** in our book. Kind of like a tattoo, except if you're into scarification, a tiny rose on your ankle just isn't going to cut it...literally.

# scat

Playing with doodie in bed. More to do with wanting to get up close and personal with someone else's feces than wanting to share your own shit. Fans consider it a way to achieve the ultimate in defilement (see **humiliation**) or to break the ultimate taboo. After all, what better way to rebel than to choose the one kink that even hardened kinksters can't abide? (It's famous for being an activity that **squicks** many in the **scene**, including **Christian Grey**.) It's like the facial tattoo of the fetish world! Surprisingly, so long as you follow the "on me, not in me" rule (the latter could get you pretty damn sick even if you eat "healthy" caca, and could also transmit infections like hepatitis), there's really nothing about scat to qualify it as **edge play**. Then again, there's really nothing about scat to appeal to 99.9999 percent of players. By the way, admiring your own work of art in the toilet bowl, or even having the urge to show it to a friend, doesn't count. See also **baby (adult)**, **enemas**, and **watersports**.

# scene

1) (*a scene*) The **BDSM** equivalent of a hook-up, during which sex (or at least sexual release) may or may not occur (see **nonsexual BDSM**). The play takes place during a predetermined, finite period of time, whether that's an hour (a visit to a professional dominatrix, a particular kinky afternoon sesh between a married couple, etc.), a day (perhaps at a BDSM retreat or just a couples naughty weekend getaway), or a year (see **slave**, **taken in hand**, and **T.P.E.**). Think of it as an improvised *play*, in which participants have *roles* (there is usually at least one **top** and one **bottom**), and they *act* out their fantasies until someone figuratively yells out "And...scene!" in order to end the action. (Guess you could call it "**play** within a play.") But when it comes to BDSM, all the world is *not* your stage: Kinky play should take place in a safe, secure environment and not at the grocery store or **airport** (see def. #2 in that entry). A.k.a. session, sesh. See also **law (the)**, **online personals**, and **role-playing**.
2) (*the scene*) The **BDSM** community: Its participants, their organizations, message boards, personal ads, and events. The term can also be modified to

refer to particular sub-categories of BDSM practices and preferences (e.g. "the **spanking** scene"). A.k.a. the **leather** scene.

## secretary

1) (*noun*) Common **role-playing** role. See def. #2 below for inspiration.
2) (*movie: Secretary*) Totally awesome 2002 movie starring Maggie Gyllenhaal and James Spader, based on the totally awesome eponymous short story by Mary Gaitskill: She's a secretary recently released from a brief stint in a mental hospital, he's her demanding lawyer boss; together they find hot sex and redemption in a full-time **BDSM** relationship (see **taken in hand** and **T.P.E.**). On the surface, *Secretary*'s story could be interpreted as a traditional fairy tale in which a poor, depressed, self-cutting **damsel in distress** needs to be saved and taken care of and provided for and told what to do by a male hero who's totally in control. But look closely, and you'll realize that (at least for the second half of the movie) this is a woman who knows what she wants and knows how to get it, conventions and social norms be damned. The last shot of the movie has Gyllenhaal, now a domestic goddess, placing a gross dead bug in their pristine, neatly made marital bed in their perfectly organized, beautifully decorated, sparkling house while now-hubby is off at work—and then she looks knowingly at the camera. Wink, wink, nudge, nudge. Probably the best depiction of a kinky lifestyle in all of pop culture (certainly better than the *Fifty Shades* books).

## sensation play 🖐

Touchy-feely erotic exchanges, in every sense of the term. Kind of like that game you played in nursery school where you closed your eyes or stuck your hand in a box and had to guess what various objects were just by using your sense of touch. Except in this case, you're using your whole naked body for the tactile experiences, you're probably **blindfolded**, and it might hurt, just a little. Bare hands on your bod feel good, no doubt; but sometimes you want to mix things up, arouse your nerve endings in new and unexpected ways, pretend you're having sex with Thumper, Edward Scissorhands, or Mr. Heat Miser.

Sensation play can include being touched, **tickled**, **teased**, or tormented with an **ice** cube, hot **wax**, a **fur** or spiked vampire glove, **menthols** like Ben Gay or Nature's Gate Peppermint toothpaste, a **Wartenberg wheel**, an **e-stim** device, fine (as opposed to coarse) sandpaper, emery boards, brushes, wire wool, 5 o'clock shadows, and other textured objects pretty much anywhere on the body except internally or on erotic **mucous membranes**. Alternating contrasting sensations can be quite a **mindfuck**. A pleasant sensation might even cross wires with a painful one, helping to lessen the latter's sting or having a Pavlovian effect on it, whereby the **pain** becomes associated with the pleasure. See the bolded entries above for their specific safety info. And please know that in our book (the one that you're holding), sensation play is not meant to **scar**, break or scrape skin, or be excruciating—it's the *softer* side of **BDSM**, i.e., just enough to feel like you're being licked up and down by your cat. We cannot endorse the more intense (read: really fucking dangerous) forms of sensation play: blade or knife play, fire play, **branding**, and play **piercing**. While we think sex is pretty damn important, it's not worth bleeding to death or singeing off your eyebrows for. See also **temperature play**.

## sensory deprivation

Restricting one's ability to see, hear, smell, talk, and/or move in order to create a unique sensual and/or psychological experience. Limiting one or more senses automatically heightens the unrestricted ones: Tie your partner to the bed, slap a **blindfold** on them, put some **MP3-player** headphones over their ears (playing a 16th-century classical piece by Thomas Tallis, perhaps?), and they'll swear you took a Tantric workshop on erotic handwork! Make your **bottom** wear an eyeless **hood** with nose holes and a mouth **gag**, and they'll be *that* much more vulnerable and dependent on you. If they've refused to obey your commands during a **scene**, put them in the basement, turn off the lights, and withhold your touch from them as punishment until they've learned their lesson. Or give them a full "out of body" experience with a blindfold, hood, gag, ear plugs, and tightly laced **sleepsack**, so all they hear is the sound of their own thoughts and all they can feel is the beating of their own heart. For some, this can be a deeply profound, moving, and even spiritual meditation. For others, it's one of Dante's levels of Hell. As with any kind of bondage, never *really* leave someone alone; make sure their breathing is and stays unobstructed; and work out a **safeword** or safe signal ahead of time: Three Morse-code moans means, "Take me out, I'm done!"

## service kink

Doing shit like mopping the floor not because it's your turn or because it's nice to help out around the house, but because that's "your thing," kinkily speaking. Perfect for those **submissives** who claim that they simply don't have the time to devote themselves to the kinky arts *and* get the dishes done. Full-time, live-in service kinksters are known as **houseboys**; the freelance kind can be found on the "Casual Encounters" section of your local Craigslist.org—perfect for free agent **doms** who'd consider it a bargain to pay their domestic help in verbal abuse and a light flogging rather than minimum wage. See also **body service** and **taken in hand**.

## service top

A **top** who doesn't mind taking directions. Why are we picturing **Anastasia's** eye roll and **Christian's** ubiquitous "smirk" right now?

## shackles

When nylon and leather **cuffs** are just too cute and fluffy, and you want something with a little more weight and muscle, go for cold, hard, steel wrist and ankle restraints. Steel shackles have that quintessential **dungeon** feel, for when you want to get medieval on your **sub's** ass. There are heavy metal **bondage mittens**, **collar**-wrist combos that act as portable stockades, even single ankle cuffs with a big weighted ball attached via chain (imagine the entertainment value you'll get out of being able to say, "I have to get back to the ol' ball and chain," and literally meaning it!).

All the usual rules of **bondage** apply, and then some; since these are unforgiving, heavy, unadjustable restraints, make sure they're not too big (you don't want your sub escaping) or too small (you don't want to cut off circulation); also make sure shackles aren't sitting too heavily on a body part and possibly pinching nerves; finally, most of these restraints are locking devices, which can make quick release tricky, so make sure you have the key handy (or even large bolt cutters). For the look of steel without any of the discomfort, try **leather**-lined collars and cuffs with a steel exterior. Shackles will cost quite a bit more, but it's worth it when you hear that oh-so-sexy clanking sound, like the ghost of Jacob Marley reminding you he needs a Scrooge **spanking** for being such a naughty, naughty money lender. A.k.a. manacles and, specifically for the ankles, fetters and leg irons.

## shaving

See **hair removal**.

## slappers

Like **paddles**, but narrower and with better sound effects. Usually made of **leather**, patent leather, or **pleather**, slappers consist of either two pieces of material or one looped piece of material that's bound into a handle at one end and left unbound at the other. It's the unbound end that—when smacked against a bottom, thigh, or upper back—makes a resounding "slap!" as the two pieces (or loop) of material knock against each other.

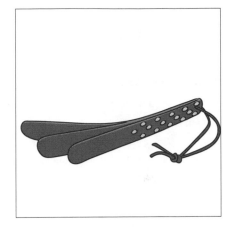

Slappers can certainly sting, but they pack less punch than most other **flagellation** tools. So if you're more into the *idea* of **discipline** than the actual *pain* of it, a slapper could be your new B.F.F. (best **fetish** friend). We like the diminutive black patent "Spanky" for playful slapping and Bare Leatherworks' longer, stiffer "Handy Slapper" for bringing in da noise and packing a punch. For something a little more badass, keep an eye out for tire-tread slappers! See **paddles** and **flagellation** for more important safety information. A.k.a. spankers.

## slapping, face

Opened-palmed smacks to the cheek. Kind of like butt **spanking**, but not usually so repetitive, rhythmic, or even loving. After all, a face slap is *personal*: You're attacking the very manifestation of their persona. And it usually has to do with punishment or **humiliation**, whether in real life or in a BDSM **scene**. Even people who appreciate a little rough-housing in bed can be thrown off by a smack to the cheek. One unwelcome slap can ruin the mood—hell, it can ruin the whole relationship—so make sure your partner is *into* a blush upon their cheek. If they are, a couple things to keep in mind:

1. Stick to the fleshy part of the cheek—avoid eyes, ears, and cheek or jaw bones.
2. Don't hit so hard that their head literally spins; in fact, it's a good idea to cradle the other side of their face with your non-hitting hand to stabilize them.
3. Once is usually enough to get your message across.
4. Even if you have blanket permission to occasionally administer a corrective

slap, make sure it's delivered in the right context—fine when they're tied up naked and acting like an **eel** against your commands; not fine when you're having lovey-dovey sex in the hopes of conceiving.

## slapping, genital and breast

Gently—*we said gently!*—smacking the penile shaft, the labia, or the boobies. This is *not* a **spanking**: The slap should be much lighter, done with only the upper parts of the fingers rather than the entire palm, and only a few times per session, max (though the labia can take a little more). If your partner's got breast or penis implant(s), forget it! Not to be confused with **dick slapping**. See also **cock and ball torture**, **cunt torture**, and **nipple torture**.

## slave

1) Someone who wants to be completely controlled by a **master** or **mistress**, either on a **scene**-by-scene basis, or in a full-time SM relationship (see **taken in hand** and **T.P.E.**). A scene slave gets off on being controlled, while a 24/7 slave gets off on actually being *owned*. The latter is said to be "under **contract**" to the master/mistress, and may have signed an actual (though not legally binding—god bless the 13th amendment) contract, just like in *Fifty Shades*. See the **T.P.E.** entry for a complete description of full-time **D/s** relationships. See also **collars**.

2) *(Archaic)* Used to be a synonym for **bottom** or **sub**, though these days some subs and bottoms will get mighty P.O.-ed if you assume that they're a slave: Slavery is considered to be a particularly extreme form of submission, and not all subs are down with that (they might even be **squicked** by it).

## sleepsacks

Tight and kinky sleeping bags for **mummification**. Many come with inside sleeves for extra immobility, external laces running down the entirety of the front for cinching, hoods, and threeway zippers and/or strategically placed flaps for easy, erotic access. **Latex** sleepsacks are super form-fitting, can be rubbed down with lubricant for extra shine, and are easy to clean (you can even pee in them if that's your piss bag!)—but they'll make you sweat like a pig in heat, so you have to watch out for dehydration and the possibility of puddles forming and leaking (whatever the bodily fluid). Some rubber sleepsacks can even be inflated with a bike pump, for a funky feeling of all-over pressure. (We must insist you *not* try to pop it with your butt like a balloon while someone is inside it, though.) If you really want to work for your bondage, grease up and try to squeeze yourself into a latex balloon about half the size of a sleepsack—it's like trying to get back *into* the womb! **Leather** sleepsacks are durable, fairly breathable, and sturdy enough for **suspension** using attached **D-rings**, but they're hard to clean, expensive, and baggy if not sized correctly (almost as bad as saggy-butt leather pants). Spandex or even the heavier-duty Darlex ones make a great my-first-sleepsack, because they're cheap, breathable, snug but not too unforgiving, and just kind of cute ('80s aerobicizing material just isn't that intimidating). A.k.a saunasack. See also **body bags** and **straitjackets**.

## slings

1) Like arm slings, except they support weary lovers instead of broken limbs. Typically made of leather or nylon, a sling straps around the back of your neck (this section is usually padded for comfort) and then around each leg—it's either attached to ankle cuffs, or loops around the thighs. Thus, the lazy fucker is suspended comfortably in the receptive missionary position:

hips slightly tilted back, legs raised and spread, knees bent.

Or, if you don't want to risk a crick in the neck, then check out something called a "Bonker," which is basically two leg straps attached to curved, slim, steel tubes that are held in place by a base board that slides between your mattress and boxspring. Way to kink up the **vanilla**! (Hard to explain the device to your kids, though.) A lover thus slung will also be particularly, er, *open* to receiving oral attention.

2) Another name for a sex **swing**.

## SM 🖌

The symbiotic relationship of **sadism** and **masochism**, or sadomasochism; the "S" and "M" of **BDSM**.

## Society of Janus

See websites listed in Appendix B.

## spanking 🖌

Hand-to-tush contact, which many consider more intimate and less scary than any other type of **flagellation**. It's **Christian Grey**'s calling card. Spanking is definitely safer for newbies, since you have much more control over (and better aim with) your own hand. Spanking can be a seasoning (a few spanks during a particularly passionate bout of intercourse to add some kinky flavor), an appetizer (spanking as foreplay before more orgasm-focused activities, like the first **vaginal balls** scene in *Fifty Shades of Grey*), or it can be a meal in and of itself (a session in which the spanking is the goal—the main course, if you will— that takes half an hour to serve and enjoy).

If you're hungry for more than just a sprinkle of seasoning, then follow the rules of any first-time flagellation: Have the spankee lie across your lap, kneel on a bed, stretch out stomach-down, or bend over something they can put their full weight on for comfort; start slowly and build up intensity gradually with your bottom's permission, varying your pressure and strokes; and contain your spanking to the lower, fleshier halves of each cheek and the backs of the upper thighs (even if you're just having a spanking snack during sex, this area should be your target)—avoid the lower back, tailbone, and back of the knees at all costs. Specific considerations for spanking include the following:

1.  Remove all bracelets and rings.
2.  Start with a butt **massage**.
3.  Follow each blow with a short massage, too, to spread out the **pain** and keep things nice 'n' warm (at least during your first few sessions together).
4.  A woman might like particular attention paid at the intersection of ass crack and crease, with the vibrations reverberating throughout the vulva, but definitely steer clear of the guy's family jewels.
5.  Remember that, because of your close proximity to your partner, spanking is especially great for pleasantly diddling their lemonade area while whacking the steps of their fudge factory 'round the corner.

For a cute site on "honey buns," with vintage photos, advice, and even "spanking cream," visit MyHoneyBun.com. SpankingBlog.com will keep you posted on all the latest breaking spanking news. And for inspiration, read *Naughty Spanking Stories from A to Z* by Rachel Kramer Bussel (and, if you can't get enough, her follow-ups, *Spanked: Red-Cheeked Erotica* and *Bottoms Up: Spanking Good Stories*). A.k.a. fanny dusting. See also **floggers**, **paddles**, **slappers**, and **arnica cream**.

## spanking benches

**Furniture** made specifically for **spanking**, usually with two padded levels (one for the knees, the other for the torso) and restraints attached. Because big boys and girls who've been bad can start to get heavy after twenty minutes bent **O.T.K.** A.k.a. Berkeley Horse, spanking horse.

## spank skirts/dresses

**Fetish wear** with an open bottom leaving the naked tush exposed for **spanking** or simply ogling. Not unlike the butt-less jeans featured in the classic 1981 Ryan O'Neal comedy *So Fine*, which were then co-opted by Prince for a disturbing VMA performance in the early '90s. Most online roads will lead you to one spank dress on the market: a short, strapless, tacky, leather number, closed in the front, completely open in the back save for a buckled strap around the waist, one just under the butt, and one over the thighs. It's not pretty. For something assless with a little more style (an oxymoron, we know), try the latex spank dress or skirt available on Syren.com.

## spatulas

It appears 1981 was *the* year of the immature sex-obsessed comedy (see **spank skirt**): That's also when preteens snuck into theaters to see Bill Murray in *Stripes* give his love interest the "Aunt Jemima" treatment—and a million spatula fetishes were born. The kitchen appliance can be used as an impromptu **slapper** or **paddle**. See also **D.I.Y.**

## sploshing

The eroticization of rolling around in wet and messy substances—condiments, whipped cream, mud, paint, shaving foam, etc.—or even just in wet clothes. In fact, this proclivity used to be called "wet and messy," plain and simple (wam for short; participants would call themselves wammers), but then a British mag dedicated to the art was launched under the name *Splosh!* and a catchy moniker was born. As the cheerful exclamation mark implies, sploshing tends to be one of the more lighthearted (even slapstick) breeds of kink—throwing cream pies is a favorite activity, for example. Some wammers like to splosh each other, while others like to combine the activity with a little **dom** and **sub** play (you'll never guess which one gets doused in ketchup). Some people like to eat the food off each other, while others prefer to **wrestle** in the wet and messy stuff. (If you're only playing with edible substances, then it might be called **foodplay** instead of sploshing.) Still others gather in groups for splosh parties: It's everything your Momma told you not to do when you were a kid, *plus* there's nudity?! No wonder so many sploshers have smiles on their faces. That said, naked food fights are not entirely risk-free:

1. Play on a plastic sheet, a waterproof mattress cover, or in the bathroom or kitchen (or be prepared for your cleaning service to break up with you).
2. Oil-based substances won't wash away quickly or easily, so think twice before applying that chili-infused drizzling oil to your partner's tender bits.
3. Oil destroys latex, so don't use oil-based substances as a **lube** if latex protection is involved (and it always should be, unless you're explicitly monogamous).
4. Test all substances on unbroken skin first, then on your mouth or external genitals, and only then inside the veegee or butthole (and do the latter at your own risk of infection).
5. When inserting a food item anywhere, always completely cover it with a condom. (Do you really want those pesticides hanging out inside you?)
6. Keep sugary items (fruit, whipped cream, chocolate sauce, etc.) out of her vagina…unless she actually *likes* yeast infections.
7. If you're allergic to peanuts, then your penis is, too.
8. When inserting a food item up the butt, make sure it has a flared base so it doesn't get sucked in and lost up there (no zukes!). And put a condom on it.
9. Don't eat anything that's been up someone's ass. And don't run with scissors, either.

A.k.a. mess fetish, wet and messy, wam.

## spreader bars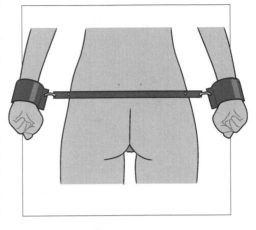

Stiff bars, usually two to three feet long, with a **cuff** at either end, used to force the wearer's ankles or wrists into a spread eagle pose during **bondage** play—most bars can be adjusted, depending on how much yoga your **bottom** practices. Spread 'em, yogi! **Christian Grey** famously uses one on **Anastasia** in the *Fifty Shades* trilogy. Many people enjoy spreading the ankles and then attaching the wrists to the center of the same spreader bar. They're handy if you don't have bedposts for attaching cuffs to. Instant self-contained bondage! Sure, your bottom could still get up and walk around if they were particularly coordinated, but they'd look mighty funny doing so. Some bars come with built-in cuffs, while others have hooks or rings to hitch to your own cuffs—because we know how "attached" some of you get to your favorite pair. (Breaking in **leather** items is the drudgework of **BDSM**.) You can even padlock the cuffs in place if you really want to send a message (though we don't recommend this for beginner play). And you can attach larger cuffs if you want the spreader bar to attach at the thighs instead of the ankles (if you're restraining one of the Olsen twins, then wrist cuffs will work just fine). If you're a **D.I.Y.**-er, you can make your own spreader bar out of anything rigid (heh heh, we said *rigid*), like a steel pipe, and some rope if you know how to tie the appropriate **knots**. See Jay Wiseman's *Erotic Bondage Handbook* for inspiration.

## squick

(*Verb, Adjective, Interjection*) To trigger an involuntary "ew," as in, "**Enemas** totally squick me," or "**Fisting**? Squick!" This onomatopoetic term has its roots in the **BDSM** community, though these days you may hear it in the **vanilla** world, too ("Tom and Katie's relationship really squicked me, I'm so glad they divorced"). Your personal squick barrier does not need to be explained or justified, so long as you are not mean to people who are *not* squicked by what squicks you. In this way, squick is fundamentally different from your-kink-is-not-ok (**Y.K.I.N.O.K.**), which implies a kind of moral judgment, or **edge play**, which suggests a paternalistic attitude (*You'll shoot your eye out!*). Squick, on the other hand, is simply a very personal, physical reaction to something that you'd rather not witness or indulge in yourself (or even discuss at the dinner table, in extreme cases); in that sense, it's more like your-kink-is-okay-it's-just-not-my-kink (**Y.K.I.O.K.,I.J.N.M.K.**). **Scat** is a particularly common squick culprit, though you might be squicked by anything in the kink world—saying "**Daddy**," fetish **clubs**, **rape fantasies**, pleather. If you are mid-**scene** and your **play** partner introduces an activity that squicks you, your **safeword** is your get-out-of-jail-free card. In 2005, squick was nominated as word of the year by the New Oxford American Dictionary, though it was narrowly beat out by "podcast." Squick could be considered the kinkster's "gross," though as with most fetish world practices, it's just a little more polite and P.C. than its vanilla equivalent.

## stereostim

Transmitting amplified (electrified) audio signals through electrodes applied to the genitals. This is not the kind of thing you can finagle on your own by messing around with the cords in the back of your stereo, unless you want to end up more deep-fried than a bucket of Colonel Sanders. No, you must buy high-quality devices made specifically for electrosex—these have audio inputs so you can safely synch up your zapping to Barry Manilow for double the torture! Serious dabblers recommend products at ErosTek.com. See **e-stim** for important safety information.

## Story of O

Classic French **BDSM** novel originally published in 1954 and written by Pauline Réage—a pen name, natch; this might have been France, but it was the '50s, after all. ("Pauline" finally outed herself a few years before her death, in 1998: She was born Anne Desclos—not quite as sexy, we know.) Our heroine, "O"—short for both "Odile," her name, and "object" (*objet* in French), get it?—is a Parisian fashion photographer who begs her lover to dominate her. During the course of this slim work, she is tied up, **blindfolded**, **masked**, **whipped**, **branded**, and given a good seeing to (all orifices) at her lover's whim. Though obscenity charges were brought in multiple countries, O stayed in print and went on to sell millions of copies, inspiring female **submission** fantasies around the globe (not to mention a bunch of appalling film adaptations). These days, those submission fantasies are more likely to be inspired by *Fifty Shades of Grey* instead.

## straitjackets

If you want to **role-play** psychiatrist and psycho, if you have a Houdini **fetish** or fantasy, if you thought Pat Benatar was just the sexiest thing on the "Get Nervous" album cover when you bought that cassette in 6th grade, if you're *really* into "American Horror Story: Asylum," or if you just think your **sub** might be a tad chilly on a cold winter's night, then the traditional institutional restraining jacket is the thing for you! You know the drill: The long, close-ended sleeves crisscross over the wearer's front and usually buckle in the back to restrict arm movement, with accidentally kinky groin straps to keep **eels** and looney tunes from wriggling free. The traditional jackets are made of off-white canvas, but you can get them in **leather**, **latex**, even black denim (for **bondage** on casual Fridays). Some come with straps for extra bondage or "tit flaps" for **nipple** attention. Variations on the theme include matching one-leg pants with booties, matching **hoods** which lace or buckle up the back with only two little nostril holes, and full **body bags** or **sleepsacks** (usually with lots of **D-rings** for suspension). Whether you're a **slave** in training or an amateur escape artist, check out Maxcita.com for all your straitjacket needs, except leather—for those, visit WartenbergWheel.com. Just remember that straitjacket play is a team sport: You might be able to get into one on your own, but you probably won't be able to get out. See also **mummification** and **Saran Wrap**.

## strap-on

A **dildo** with a flared base that's held in place by a **leather**, nylon, vinyl, or **rubber harness** so you can wear it like it's your very own dong. Handy for **role-playing** (*now* who's your **daddy?**), **femdom** (e.g. strap-on blowjobs), punishment (e.g. strapping on a much bigger cock than your god-given one), or just plain anal sex (see the **anal play** entry for important back-door safety rules). In all of these scenarios, the dildo would probably be strapped in approximately the same place as the real thing, using either a single-strap **harness** that fits exactly like a G-string (and is therefore pretty impractical for men, because, duh, there's

already a nonsilicone willy in the way) or a two-strap harness that fits exactly like a jock strap (making it perfect for guys and a great alternative for women who are anti-buttfloss). Most harnesses feature either buckles or **D-rings**—buckles look more hardcore and won't loosen mid-sesh (*so* embarrassing); D-rings might slip a little, but they can also be easily adjusted on the fly (handy for beginners still getting used to the fit of their setup). As a clitoral aside, many harnesses contain handy pockets designed to fit a miniature **vibrator** or **bullet** (yay).

Or, for a very different kind of strap-on play, you could make your **bottom** wear a face harness—basically a ball **gag** with an O-ring that holds a dildo, making your bottom look like a XXX unicorn or a stem-cell scientist's research project gone horribly, *horribly* wrong. For obvious reasons, these devices are usually named something like the Humiliator. (See the attachment gags section of the **gags [mouth]** entry for more ways to be wicked with this kind of harness.)

As far as your fake frankfurter goes, you should splurge on one made of 100% silicone. Silicone schlongs are easy to clean, they retain body heat (so as not to feel like a speculum in there), they're durable, they don't get sticky or tacky, they're non-toxic (i.e. no potentially carcinogenic **phthalates** that can be found in cheaper jelly dildos), and they're nice and firm, while still having a bit of lifelike give.

On a final note, we're going to go out on a limb here and say that, ahem, size *does* matter. A little bit. But just because you *can* go large, doesn't mean you should jump in at the, er, deep end with a 12-inch glow-in-the-dark dildo. As a general rule, vaginas can take more girth than length—too much of the latter (especially if it has a pointy end) might poke at her cervix (yowza!). Bums, on the other hand, can handle plenty of *length*; it's the girth they need to work up to. Plus, don't forget that dildos have to travel past a few inches of ass cheek before getting in, so a too-short dildo can easily pop out of a bum. And bear in mind that once your dildo is strapped into a harness, you'll lose at least half an inch. (Though there's no need to tell your boyfriend this when he's congratulating himself on the epic dildo he just submitted to.)

## sub

A **submissive**. How's that for a Dictionary.com definition? See **submission**.

## submission 🐾

While **bondage** and **discipline** sometimes lead independent lives, submission can't leave home without **domination**: **D/s** is essentially the psychological element of **BDSM**—the **power exchange** that takes place in just about all kinky **play**. A submissive (or sub) gets off on yielding control—but first you have to find a **dom** who's willing to take said control (it's not just bottoms who have to give **consent**, remember?). A sub is always a **bottom**, though a bottom doesn't necessarily have to be a sub. Sure, the terms are often used interchangeably (and therefore incorrectly, sticklers would say), but there are plenty of bottoms out there who get off on the *sensations* of being, say, **spanked** without feeling particularly submissive about it. **Vanilla** types might view the distinction between "taking it" and "submitting" as quibbling over semantics—in which case they're advised to steer well clear of any kink-related message boards, where debates such as this can rage on for years.  See also **humiliation** and **slave** (def. #2 in the slave entry).

## subspace 🐾

**Submissive** head space. This trance-like state can be the result of getting so into character during a **role-playing scene** that you actually become a **slave**/patient/ **secretary**/**pony**/dog/Republican. But more often it is the result of the endorphin rush produced by a good **spanking** or **whipping**, etc.—at this point the **bottom** may be unable to distinguish pleasure from **pain**. That's usually a good thing, though the responsible **top** should watch out for their bottom drifting into *deep* subspace, at which point they may no longer know their own name, let alone their **safeword**. E.L. James is surprisingly eloquent on the topic of subspace in the *Fifty Shades* series: She doesn't use this actual term, but **Anastasia** frequently, to her own surprise, goes into a kinky trance. A.k.a. bottom space.

## suspension of disbelief 🐾

A must-have for engaging in **BDSM** without cracking up uncontrollably (or for making it through the entire *Fifty Shades* trilogy). Deep down you know you're not *really* a schoolgirl, or an Egyptian slave, or a **pony** named Hoof Hearted who has to wear a bit and pull a wagon naked. But the more you can get into character and really *commit* to that role, the more enjoyable your **scene** will be. It's like pretentious method actors who never break character while on set, even after the director has yelled "Cut!": For a while, they truly believe they *are* Capote or Tootsie.

## suspension play

A very high risk form of **bondage** that involves suspending your **submissive** from a ceiling, rafter, kids' climbing frame, etc. The sub will typically be suspended by a combination of ankles, wrists, and a chest **harness**, or in some way bound and unable to escape—in other words, just screwing in the hammock doesn't count as suspension play. Thus hanging, your **bottom** will feel a heightened (and not entirely unwarranted) sense of vulnerability, not to mention a rather pleasant feeling of objectification. Subs may be suspended horizontally, vertically, or even upside down, the latter being the most dangerous. During *partial* suspension, at least one body part (maybe a foot or the upper back) remains on the ground. Practitioners use specially designed suspension **cuffs**, which are meant to distribute weight more evenly and thereby prevent circulation, joint, or nerve damage.

Unfortunately, there is the niggling issue of "harness hang syndrome" to deal with—this was discovered back in the '80s after the deaths of a number of French cavers: Suffice it to say that motionless suspension can lead to serious blood circulation issues, which can lead to full-blown death. And then there's the distinct possibility that your ceiling hook isn't quite as securely mounted as you thought. Even uber-expert Jay Wiseman won't go near the subject of suspension bondage in his *Erotic Bondage Handbook*, which is more than enough for us to classify it as **edge play**. If you want to play around with the *idea* of **suspension play** but aren't prepared to explain a hanging corpse, then check out **door jamb cuffs** instead. See also **human furniture**.

## swings

Sometimes referred to as **slings**, swings are contraptions that suspend someone (not usually from a blossoming apple bough) for the purposes of gravity-defying sex. The most common swings look kind of like hammocks and are made of a large, sturdy piece of leather or nylon which is hung by chains from a ceiling beam or doorframe—the lucky swinger then reclines for a good seeing too.

(**Fisting** is a common swing activity, because if you're going to take someone's fist up to your colon, then apparently it helps to be cold-chillin' when it happens.) Or, if you're Pamela Anderson, you just lie back, suspended above a grand piano, and listen to Tommy Lee tickle the ivories (if you can believe it, that's actually not a euphemism).

If you don't fancy drilling big holes in your ceiling (*It's nothing, Mom, we were just trying to hang that planter you gave us*), check out door swings: No hardware or assembly required! They hook over a door and are held in place when you close the door (just like over-the-door towel hooks), and then can be packed under the bed when Mom comes to visit. Alternatively, a *body* swing (see illustration) is suspended from your partner's neck, for standing-up sex that's easy like Sunday morning. Some swings come with **cuffs** or stirrups to add a dose of **bondage** to the mix, while others are a series of straps (supporting the back and butt, or waist and thighs) rather than a solid piece of fabric, e.g. the Pleasure Swing (if you can get over the animal print).

If your swing leaves your head hanging, you might want to accessorize with a supporting head harness (like a mini hammock for your noggin, different from the kind of head harnesses that hold ball **gags**), which attaches to the main contraption...assuming that comfort is a goal.

On a final note, many swings are designed to support the weight of two: Hang it from the front porch, grab a glass of pink lemonade each, and you're guaranteed to never again get invited to your neighbors' annual bean-burger cook-out. See also the Bonk'er in the **sling** entry.

## switch

1) Someone who can be either a **top** or a **bottom**, or a **dom** or a **sub**, depending on their mood, their partner, the activity, or the direction of the wind. Remember, **Christian Grey** began his kinky life as a submissive to **Mrs. Robinson**, and he reverts back to that **subspace** when he's trying to prove his love to **Anastasia**. A.k.a. switch-hitter.
2) A whipping stick. See **cane**.
3) A pretty good Will Smith song for dancing and/or rhythmic **flogging**.

## taken in hand

A domesticated, almost suburban version of **T.P.E.** A taken in hand relationship typically comprises a heterosexual couple, usually married, who have mutually agreed to let the man wear the pants in the family (which includes deciding when the woman's come off). The gal isn't necessarily **submissive**, but the guy is definitely **dominant**. Being taken in hand is not about **role-playing** or about following a community protocol, but about figuring out your own way to keep things spicy based on this basic, extremely retro power dynamic. Maybe the man always opens the car door and buckles the seatbelt for her, or he always dresses her, or he makes all the decisions of the house, or he **spanks** her. Kind of like a Southern Baptist wife who graciously submits to the leadership of her husband, but in this case that submission is always a turn-on for her. TakenInHand.com is a well written, stylishly designed site dedicated to the topic, with articles such as "The Erotic Power of the Unshackled Man" and "When **Rape** Is a Gift." It will make your inner feminist throw up a little in her mouth. And yet you'll find yourself asking, "How can something so fucked up sound kind of sane?" A.k.a. **Christian Grey**'s idea of a "happily ever after."

## tamakeri

Ball-kicking **fetish**. Do we even need to bother telling you that this is a Japanese thing? In tamakeri porn, which is rather popular with **masochistic** young men, a woman will kick a man's saddle bags hard enough to make a slapping sound (we'd posit that the sound effects are added after the fact, but again, this is Japanese porn we're talking about here). If we had cojones, we'd no doubt be **squicked** by this particular proclivity; lacking testicular **empathy**, we're just plain confused. Then again, we'd never eat fermented squid guts, either. A.k.a. ballbusting. See also **bukkake**, **slapping**, and **spanking**.

## teasing

One of the best forms of erotic torture around: No props necessary, no chance of serious injury, and no money down! Love and sex are always more satisfying when there are obstacles to achieving them—you feel like you really *earned* them. That's why teasing in a **BDSM** context can be great for long-term couples who know they're a sure thing for each other: It creates the *illusion* of adversity and challenge. Tie up your partner and touch everything *but* their naughty bits; withhold the pleasure of your tongue until they tell you everything you want to hear; don't give them an orgasm until they submit to a light **spanking**. The possibilities are as limitless as your imagination. And that's one to grow hard on.

## temperature play 🐾

Turning the heat up or down on the skin in order to turn the heat up in the bedroom (or **dungeon**, as the case may be). Tools for this particular brand of **sensation play** include hot **wax**, **ice**, **menthols**, **e-stim** devices, hair dryers, wet towels warmed up in the microwave... You can even take a sip of ice cold water or hot herbal tea right before an oral administration to send chills up their spine or make them feel warm and cozy. Extreme forms of T.P. include fire play and **branding**, otherwise known as "bad ideas." Please see the entries bolded above for their specific safety info.

## therapy 🐾

The treatment of psychological disorders. Some see a shrink, some self-medicate, and some like to "explore their issues" via **BDSM** play. A rape victim might act out a **rape fantasy** at the scene of the crime, an incest victim might have her "**daddy**" repeat things her real daddy once said or did, a child abuse survivor might take part in a prepubescent **age play** scene in order to regress to happier times, a domestic violence victim might tie up a partner who is pretending to be her ex and beat the crap out of him. You know, heavy shit. The idea is that by revisiting the situation in a controlled environment, you might be able to move on from it. But given that we are not licensed professionals, and given that a mind is a terrible thing to break (and typically slower to heal than a broken heart), we'd have to classify this as **edge play**. If you want to use BDSM as healing therapy, then you better have a seriously understanding partner and a seriously qualified shrink to guide you through it. (For the latter, see Kink Aware Professionals in the Surfing Suggestions list, Appendix B.) And be prepared for brand new pain, post-traumatic stress disorder, depression, flashbacks, blinding rage, debilitating grief, and possibly a very confused and/or hurt partner. Personally, we like the couch.

In fact, even if you're suffering only a few minor issues of self-worth, you should play with caution—heavy kink, like **humiliation**, can be an awesome **mindfuck** if you've got your shit together, but potentially disastrous if you don't.

However, if you'd simply like to work on a few points of self-improvement —say, being more proactive in bed, or being a more vocal shag—then BDSM can certainly come to the rescue. The trust and communication required to play around with **power** in the bedroom can be an incredibly bonding experience, and if you find that more therapeutic than *Chicken Soup for the Kinky Soul*, then we'd be fools to stop you.

Also, if you are a survivor of some kind of sexual or physical abuse but have been working through this with someone more qualified than either of us, and if you feel that the experience is as behind you as it ever will be, then what you do in your sex life is up to you. (We suppose that what you do in your sex life is *always* up to you, but we do worry about you, Dimples.) If you're titillated by kinky experiences that mimic past abuse, don't beat yourself up about it (leave that to your **top**, badum-ching!). Seriously, though, you wouldn't be the first person to get off this way. And there's a world of difference (a decade of therapy, say) between playing like this, and taking part in a **scene** in the hopes that it'll fix you. Either way, though, make sure you both know your **safeword** and, as with any **scene**, decide in advance how far you're willing to go.

On a final note: Rumors abound in the **vanilla** world that kink is for head cases, and that you must have been seriously abused in the past if you get off on pain (and the ***Fifty Shades*** trilogy only helped fan these rumors). While we are the first to admit that the kink community can sometimes be deficient in both humor and fashion sense, we must defend its sanity. Sometimes a **flogger** is just a flogger.

## ticklers

Devices that elicit *intentional* giggles—feathers, soft brushes, strands of rubber or light chains, a well-trained spider, etc. May be used as foreplay, in **sensation play**, or for full-on **tickling** fetishism. You could swipe the feather duster from your mom's cleaning supplies closet, or you could be a tad classier (not to mention hygienic) and buy a down feather teaser (e.g. LELO's Tantra Feather Teaser pictured on the back of this book, available in purple, red, or black). See also **D.I.Y.**

## tickling

1) What junior high schoolers do to each other when they really want to get it on but are too shy to make a move, much like the classic backrub.
2) A cutesy form of foreplay.

3) A rather cheery **fetishism**. This kind of tickling could be considered a subset of **resistance play**, and, like all fetishes, boasts its share of dedicated websites (such as TicklingForum.com) and pornos. Tickling may also be involved in **age play**, e.g. adult **babies**. If you think of tickling as a non-violent means of painful pleasure or punishment (and rumor has it the Romans used it as torture), then it makes sense that it's part of the **BDSM** family. That said, it's often thought of as the redheaded stepchild of the **scene**, perhaps because of all the giggling involved (many people take their kink *very* seriously... some— not us, of course, ahem—might say a little *too* seriously). And in case you were wondering, even tickling fetishists can't tickle themselves. A.k.a. tickle torture.

## tie 🐾

Handy bondage item in your closet—even kinkier if the **dominant** has been wearing it all day. Kinkier still if the dom wears that tie to the next dinner date or neighborhood cocktail party, à la *Fifty Shades*. Just make sure to leave ample space between the tie and the limb, as knots can tighten under pressure. Keep a pair of **medical scissors** handy just in case. See **bondage safety** for more tips.

## *Tie Me Up, Tie Me Down*

The 1990 Pedro Almodóvar film starring Antonio Banderas as a recently released mental patient who hunts down a pornstar he once slept with and keeps her in **bondage** until she falls in love with him, Stockholm Syndrome-style. Which brings us to three points: A) This is not **safe, sane, or consensual**. B) This is not considered proof that, deep down, all kinksters are a little bit nuts (see **therapy**). And C) If this happened in real life, Melanie Griffith would *so* be the one putting your ass in bondage. Antonio has **bottom** written all over him.

## top 🐾

(*Noun*) The one doing the doing to in any **BDSM** scenario (the **bottom** is the one being done to). The term top derives from the gay male community, wherein "top" means the partner doing the penetrating. In BDSM, however, the top will not necessarily get to do any penetrating (you could top for years without getting to wield so much as a baby carrot). Also, the top might not be *literally* on the top, à la missionary sex, and he or she doesn't have to be in a particularly **dominant** mood either (though the two frequently go hand in hand, kinda like the Religious Right and side parts). Rather, the top is simply the one providing the stimulation, whether that "stimulation" takes the form of a **spanking**, a verbal lashing (see **humiliation**), an icy-hot rubdown (see **temperature play**), or a good ol' tongue licking delivered to someone who's, say, tied up. Sometimes a top might even take explicit instructions from the bottom, either before or during the scene—this is known as being a **service top**. However, if the bottom does this in a pushy or whiny way ("No, not *there*, numbnuts") they might be written off as a **do-me queen** (see also **topping from the bottom**).

Topping is not necessarily a permanent state: Partners frequently trade places from one session to the next, or even—for particularly versatile **switch**-hitters—mid-sesh. Finally, some people assume that you have to be a bitch in the boardroom to make a good top, while others think that it's the shy mousy types who come out at night armed with their **whips** and **chains**. We say, who invited all the assumers to the party? We do know one thing, however: Ann Coulter? Total do-me queen. A.k.a. The pitcher. See also **bottom**, **bottoming**, **topping**, and **topping from the bottom**.

## topping

Being the **top**.

## topping from the bottom 🔖

Attempting to control a scene when you're supposed to be in the **submissive** role (i.e. it's not called topping from the bottom if your partner has already agreed to be a **service top**). If you don't want to be a service top, then don't take that shit from your **bottom**! Cesar Millan, a.k.a. the Dog Whisperer, likes to say that there are no bad dogs, only bad owners, meaning, your pet is only being annoyingly alpha because you don't know how to play that role yourself. We think tops could learn a lot from Cesar. (And don't give us that look—it wasn't our idea to make the bottoms wear **collars** and **leashes**.) But like we said in the **do-me queen** entry, if you're just dabbling in **BDSM**, we see no real harm in directing your top so that you can, as the Burger King once said, have it your way. A.k.a. topping from below, pulling an **Anastasia**.

## T.P.E. 🔖

Short for total power exchange, it's the most extreme form of **power play**: A long-term **BDSM** relationship in which the **submissive** gives up *all* control to the "**master**," not just for the duration of an afternoon **scene** of eroticism, but indefinitely (or until their "**contract**" runs out) and regarding all aspects of their existence (when, where, and how you look, talk, eat, sleep, exercise, shop, shit, fuck…). Basically, the last choice the sub makes is to enter into the relationship and after that, whatever Master says goes. This is the kind of set-up **Christian Grey** initially proposes in *Fifty Shades of Grey*. Typically, there are no **safewords**, negotiations, backtalk, or mentions of headaches. If Master says go play in traffic naked or accept this Saab 9-3 convertible as a gift, you do it—trusting that Master has your best interests at heart. True T.P.E. is rarer than a legitimate Chupacabra sighting because it requires 24/7 diligence by both parties, the unwavering and unquestioning devotion of the sub, and the top's complete responsibility for the sub's finances, health, well being…basically, their life. While both parties may have signed an actual **contract** to seal the deal, it won't hold up in court should the slave suffer from **role fatigue**, take off their **collar**, and hit the road. (Newsflash: Slavery is illegal in the U.S.) But then some would argue it wasn't a true T.P.E. to begin with. A.k.a. absolute power exchange, complete irrevocable submission (CIS).

"Intimacy is based on shared vulnerability...
nothing deepens intimacy like the experiences that we share
when we feel flayed, with our skins off, scared and vulnerable,
and our partner is there with us, willing to share in the scary stuff."

— Dossie Eastman and Catherine Liszt, *The Ethical Slut*

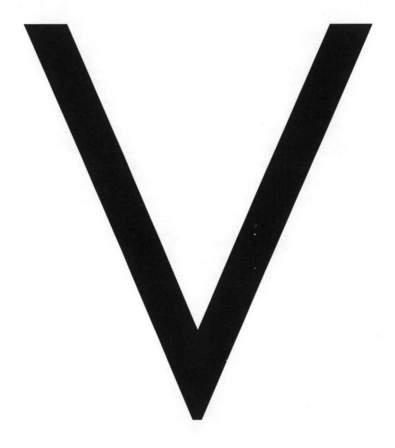

## vacuum beds

Ever wonder what it would feel like to be laminated like your library card, vacuum-packed like a snobby bag of Seattle coffee beans, or cryogenically frozen like Han Solo? Well, here's your chance: A bed-sized frame which can seal you between two layers of clear, translucent, or opaque colored latex for total immobility. There's a breathing hole you align your mouth with, but all retailers recommend using a hollow tube gag that fits inside your

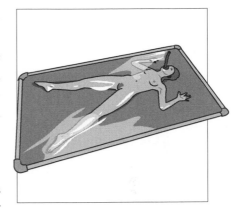

mouth and sticks well outside the bed so there's no fear of the hole slipping and you suffocating. Once you are positioned comfortably between the sheets, your lovely assistant will need to zip up the two layers and then attach a high-powered vacuum cleaner (not included) to the tubing at the bottom to suck all the air out, immediately shrink-wrapping you like a software package. Unfortunately, you have to keep the vacuum running to keep the thing sealed, which makes it hard to hear distress signals and the Yanni you might be playing on the stereo. (Swear to god, we found Yanni as recommended music for bondage scenes on one **fetish** website!) You have to be *really* into **mummification, sensory deprivation,** or **latex** to invest in one of these babies, 'cause they ain't cheap (about $300-800) and they won't fit in your carry-on, either. They also make vac boxes or cubes that allow you to be shrink-wrapped while in a kneeling position. A.k.a. vacrack, vac bed, vac sack, suction bed, suck bed, or Sucky Bed when you buy at Baroness.com.

## vaginal balls

Balls or beads inserted into the vagina. They can be free-floating, or connected by a cord. They can be hard and shiny, or made of softer material. Inside each is a weight that moves when a woman moves, causing her vaginal muscles to involuntarily contract.

In *Fifty Shades of Grey*, Christian and Ana use the classic "Ben Wa" or "Geisha" balls, which are those silver numbers with the fabric thread. If you ask us, they're old-fashioned and outdated, cold and not easily cleaned. Much better, in our opinion, are modern versions like Luna Beads, which are made of body-safe, phthalate-free materials that are easily sterilized. Luna Beads also come with balls of different weights, so you can mix and match in the silicone harness to customize the product for your own needs. We think the black version, called Luna Beads Noir (pictured on the back of this book), has a particularly *Fifty Shades* feel.

While *Fifty Shades* would have you believe vaginal balls are an orgasm generator, the sensation most of them radiate is super subtle. They are actually geared more towards future orgasms you'll have *without* them inserted. Here's why: Items like Luna Beads work to strengthen your pelvic floor muscles—just by having them inside you, you'll automatically start doing your Kegel exercises, probably without even noticing you're doing them! The weighted balls inside each bead move as you move, prompting unconscious muscle contractions that result in an efficient workout with minimal effort. And strong pelvic muscles mean all sorts of good things:

- Better blood flow to the area, which means more sensation for you, which can increase your libido and lead to more satisfaction during stimulation (yes, we're talking longer, stronger orgasms).
- Fuller, deeper and more satisfying sensations for both partners during intercourse.
- More bladder control and fewer pelvic floor disorders—problems which affect 1/3 of women worldwide.
- Easier vaginal childbirth.
- And a faster return to tone and tightness after giving birth.

In fact, a woman can wear vaginal beads and pretty easily forget about them. That is, of course, unless she's got a hot 27-year-old billionaire **spanking** her at the same time.


## vampirists

Extreme *Twilight/True Blood/Buffy* fans. Members of the vampire subculture may (or may not) be into magic, **bloodplay**, Anne Rice novels (before she found Jesus), Robert Pattinson, Victorian dress, goth shit, and psychic energy sucking. Those who actually drink blood are called sanguinarians. But contrary to popular belief, they don't actually bite; rather, they cut and suck, for myriad reasons: Biting causes way worse scarring and bruising, hurts more (vamps aren't necessarily into **pain**), takes longer to heal, is less accurate, and has a greater risk of infection than cutting with a sterile scalpel or razor. We're getting faint just writing this, which means it's a form of **edge play** in our book—so restrict your vampire **role-playing** to psychic energy sucking, giving hickies that don't break skin, and wearing black trenchcoats and sunglasses at night. By the way, did you know that *Fifty Shades of Grey* began its life online as *Twilight* fan fiction? Maybe that explains why Christian was so cool about removing Ana's tampon...

## vanilla

The opposite of **kink**. In other words, vanilla sex is all the rutting you do that *isn't* in this book. No **blindfolds**, no **whips**, no **chains**, no **bondage**, no **role-playing**, no **leather**, no **pain**. Also, no secret passwords, no funny outfits, and no life-threatening **edge play**. When serious kinksters say that something is vanilla, they're not usually being very nice. Then again, when we say that vanilla sex requires no secret passwords or funny outfits, we're not being very nice either. Vanilla, Chunky Monkey, Cherry Garcia, Hershey Highway...it's all just ice cream when you melt it over each other and lick it off (see **sploshing**). We can't imagine a world without at least a hint of kink—and we especially can't imagine long-term monogamy without it—but there are some days that would be unbearable without a little vanilla comfort sex to help us through. Can't we all just get along?

## vegan gear and toys

Erotic cruelty supplies made cruelty-free (i.e. no **leather**, suede, **fur**, or **sploshing** with meat or dairy). If you're a vegan who's getting into **BDSM** (a.k.a. a **leather vegan**), you can find **bondage belts**, spiked **collars**, neck-to-wrist **cuffs**, **floggers**, and more all made of synthetic materials. They may not have that fresh dead cow smell or be able to inflict as much **pain** in the **whipping** department as leather, but if you're more into the psychological rather than physical aspects of shit-kickings (and you also know cows are just as smart as dogs), then pleather is for you! You can shop at TheVeganSexShop.com, where six percent of profits go to charities; in fact, you can choose which charity you'd like each of your kinky items to support: PETA, Vegan Outreach, Code Pink, or the Human Rights Campaign. Some mainstream shops also feature vegan-friendly sections—if that's important to you, then just ask when you're browsing!

## vibrators

Electric toys whose vibrations provide sexual stimulation when applied on, near, or in erogenous zones. They're pretty mainstream when it comes to women's quality alone time. But add them to partner play, and they suddenly become a whole lot kinkier. There's just something about another person being in total control of the speed, vibration patterns, and pressure of a vibe that transforms it into a useful **BDSM** prop (whether or not you're **role-playing** a scene featuring a Victorian doctor and a patient suffering from "hysteria").

While it's tempting to think of a vibrator as a penis substitute, during partner play it's best to think of it as an extension of your hand. Take the toy wherever your hand likes to roam on your partner's landscape: thighs, mons, labia, clitoris, nipples even. If your hand likes to roam *inside*, make sure you pick a vibe that can safely go there—if a toy is designed for insertion, then the instructions will say so. And if a toy *doesn't* come with instructions, then you shouldn't be inserting it anyway!

You may find that holding a vibrator directly over your partner's clitoris is too much for her—that little man in the boat is a sensitive little fella. If he and his owner aren't into **cunt torture** whereby "too much" is actually a good thing, then start with the lowest setting on your toy (if it has options—and most vibrators do these days, yay progress!), move it to your partner's mons or labia (the nearby clitoris will still benefit from the vibes), or hold it over clothes or a blanket to help disperse more mellow vibes throughout her genital region. Experiment with moving it around or keeping it in one place. **Teasing** is always a good option for kinky play, at least initially.

By the way, external vibration isn't just for females: A guy might enjoy you running a vibe up and down the shaft of his penis, curved around his balls, or pressed into his perineum (it's like a baby step toward a vibrating **butt plug**!). And either of you might enjoy a little nipple vibration or some buzzy thigh stimulation. If you want to keep using the toy throughout intercourse (like we've said before, there's absolutely no shame in it), rear-entry or woman-on-top positions work best. However, if the penis or **dildo** owner dons a vibrating **love ring**, you can do it however the hell you want! Go nuts and do it missionary style!

A few considerations when choosing a vibrator for partner play: It's best not to foist a 12-inch penis-shaped vibe with realistic veins on him lest he get an inferiority complex—if that's your bag, drop really subtle hints and hope he picks one like that out himself for use on you. Diminutive vibes like **bullet vibrators**, pebble-like vibrators (e.g. LELO's Lily), and **finger vibes** (e.g. PicoBong's Ipo) are less likely to be a buzz kill (as it were). And for big powerhouses that won't hurt his ego, opt for "back massagers" or **wands**.

All of the aforementioned toys are usually for external use only, so if you want to go deep, get a classic penetrator (i.e. just your basic slimline vibrator, about the size of a penis, though they rarely resemble penises), a G-spotter (e.g. PicoBong's Moka), a full-bodied vibe with impressive girth (like the Elise 2 pictured on the back cover), or, if you don't want to do any of the work yourself, a dual action vibe that practically does the dishes too (e.g. PicoBong's Kaya or LELO's Ina 2, also pictured on the back). Some other things to keep in mind when picking out a vibe:

- Look for ergonomic designs made from phthalate-free, hypoallergenic, non-porous materials—they're best for your bod.
- Go battery-operated if you don't want a pesky cord getting in the way, or better yet, get something rechargeable so the earth doesn't have to be another thing you're torturing.
- For those of you who might like to have a **scene** in the shower or bath, invest in a *fully* waterproof toy.
- If you don't want the machine-made vibrations to stop once intercourse commences, there's a revolutionary new kind of internal vibrator, shaped like a flattened letter C, that's worn *during* penetrative sex (e.g. the Tiani 2). These vibrators—which are typically waterproof and rechargeable and come with an optional wireless remote control—provide simultaneous internal and clitoral stimulation during intercourse. Holy mother of invention!
- When buying something at a bricks-and-mortar store, turn it on right then and there to test it out. Smaller vibes are typically quieter and buzz less vigorously, though there's not always a direct correlation. For example, all the toys at LELO.com—even the biggest ones—are quiet as a mouse, and yet they all buzz with zeal, too. In this regard, you usually get what you pay for: More expensive toys are more likely to be powerful without being wake-the-neighbors loud. Hint: A noisy toy can be drowned out by cranking up the volume on your **MP3 player**.

Finally, a random safety tip: Never use your vibrator on unexplained calf pain. (It's because of the danger of dislodging a blood clot that might be causing said pain.)

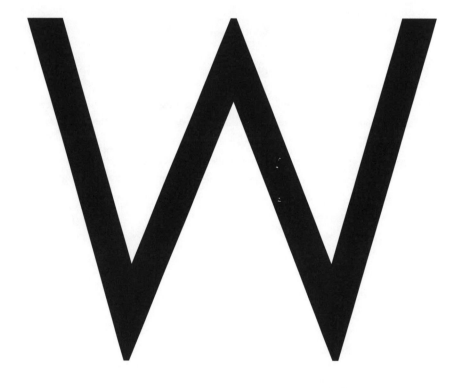

## wand vibrators

Often sold as "back massagers," these big boys are for external stimulation only, usually of the clitoris. They pack such a powerful punch that the recipient of its vibrations may get over-sensitized. Which, if you're into sensual torture, could be just the tool for you. The most famous is the **Hitachi Magic Wand**, though we prefer the beautiful new line of "Smart Wands"—they pack the same punch but, unlike most Hitachis, are cordless, rechargeable, and waterproof! See also **vibrators**.

## Wartenberg pinwheels

Stainless steel neurological **medical** devices designed to test nerve reactions as they glide across skin. The pinwheel is incredibly popular in many forms of **BDSM** play—not just medical **role-playing** (even the relatively **vanilla** outlets often sell them). The device looks a little bit like a miniature pizza cutter, except that it has evenly spaced pins on the

wheel that stimulate the skin as the wheel rolls across your body—the sensation can vary from ticklish to stinging, depending on the pressure you apply, and can leave your skin feeling tingly and even a little itchy. Don't push too hard: The point is *not* to break skin. (For the record: A pizza cutter makes a terrible sex toy!) Many pinwheel enthusiasts like to make their patient wear a **blindfold**, too, though it's not really standard hospital practice—we won't tell the registrar.

## watersports

1) Peeing as a sexual act. Some people like to pee on each other (neat freaks do it in the shower). Some like to pee right into each other's mouths. Some get off on peeing in public (just make sure your local fetish **club** is down with that before you unzip). And some may incorporate watersports into **humilation** play, forcing their partner to pee their pants, wet the bed, or drink their (the **master's**) own pee (see funnel **gags**). For connoisseurs, it's a way to demonstrate complete devotion to their partner's every bodily part and substance. (Okay, *almost* every one—see **scat**. Now see **squick**, 'cause we know you're thinking it!) Golden showers—as this proclivity is also known—

are not the same thing as female ejaculation, which is not pee and is not particularly kinky either, unless you make it so. As with scat, the golden (heh heh) rule is "on me, not in me," because, contrary to popular belief, pee is not *completely* sterile and could conceivably transmit an infection like hepatitis (and you certainly wouldn't want to get it in any open wounds, either). The more water you drink, the weaker, and therefore more benign, your pee will be. As with scat, this was firmly on **Christian Grey**'s no-go list, much to Ana's relief.

By the way, if you're looking for a solution to a *really* wet spot (be it pee or female ejaculation), check out the Liberator Throe Blanket—it's waterproof, with one silky side and one plush side. For a cheaper and more **D.I.Y.** solution, try a product designed for incontinent rabbits (seriously!): a soft, quilted cotton pad with waterproof material on the reverse side. It's completely washable and holds two cups of liquid! For sale at CatFaeries.com. See also **baby (adult)** and **enemas**.

2) Waterskiing, windsurfing, et al.

3) Sex at a Six Flags water park.

## wax, hot

The M.V.P. of **temperature play**. Scented and colored candles often contain plasticizers, which make them burn very hot—i.e., way too hot to be safe. Black candles and beeswax candles burn the hottest of all. We know black is the new, well, *black* for **BDSM** activities, but you're better off with the plain white paraffin candles sold at grocery and hardware stores for emergencies. Better still are soy candles, which burn cleaner and at an even lower temperature than paraffin. The very best in terms of safety (and the least hardcore in terms of sensation) are scented **massage** candles like those made by LELO, whose liquid wax turns into a body oil when rubbed, without any messy buildup (pictured on the back cover). Most sex toy shops carry massage candles in various scents like vanilla, lavender, mango, cucumber, and sandalwood, though we would recommend unscented, since the smell of the more affordable scented candles can be overwhelming.

Whatever candle you choose, here's how to **play** with it: Blow the candle out before dripping the wax (not a candle that's been burning for hours or else it'll be too hot); test the wax on the back of your hand first; hold above your target area (the higher you hold the candle, the cooler the wax will be when it finally touches down); when the wax hits the skin, rub it in to disperse the heat; do not drip the wax on your partner's face, orifices, or hairy areas (unless they're prepared for **hair removal** the hard way). Alternate with **ice** for extreme **sensation play**.

## waxing

See **hair removal**.

## wigs

The quick, easy, commitment-free way to dabble in **role-playing**, without any of the complicated **fetish wear**, the esteem-crushing **humiliation**, or the messy cleanup! You don't even have to pretend to be someone you're not. Simply changing your appearance with a mop of long black tresses when you're a shorthaired blonde can be enough to make you *feel* different: maybe sexier, naughtier, bolder, more **dominant**... (Don't tell us you haven't had some of the hottest sex of your life on Halloween.) And if you believe that guys are hardwired to want sexual congress with many different women (which is why, some would argue, monogamy is apparently so difficult for some of them), then this is a simple way to sort of trick their natural instincts and satisfy their urge for variety. Yes, we can only in good conscience recommend wigs as option for *women* (gay or straight), because we have yet to see a wig that looks good on a man...unless he's a drag queen or Brad Pitt.

## whips, multi-tail

**Cats** or **floggers**. Please see these entries, as well as **flagellation**, for details and important safety information.

## whips, single-tail

Indiana Jones's favorite accessory. But we don't care if you've got the whole Raiders outfit down (from the hat to the idol) for a little **role-playing**: You *cannot* use bullwhips as kink equipment. Not unless your day job is cattle herder, your part-time job is **dominatrix**, and you have a doctorate in whip wielding. It's just too dangerous. To mix movie metaphors, it's the Red Ryder BB Gun of the **BDSM** world: You'll whip your eye out! For more manageable **flagellation** tools, see **cats** and **floggers**. A.k.a. bullwhip.

## whiplash

Any kind of neck injury caused by an enthusiastic and sometimes involuntary physical response to a hard blow from a **flagellation** device, whereby the one being flagellated quickly snaps their neck back in **pain** and/or ecstasy. Another good reason to put your **bottom** in a thick posture **collar**.

## wrestling

1) A **fetishism** that may be as simple as a bit of rough and tumble before bed or as elaborate as a **scene** involving headgear, booties, and a regulation leotard (or "singlet," if you want to be all official). It can take the form of **resistance play**, **domination**, **sploshing** (think mud, oil, etc.), **age play** (think two guys in diapers who don't feel like playing with **mommy**), or just plain voyeurism (think cat fights on film). Just as the majority of WWF fans are straight men, the majority of erotic wrestling fans are het dudes, too (coincidence?), so some pro **dommes** specialize in half nelsons and neck scissors. (If the Amazon has neither the heft nor the skills to take him to the mat, he'll probably let her win just for looking so good in a Lycra onesie.)

2) What college guys do in dorm rooms when they really want to get it on but are too repressed to make a move.

"Power is the ultimate aphrodisiac."

—Henry Kissinger

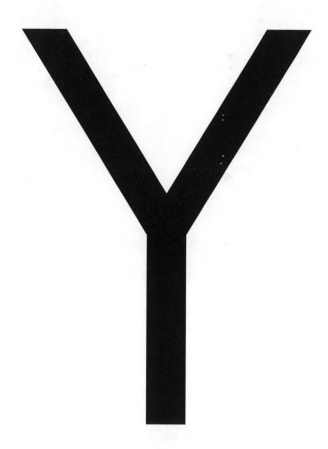

## Y.K.I.N.O.K.

An abbreviation for "Your kink is not OK." The term refers to judgmental statements made by narrow-minded tight-asses who believe that sexual practices they either don't engage in, don't understand, or don't consider "normal" are just plain wrong. (In other words, at least half the sexually active people in this country, including **Anastasia Steele** in the opening chapters of *Fifty Shades of Grey*.) Of course, you're free—indeed, *encouraged* by most serious kinksters—to call anything that isn't **safe, sane or consensual** "not okay." But if something just **squicks** you, then don't be a prude about it. The term is thought to have been coined in the Usenet newsgroup alt.sex.bondage back when the Internet was just in diapers (the baby kind, not the adult kind).

## Y.K.I.O.K.,I.J.N.M.K.

An abbreviation for "Your kink is OK, it's just not my kink." The politically correct version of **Y.K.I.N.O.K.** The term expresses the widespread acceptance by most serious kinksters (and *eventually* Anastasia in the *Fifty Shades of Grey* series) of other people's preferences, practices, and **fetishes**, even if said kinksters don't get them or are **squicked** by them. Interchangeable with Y.K.I.N.M.K. ("Your kink is not my kink"). A.k.a. Can't we all just get along?

## Y.K.I.O.K.,B.M.I.B.

An abbreviation for "Your kink is OK, but mine is better."

## Y.K.H.M.K.F

An abbreviation for "Your kink hit my kink first."

## Y.K.G.G.W.C.

An abbreviation for "Your kink goes great with chardonnay."

## Y.K.T.L.C.

An abbreviation for "Your kink tastes like chicken."

## Y.G.Y.K.I.M.P.B.

An abbreviation for "You got your kink in my peanut butter."

## you're with me, Leather

1) The pick-up line ESPN sportscaster Chris Berman allegedly once used on a woman in a bar. Apparently she was being chatted up by another gentleman when Berman, all **dom** and shit, walked up to them and dropped his mad charm on the little lady. Practically **taken in hand**, she immediately got up and left the bar with the D-celebrity. Her pants were, of course, made of any **power player**'s material of choice: **leather**.

2) The best ironic pick-up line for any **BDSM** event, in our opinion.

*"Holy fuck."*

—E.L. James, *Fifty Shades of Grey*

## zippers

A **D.I.Y.** kinky toy made by stringing a bunch of clothespins to a cord or light **chain**. Attach these clothespins to your **bottom**'s body (with their permission, of course), then "unzip" them in one fell (agonizing) swoop by yanking on one end of the cord. Not advisable if you've got thin walls, overly "concerned" neighbors, or a particularly vocal bottom. See also **nipple torture** and **pain**.

# Appendix A
# Shopping Advice

Looking to renovate your **dungeon**, kink up your porno collection, invest in a new **flogger**, order a custom-made **gimp suit**, or just buy your very first **vibrator**? Your best bet is to visit your local bricks-and-mortar sex shop—that way you can turn on a vibrator to test its strength and noise level; you can see exactly how big that **dildo** is; you can try on those cuffs; you can find the **paddle** that fits just so in your hand; you can ask the friendly assistant how something works (and if there's no friendly assistant offering to help, then you shouldn't be shopping there!). We recommend women-friendly stores that put an emphasis on education and eco-friendliness—try checking your local alternative weekly paper for listings (or, failing that, Yelp.com).

If you'd rather shop online, the same advice holds true: Look for stores that are responsible (for example, easy to contact), informative (for example, about what their toys do and what they're made of), and forthright (for example, about their returns policy). There are quality sites that specialize in **BDSM** gear (like Stockroom.com), but newbies might appreciate general toy stores with non-intimidating, pastel-colored designs (like Babeland.com, GoodVibes.com, and EdenFantasys.com)—they'll have a smaller selection of kinky products, but most items will be appropriate for dabbling. You can also buy many products directly from the source; for example, LELO.com sells all their own toys. There are literally hundreds of online outlets selling sex toys, including online versions of your little corner sex shop—so do a little digging until you find one that meets our standards, and suits your wants and needs. A good rule of thumb is this: If you don't feel comfortable browsing the site, then don't buy there! Your best friend's favorite place to shop for toys might not feature nearly enough leather for you (or way too much **leather**, if you're a kinky **vegan**). JanesGuide.com is kind of the Consumer Reports of sex websites—it's a good place to look for ideas.

Wherever you shop, whether online or in person, just make sure it's a place you trust not only with your credit card information but also your genitals! Look for places that stock respected brand names, i.e. toy companies that care about using materials that are both body-safe and green; provide warranties and care & cleaning instructions with their items; and create designs that are pleasing to both the eye and the body. **LELO** is a good example of this type of company, which is why we worked closely with them when writing this book and why we recommend so many of their products. Founded in Sweden in 2003, they have transformed the look, feel, and function of bedside accessories, bringing a new level of luxury to the field. We like to think of them as the Apple of the sex toy world (and we're die-hard Mac fans all the way). Like us, LELO's team believe fervently in safety, quality, and aesthetics—the trifecta of any decent intimate lifestyle product! So whatever **blindfold**, feather **tickler**, **love ring**, **flogger**, or other kinky accoutrement you buy, please do make sure it measures up. And insist that your favorite shop stock it!

Remember, sex toys, kinky or otherwise, are all about *loving* your body— and your partner's body—in every sense of the word.

# Appendix B
# Surfing Suggestions

Want to learn how to tie a **knot** or wield a **whip**, find a shrink who specializes in kink, or just connect with like-minded pervs? The following websites should help. A note of caution: While we don't list purely hardcore porn sites, some of these destinations are not for the faint of heart. And design snobs be warned: Many of them look like they haven't been updated since 1997.

**AdultFriendFinder.com**
One of the oldest adult dating sites on the block—find a **fetish** partner, a new **slave**, a dirty IM-er, or a **pinch-hitter** for that threeway you've been meaning to get around to. Just watch out for the "professionals" who post on here—they're not just looking to become your kinky new best friend (the same goes for any adult personals site).

**Alt.com**
Kinky **online personals** with a *very* specialized **fetish** search feature.

**BDSM Folks I Can Do Without**
**Xeromag.com/fvbdfolks.html**
If you're feeling a little **scene**-d out, this list will crack you up.

**Bondage.com**
This deeply purple site has been around forever (if you couldn't tell from the prized URL) and offers photos, stories, discussion forums, and online personals—you'll have to pay for the photos, vids, and full access to the personals, but the stories, columns, and community areas are all free. It began out of (where else?) San Francisco, but has since gone national.

**BondageCafe.com**
Alright, so it's a paid service (about 20 bucks a month), but compared to all the other P.P.V. sites out there, this one actually seems to have a personality, a sense of humor, and a bit of a personal touch (which is not the same as saying that the ugly dude at the party is "all personality"). The free preview is, thankfully

more tame than most kink-porn sites (yay, no body fluids!)—but it's still porn, still kinky.

**ClarisseThorn.com**
The blog of the internationally respected feminist **SM** writer.

**CraigsList.org**
Free online classifieds the world over, which feature the popular "Casual Encounters" section, for when you're in need of a cleaning **slave**, an afternoon **top**, or a human toilet. See **service kink** entry.

**DarkConnections.com**
**BDSM** for people of color: **online personals**, message boards, chat, **munches**, links, advice, a **pro dom/me** directory, photos, kinky games, and even naughty voicemail messages.

**DarkerPleasures.com**
BDSM stories and ebooks, some with a focus on the tata "torture." See **bondage (breast)**.

**EMandLO.com**
Home of yours truly, we blog daily on love, sex, and everything in between, offering advice on topics both **vanilla** and kinky. And we have a strict no-nudity policy: We're about education, not titillation.

**The Eulenspiegel Society**
**TES.org**
Founded in 1971, The Eulenspiegel Society is the oldest **BDSM** group in the nation. This New York-based non-profit organization fights for the kinky rights of **SM**-ers, and like Janus in San Francisco (see below), considers itself a support and education group. They host special interest groups for locals (e.g. **Spanking**, **Switchables**, etc.) and are very welcoming to beginners.

**FetishExchange.org**
Lots of free info on a whole range of **BDSM** topics, but also lots of links to straight-up, in-

your-face, kinky porn with the warning, "Not for the meek."

**FetLife.com**
A free social network for the **BDSM** and **fetish** community. It's *the* place to meet like-minded souls—our favorite kinky expert Jay Wiseman has said so, and the dude knows of what he speaks.

**FoxyFurniture.com**
If you're looking for dungeon **furniture** that can be disguised as a hat stand or a planter when the neighbors are over, this is the site for you. They no longer sell direct, but offer all the plans for free if you're handy with a table saw.

**Groups.Google.com**
If you have no idea how to get onto Usenet (it's a '90s thing), this site will give you easy access to classic kinky discussion groups like soc.subculture.bondage-bdsm, alt.polyamory, soc.sexuality.spanking, and more. Type in your fetish of choice and see what comes up.

**Groups.Yahoo.com**
Web-based discussion groups, that range from saintsindiapers ("A safe place for Latter Day Saints diaper wearers, their spouses, family, and friends to discuss infantilism and the LDS faith") to xenas_playground ("A **role-playing** group for fans of both Xena and **spanking**"). Because you're only *truly* pervy if you start a Yahoo Group for your **fetish** and no one else joins in.

**HouseofGord.com**
Super intense bondage photos and video with some unintentionally hilarious running commentary. There's a free tour—that may be all (or much more than) you need. See **human furniture** entry.

**IsabellasRecordings.com**
Isabella is a certified clinical hypnotherapist, a phone sex **mistress**, and a consummate **dirty**

**talker**. Take tips from her numerous MP3 recordings or get a free kinky ring tone. Seriously, they're hilarious: Try the **slave** ring tone if you're a chronic screener ("Pick up the phone slave, get down on your knees and crawl..."). Or, if your boyfriend cheats on you: switch his mobile to the panty ring ("Hi panty boy, now that your phone is ringing everyone's going to know that you're wearing panties!").

## JanesGuide.com

The Consumer Reports of the online sex world: A well respected, comprehensive guide to every kind of X-rated site imaginable, from hardcore porn to high-brow erotica (and Jane always warns you if you'll be asked to whip out your credit card). In the review index, check out the Adult Products and **Fetish/BDSM** categories. There's even an entire section dedicated to **corsets**! (Including the awesomely titled FairyGothMother.com.) Their regional guide offers state-by-state listings of BDSM events.

## Kink Aware Professionals
## Resources/KAP section of NCSfreedom.org

Non-profit referral service for kinksters, hosted by the National Coalition for Sexual Freedom (see below): Find medical, legal, and psycho-therapeutic pros who aren't going to blush or cringe when you explain exactly how you got that bruise/weapon/heartbreak.

## KinkTalk.com

Another forum for talk about...you guessed it!

## KinkyRopes.com

Information you can use to enhance your sex life with the practice of erotic **rope** bondage. Includes events listings, online tutorials, and products.

## LELO.com/news

This blog provides tips on using LELO products alongside smart and funny advice about everything from sex after childbirth to the benefits of prostate massage.

## MaybeMaimed.com

A blog promoting sexual freedom from a submissive man's perspective.

## MistressAbsolute.com

We met Mistress Absolute when we interviewed her for our UK TV show. She's a London-based professional **dominatrix** and she totally rocks—she's smart, funny, and manages to take her profession seriously without taking herself too seriously. Also, she takes no shit, though we guess that kind of comes with the territory.

## MistressMatisse.blogspot.com

Diary of a professional **dominatrix** who used to be a columnist for the *Seattle Stranger* (where she hilariously reported on some of the phone calls she received). Her professional website is MistressMatisse.com, but if you're just there to gawk, then her blog is far more entertaining. She doesn't update it much these days, but her Twitter feed @mistressmatisse is active and worth checking out.

## MistressMorgana.com

Possibly the most attractive **BDSM** website we've ever seen! Mistress Morgana is a San Francisco-based **pro domme** who runs numerous classes and events, both in San Francisco and in New York: **cross-dressing** for boys, **bondage, cock and ball torture**, etc. She also runs a Kink Consultancy Service where she works with couples who want to get their kink on, women who want to learn how to **dom**, or people who just want to know what to do when someone you love is kinky (if you're in a fly-over state, she gives good phone, too). And then there's the actual pro domme stuff, which all takes place in her well-appointed **dungeon**. It's a great glimpse into the world of a pro domme with the most down-to-earth FAQ we've ever read. And the gallery contains a ton of classy (and nudity free!) pics of Holly Hunter-lookalike Mistress Morgana in full kinky attire.

**MyHoneyBun.com**
Cute site dedicated to all things **spanking**.

**National Coalition for Sexual Freedom**
**NCSfreedom.org**
The ACLU of the kink world, this organization is "committed to creating a political, legal, and social environment in the United States that advances equal rights of consenting adults who practice forms of alternative sexual expression." Their primary focus is the **BDSM**, swing, and polyamory communities. See **law (the)** entry.

**National Leather Association**
**NLA-i.com**
A communication, information, education, and support network for all members of the **Leather/BDSM/Fetish** community. See **law (the)** entry.

**PowerExchange.com**
The online home of a San Francisco **BDSM** club of the same name, and also host to kinky **online personals** (gay and straight)—primarily in San Fran, but expanding nationally, too. Another site that features loud intrusive music, so turn down the volume on your computer if you've got nosy cubicle-mates.

**RopeFashions.com**
Rope **bondage** tutorials from an incredibly sweet, average looking **D/s** couple. See **rope** entry.

**Rubberist.net**
An online support community for **rubber** fetishists.

**SmartStim.com**
Free online community for **e-stim** players or wannabe players.

**Society for Human Sexuality**
**Sexuality.org**
A great source of **BDSM** info culled from around the web, plus guides to getting your kink on in Seattle, Portland, San Fran, Vancouver, and the West Coast (we guess the Greenwich, Connecticut, guide is still in the works). Worth visiting just for the archived Alt.sex.bondage FAQ.

**Society of Janus**
**SOJ.org**
San Francisco-based **BDSM** support and education group. It was founded in 1974, making it the second oldest BDSM group in the US (after the Eulenspiegel Society in New York, see above). For locals, the site offers a calendar of local kinky events; for the rest of you, it's a fount of kinky info (plus they include a directory of groups across the country that they're affiliated with).

**SpankingBlog.com**
For all the latest **spanking** "news."

**TakenInHand.com**
A website dedicated to domestic **T.P.E.** relationships that reek a little of the '50s. Even if you find the philosophy offensive, the design and quality of writing is anything but. See **Taken in Hand** entry.

**TheBDSMeventspage.com**
An impressively detailed state-by-state guide to local **BDSM**, **leather**, and swinging events and organizations, from North Alabama Spanking and Social Alternatives (NASSA) to the Virginia **Power Exchange**, from Boston's **Fetish** Flea Market to Oklahoma's Mr. Leather (we are *so* there).

**The-Stampede.com**
One of the nation's largest organized **pony play** and **animalism** groups.

**TicklingForum.com**
Free forum for **tickling** fetishists.

# Appendix C
# Reading List

If you're looking for further kinky information, instruction, or titillation, here are some good books to start with.

*The Adventurous Couple's Guide to Strap-On Sex*
*by Violet Blue (Cleis)*
Full of ideas on positions, toys, **harnesses**, **role-play** scenarios, and reading your partner like a dirty book. Look, ma! No hands.

*Anything for You: Erotica for Kinky Couples*
*edited by Rachel Kramer Bussel (Cleis)*
Rachel Kramer Bussel is a one-woman machine when it comes to erotica anthologies —if you've got a kinky preference, chances are, she's edited a book about it.

*Back on the Ropes*
*by Two Knotty Boys (Green Candy Press)*
This book features 750 full-color photographs demonstrating everything from basic **knots** to advanced sensual **bondage** techniques. You might also want to check out their earlier book, *Showing You the Ropes*. (Oh how the puns abound in this world!)

*Best Bondage Erotica / Best Bondage Erotica 2*
*edited by Alison Tyler (Cleis Press)*
See **communication** entry.

*Best Fetish Erotica*
*edited by Cara Bruce (Cleis Press)*
See **communication** entry.

*Best Women's Erotica 2012*
*edited by Violet Blue (Cleis Press)*
Flip through until you find the fantasy that takes your fancy.

*The Better Built Bondage Book: A Complete Guide to Making Your Own Sex Toys, Furniture and BDSM Equipment*
*by Douglas Kent (Mental Gears Publishing)*
If you can get past the cheesy photography and the price tag, you'll be able to connect with your inner kinky Bob Vila.
See **D.I.Y.** entry.

**The Big Bang: Nerve's Guide to the New Sexual Universe**
*by Em & Lo (Plume)*
Our very first sex book! Includes in-depth how-to info on kink-lite topics such as **strap-on** sex and **fisting**.

**Bob Flanagan: Supermasochist**
*by Andrea Juno & V. Vale (powerHouse Books)*
The life story of a performance artist/public masochist who used kink to deal with the pain of his cystic fibrosis. See **masochism** entry.

**The Claiming of Sleeping Beauty series**
*by Anne Rice writing as A. N. Roquelaure (Plume)*
The original *Fifty Shades of Grey* erotic trilogy from the 1980s. It follows the story of Sleeping Beauty, except she isn't woken up by a kiss, if you know what we mean. Then she becomes a sex slave to her prince and his whole court. Fairy tail ensues. Way kinkier and way better written than *Fifty Shades*.

**Come Hither: A Commonsense Guide to Kinky Sex**
*by Gloria G. Brame (Fireside)*
We love this book! The design is funky and the writing is down-to-earth, informative, and engaging. Definitely written for the kink beginner, this book even has quizzes to help you figure out and understand your very own kink.

**Different Loving: The World of Sexual Dominance & Submission**
*by Gloria G. Brame, William D. Brame, and Jon Jacobs (Villard)*
Gloria Brame worked on this book before she wrote *Come Hither*; this one is intended for people already in "the scene." It's not as easy to dip in and out of as *Come Hither*, but it contains some fascinating kink **history** and numerous interviews with self-professed kinksters of every breed. A great behind-the-**scene** (heh) look at kink.

**Erotic Bondage Handbook**
*by Jay Wiseman (Greenery Press)*
Jay Wiseman is the Papa Smurf of the **bondage** world. Ask anyone in the kink world where you should go to brush up on your restraining skills, and they'll send you here. He's been in the **scene** since there *was* a scene, so beginners may find his way of talking a little, you know, *scene-y*. But if you want to learn mad **rope** skillz, you won't meet anyone who is more responsible, enthusiastic, knowledgeable (especially on the medical side of things), and just an all-around nice guy.

**Exhibitionism for the Shy**
*by Carol Queen (Down There Press)*
Let us count the ways we love Carol Queen: She is smart, sweet, funny, saucy, and responsible for some of the best sex advice we've ever heard. If you can't imagine ever raising a **paddle** and telling your partner they've been a bad boy/girl/puppy, but you'd really *like* to be able to imagine yourself talking like that, this book is a great place to start. See also the **dirty talk** entry.

**FetishSex: A Complete Guide to Sexual Fetishes**
*by Violet Blue (Digita Publications)*
If Violet Blue hasn't heard of it, it's not a **fetish**.

**The *Fifty Shades of Grey* trilogy**
*by E.L. James*
Oh, just read them already. Start on page 80.

**Flogging**
*by Joseph W. Bean (Greenery Press)*
Let's just say that this man knows a *lot* more than we do about **flogging**.

**Get This Party Started! 50 Naughty Games for Twosomes, Threesomes, Foursomes, and More**
*by Frances Hill (Chronicle)*
Never again will you need to ask yourself, *How do I turn this drunken after-party into a full-on, shock-the-neighbors orgy?*

**Good Porn: A Woman's Guide**
*by Erika Lust*
A smart, feminist guide to high-quality porn made with a woman's pleasure in mind (it's rarer than you might think).

**A Hand in the Bush: The Fine Art of Vaginal Fisting**
*by Deborah Addington (Greenery Press)*
See **fisting** entry.

**Intimate Invasion: The Erotic Ins & Outs of Enema Play**
*by M.R. Strict (Greenery Press)*
See **enema** entry. Out of print but used copies are available at AbeBooks.com.

**Justine**
*by Marquis de Sade (many publishers)*
See **Marquis de Sade** entry.

**The Kama Sutra Deck: 50 Ways to Love Your Lover**
*by Julianne Balmain (Chronicle)*
If you think kink is a '70s thing, then you don't know your *Kama Sutra*. This card deck is a saucy reminder that people have been getting their kink on for a *loooooong* time.

**The Kinky Girl's Guide to Dating**
*by Luna Grey (Greenery Press)*
See **online personals** entry.

**Learning the Ropes: A Basic Guide to Safe and Fun S/M Lovemaking**
*by Race Bannon (Daedalus)*
This very brief book is particularly strong on the "headspace" aspect of kinky play, i.e. fantasy, **role-playing**, **dirty talk**, etc.

**Lovers' Massage: Soothing Touch for Two**
*by Darrin Zeer; illustrations by Amy Saidens (Chronicle)*
Bone up on your hands-on **sensation play**. Besides, nothing says "the face **slap** was just pretend" like a loving **massage**.

**The Loving Dominant**
*by John Warren and Libby Warren (Greenery Press)*
A beginner's guide to heterosexual male **dominance** in a **BDSM** context.

**The Mistress Manual: The Good Girl's Guide to Female Dominance**
*by Mistress Lorelei (Greenery Press)*
How to get all **Christian Grey** on your boyfriend. Necktie optional.

**My Secret Garden**
*by Nancy Friday (Pocket)*
See **rape fantasy** entry.

**Naughty Spanking Stories from A to Z**
*edited by Rachel Kramer Bussel (Pretty Things Press)*
Like **spanking**? Like erotica? You'll love this!

**The New Bottoming Book**
*by Dossie Easton (Greenery Press)*
The how-to's and the why-to's of being the **bottom**, **BDSM**-style, from the author of the renowned *Ethical Slut*.

**The New Topping Book**
*by Dossie Easton (Greenery Press)*
A companion guide to the title immediately above: The how-to's and the why-to's of **topping** your partner, **BDSM**-style.

**Play Piercing**
*by Deborah Addington (Greenery Press)*
See **piercing (play)** entry.

**Please, Ma'am: Erotic Stories of Male Submission**
*edited by Rachel Kramer Bussel (Cleis)*
You *will* enjoy this, because she says so.

**Please, Sir: Erotic Stories of Female Submission**
*edited by Rachel Kramer Bussel (Cleis)*
You *will* enjoy this, because he says so.

*Queer Pulp: Perverted Passions from the Golden Age of the Paperback*
*by Susan Stryker (Chronicle)*
A historian's overview of kinky pulp paperbook fiction, from authors like W. Somerset Maugham and Truman Capote all the way down to the low-brow no-names who churned out titles like *Hot Pants Homo* and *Women's Barracks*.

*Screw the Roses, Send Me Thorns:*
*The Romance and Sexual Sorcery of Sadomasochism*
*by Philip Miller and Molly Devon (Mystic Rose Books)*
If the title didn't clue you in, this book is actually pretty funny, which is refreshing in this genre. The book focuses on male **dominant**/female **submissive** relationships, because that was Philip and Dolly's deal (until he died a few years ago)—however, most of the how-to info applies across the board.

*The Seductive Art of Japanese Bondage*
*by Midori (Greenery Press)*
A how-to for advanced **rope** players by one of the biggest names in the world of kink., illustrated with full-page photography. See also the **Japanese rope bondage** entry. Kinksters covet the hardback edition of this book—it's kind of a holy grail—but the paperback edition is much easier to get your hands on. As it were. Dita Von Teese models.

*Sensuous Magic:*
*A Guide to S/M for Adventurous Couples*
*by Patrick Califia (Cleis Press)*
Not quite as down-to-earth as *Come Hither* (after all, Califia calls kink "sensuous magic"— if you find all the omming in yoga class a little much, then this book may not be for you), but still a great introduction to the world of **BDSM** and its philosophies. The how-to info is interspersed with mini erotic vignettes for inspiration.

*SEX: How to Do Everything*
*by Em & Lo (DK)*
Named one of the top 10 sex guides ever written, along with the *Kama Sutra* and Ovid's *Art of Love*, by the *Guardian* in 2012. The book includes step-by-step, illustrated instruction, with a full chapter dedicated to kink for dabblers.

*Sex Toy: An A-Z Guide to Bedside Accessories*
*by Em & Lo (Chronicle)*
Entries for **clamps**, **cock rings**, **harnesses**, **pumps**, **strap-ons**, and **cock rings** are included alongside more **vanilla** sex toys, like the Pocket Rocket, the Rabbit Habit, and the Hello Kitty vibrator.

*The Sexually Dominant Woman*
by Lady Green (Greenery Press)
Because not all tops sport a grey **tie** and a steely grey gaze, **Christian**.

*Shibari You Can Use: Japanese Rope Bondage and Erotic Macramé*
*by Lee "Bridgette" Harrington (Mystic)*
Includes instruction on creating: Shinju (chest **harnesses**), Gyakuebi (Asian style **hogtie**), Ebi or Kuri (Shrimp or Ball ties), **rope** corsets, **strap-on** harnesses, and **crotch ropes**.

*The S&M Feminist*
*by Clarisse Thorn (Amazon Digital Services)*
A collection of the best essays by this feminist **SM** writer who's lectured internationally and written for the likes of the *Guardian* and Jezebel.com.

*SM 101: A Realistic Introduction*
*by Jay Wiseman (Greenery Press)*
Incredibly detailed safety and how-to information from the king of kink.

*The Story of O*
*by Pauline Réage (many)*
See **Story of O** entry.

*Sweet Life: Erotic Fantasies for Couples*
*edited by Violet Blue (Cleis Press)*
See **communication** entry. See also her follow-up, *Sweet Confessions: Erotic Fantasies for Couples.*

*Tarnsman of Gor (et al)*
*by John Gorman (Wildside Press)*
John Gorman's 26-book *Chronicles of Gor* series is pulp **BDSM** science fiction with a cult following—devotees of the Gor way of life (essentially, male **domination** and female **submission**) call themselves Goreans and may be in full-time **master-slave** relationships. If your problem with BDSM is that it just doesn't feel enough like D&D, then Gor could be for you.

*The Ultimate Guide to Sexual Fantasy*
*by Violet Blue (Cleis Press)*
**Role-playing** examples, fantasy suggestions, and how-to info, including advice on stripping, **dirty talk**, and how to ask for a **spanking**. See also **communication** entry.

*Trust, the Hand Book: A Guide to the Sensual and Spiritual Art of Handballing*
*by Bert Herrman (Alamo Square Distributors)*
See **fisting** entry.

*21st Century Kinkycrafts*
*edited by Janet W. Hardy (Greenery Press)*
How to turn everyday household items into **bondage** equipment, **dungeon** toys, sex gadgets, and even safer sex supplies. See **D.I.Y.** entry.

*Venus in Furs*
*by Leopold Ritter von Sacher-Masoch (many)*
See **fur**, **history of kink**, and **masochism** entries.

*Vox*
*by Nicholson Baker (Vintage)*
See **dirty talk** entry.

# Acknowledgments

Endless thanks to our former intern, Vanessa Martini, who sacrificed her innocence to help us research this book. You are wise and professional beyond your years.

Thanks to Ignas Gee, our main man at LELO.

Much love to Rob and Joey, who would like to state for the record that they weren't our guinea pigs for *every* entry in this book.

And apologies to our children for when they accidentally stumble across this book. Please know that it is possible to write about something without actually having experienced it.

# About *the* Authors

Em & Lo are the Emily Posts of the modern bedroom, and have penned six books on the topics of sex and love, including *Sex: How to Do Everything*, which the *Guardian* named one of the ten best sex guides of all time, alongside *The Kama Sutra* and Ovid's *Art of Love*. Em & Lo have written features for numerous magazines, including *Glamour*, *Details*, and *Marie Claire*; and have penned columns for *New York Magazine*, the *Guardian*, *Men's Journal*, and *Metro*. They hosted a ten-episode television series called "SEX: How to Do Everything" which premiered in the UK in 2009. And they dish about sex, love, and everything in between on their daily advice blog, EMandLO.com.

# About *the* Illustrator

Illustrator Arthur Mount (ArthurMount.com) has been in the biz for nearly twenty years, regularly publishing work around the world (including three of Em & Lo's previous titles). His other clients include the *New York Times*, *Wired Magazine*, Harley-Davidson, and NASA.

Made in the USA
San Bernardino, CA
11 January 2014